French Fine
Wines

French Fine Wines

Steven Spurrier

Foreword by Alexis Lichine

Willow Books

Collins
8 Grafton Street, London W1

1984

For Michael Broadbent and the late Martin Bamford,
fine wine personified

Willow Books
William Collins plc
London · Glasgow · Sydney
Auckland · Toronto · Johannesburg

First published in Great Britain 1984

Spurrier, Steven.
French fine wines.
1. Wine and wine making – France
I. Title
641.2'2'0944   TP553

ISBN 0-00-218116-9

Designed and produced by
Robert Adkinson Limited, London

Editorial Director Clare Howell

Editor Hilary Dickinson

Design Rose & Lamb Design Partnership

Cartography Ann Lamb

Phototypeset in Baskerville by
Dorchester Typesetting Limited, Dorchester

Colour and black-and-white illustrations originated by
East Anglian Engraving Co. Ltd., Norwich

Printed and bound in Belgium by
Brepols, Turnhout

Contents

Note: Measurement conversion

*Measurements of volume and area have been expressed in
hectolitres (hl) and hectares (ha):
1 hectolitre = 26.4 U.S. gallons
1 hectare = 2.471 acres*

Foreword

Among those who have popularized French wines in the past decade, few have done more than Steven Spurrier. This is not as easy as it sounds. One would think that excellence in anything as pleasurable as drinking fine wine should hardly need an advocate or champion, especially in France – after all, although we do not raise a glass of Château Latour or Montrachet at every meal, we have known them to be monuments to excellence for as long as wine has had a place in our lives.

Where is the sense of discovery then? Steven Spurrier has had the gift to be able to seek out that adventure, in at least two ways. Firstly, because he brought a new and even down-to-earth perspective to French wines, he has been able to lead people both through his writing and through tastings and courses at the Académie du Vin in Paris and now in London. Secondly, he has been able to communicate the qualities of the best-known, most venerable of French wines – those under consideration here – with an honest lack of pretension that can only come from true expertise and, thankfully, he doesn't pull punches.

He can encapsulate and identify with ease and grace, skills which can only come through connoisseurship acquired over a long period. Here, Steven Spurrier has performed a fine task.

Alexis Lichine

Introduction

France is the country with the widest range of fine wines in the world. French, or French-adopted, grape varieties are planted in every country which produces wines of quality, and in most cases French wine is used as a benchmark by which others are judged.

Despite remarks about the greatness of past vintages, current over-production and softer wines to satisfy market demand, there are more fine wines coming out of France than ever before. Yet progress in fighting disease in the vineyards and enormously improved vinification techniques would not have brought this about in the absence of three factors: the increase world-wide in the interest in and demand for fine wines; the strong and constant competition from other countries; and the willingness of the French to react and change. It is the chain reaction resulting from a much larger public which in turn encourages growers to re-invest in land and equipment, thereby improving their products which has broadened the base of quality wines and even saved a few *appellations* from extinction.

A fine wine may be described briefly as a wine of quality. Since this book is concerned, firstly, with the French regions and *appellations* and, secondly, with the individual fine wines within these *appellations*, I have expanded the definition to wines of potential quality. There are many wines in this book which also appear in the companion volume, *French Country Wines*. The reason is that in instances where quality has been slipping (the Beaujolais Crus), the wine is still the finest expression of the Gamay grape; where the wines had generally been overlooked (Chinon, Bourgueil), and now should not be; or where the wine, however little known (Montlouis, Saint-Péray), still has a 'hand-made' individuality.

The aim of this book is to list the better French wines by region and by *appellation*, describing the taste and characteristics of the wine and listing the finer producers. The selection of individual wines and growers aims to point out the better wines in each region, since these wines honourably represent their *appellation*. The book may thus be used both as a source of information and a buyer's guide. There are three main excuses for not making, selling or buying the best wine possible: lack of interest, lack of information and lack of money. I hope this book may overcome the first two.

Steven Spurrier

The Definition of Fine Wine

Fine wine has been defined as a wine of quality. What goes into making this quality is a mixture of six main elements, each of which gives the wine its particular style; the failure of any one of these will severely compromise the result. These elements are the soil, climate, grape varieties, care of the vineyards, vinification and ageing, and the human factor. Of these, the most important is the human factor, since it is only through continuous dedication to quality, with all the involvement, expense and risk that this entails, that really fine wine can be made.

The soil is plainly the basic element, as if the land is unsuitable for grapes, or much better suited to other crops, wine will not be made. It is said that a vine has to suffer to produce fine wine. What *is* true is that the vine should not find all it needs on the surface and should be forced to put down deep roots into the subsoil to tap the water and mineral deposits that are there. The soil is responsible for the 'soul' of the wine, its base of character that can be altered by all the other elements. The geological make-up of the soil is complemented by the exposition and with exceptions (the Médoc, Châteauneuf-du-Pape), the finest wines come from vines planted on hillsides.

The second part of the equation that makes up the French concept of *terroir* is the climate. Fine wine is made in areas with a long ripening period. The weather during the year will determine the character of the vintage, but each region has its intrinsic climate: the soft, luminous days in the Loire Valley, the cold winters and dry summers in Alsace, and the humid mornings and sunny days (with luck) in Sauternes all contribute to the style and complexity of their wines.

Given a particular soil and climate, certain grape varieties will work better than others. The laws of *appellation* in France have recognized the selection that had been made over centuries of wine-making, and the grapes that may be planted are strictly controlled. Fine wine comes only from *cépages nobles*. However, certain *porte-greffes* or grafts take better in certain soils and, within the same grape family, different strains will produce volume at the expense of quality: for instance, the Pinot *droit* in Burgundy is largely inferior to the Pinot *vrai*, but is more regular. The selection of *porte-greffe* to soil is not considered often enough as a danger or aid to quality.

Work in the vineyards follows a year-long cycle, and a badly run vineyard will be evident by the state of the vines. Vineyards do not have to have a 'manicured' look, although the best-tended vines tend to produce the finest wines, but the vines have to be pruned, tended throughout the growing season and kept free from disease. Vinification, now recognized as the key element in really fine wine, is merely the careful treatment of ripe, healthy grapes. Modern techniques and oenological research have given wine-makers greater control over the wine and diminished the quantity of spoiled wines. Cleanliness and attention to detail are more important than even the most advanced equipment, but many producers quite rightly spare no expense to make the finest, most polished wine they can. Once fermentation is over, the manner of ageing and time of bottling play a great part in the future of the finished wine.

Dominating all this is the human element; really fine wines cannot be made without the presence of a total commitment. This is true at all levels, from Gérard Chave's Hermitage, through Nuits-Saint-Georges of Gouges or Rion, to the wines currently made at Château Margaux and Lafite. Fine wine always takes more effort, requires more sacrifices and is justifiably more expensive than the alternative, since while fine wine can be produced in large amounts, it can never be mass-produced.

A final characteristic of fine wine (apart from being good to drink) is its rarity and investment potential. There are certain excellent wines, Condrieu for example, that should be drunk young, but most quality wines improve with age. This is often fuelled by fashionability, certain wines being more prestigious than others. Yet fine wine, even if it is in relatively short supply, is not rare; mature fine wine is. As for fashionability, this has a great impact on what are perceived as fine wines. Some wines are always in fashion (Claret, white Burgundy), some come and go (Sauternes) and some, not widely known due to a small production, can develop an almost 'cult' following (Côte-Rôtie). As some wines fade from the public eye, others are discovered, and as long as the commitment to quality by the producer is compensated by present or future recognition, the concept of fine wines will remain.

The Appellation Contrôlée System

The French system of Appellation d'Origine Contrôlée (AOC) is the basis of all controls on wine production in Europe and is now even being accepted as necessary in America. It is, quite simply, a system of controls on the origin of the wine, so that the wine in the bottle corresponds to the name on the label. If the controls are adhered to (and if they are not, then the wine loses its right to the *appellation*, and may not be called by its name), the wine will correspond to a style or type. This style will be lighter or more intense according to the character of the vintage, more or less 'typical', and better or worse according to the quality of viticulture and vinification, but the type should still be evident. The human element, by far the most important factor in the production of fine wine, cannot be controlled, since a wine producer can search for or disregard quality as he pleases, but the AOC system provides the framework for his efforts. Since the fine wines of France are almost without exception AOCs, it is important to know what actually is controlled. These come under eight headings:

1. The area of production. The land on which vines may be planted to benefit from the *appellation*: vines planted outside the exact region or within the region but on land deemed unsuitable do not conform.

2. Variety of grape. In some cases only a single variety is permitted (Bourgogne, Hermitage), in others, several complementary grapes (Médoc, Châteauneuf-du-Pape), with the proviso that if hybrid grapes are planted anywhere in the vineyard, the *appellation* is completely lost, and if non-permitted *vitis vinifera* grapes are planted in a particular parcel, the *appellation* is forfeited for wines from that parcel. Finally, grapes from newly planted vines may only be used in AOC wine from the *quatrième feuille* or their fourth vintage.

3. Degree of alcohol. All AOC wines must have a minimum degree of acohol and in some cases a maximum. This minimum may be attained by the natural sugar in the grape aided by chaptalization which is strictly controlled to a maximum of 2° in most regions of France and forbidden in the southern Côtes du Rhône and the Midi.

4. Yield per hectare. Each *appellation* has a maximum permitted yield per hectare. This is known as the

rendement de base (basic yield) and is fixed by decree by the INAO. There has been a recent tendency by the INAO to increase these basic yields. Further, the local Syndicats can apply for an augmentation or reduction (never yet applied for) in the basic yield depending on the quality and quantity of the crop. This is known as the *rendement annuel* (yearly yield). On top of this, each *appellation* can apply (but it is refused in the case of Grand Cru wines) for a further increase of up to 20% on the *rendement annuel*, known as the *plafond limité de classement* (PLC). In some cases, AOC Bordeaux for example, these two reclassifications can result in the basic yield being increased by as much as 60%. While this appears dangerously high, it must be added that any producer declaring wine in excess of the *rendement annuel* + PLC will lose the *appellation* for the whole crop.

5. Methods of viticulture. Control of the number of vines per hectare, the type of pruning, in some cases the method of picking (by successive *tris* for Sauternes), and whether or not the grapes may be destalked prior to fermentation.

6. Methods of vinification. Prohibition of the use of concentrated musts in most *appellations* and of *vinage* (addition of alcohol to the must) in all wines. Acidification and de-acidification are permitted under the control of the local *Station Oenologique*.

7. Analysis and tasting. Since the 1979 vintage, all AOC wines must be submitted to a tasting panel made up of members of the local Syndicat and representatives of the INAO. Those that do not pass are declassified but may be represented. A second declassification is final.

8. Bottling. Bottling in the region of *appellation* (i.e. if wines are shipped out of the region in bulk, they lose the *appellation*) has been obligatory in Alsace since 1972 and in Champagne since 1919. All AOC *méthode champenoise* wines are fermented in the bottle and thus naturally bottled in the region of origin. It should be noted that the higher *appellations* of Premiers and Grands Crus are, with the exception of all the Crus Classés of Bordeaux based on geographical *climats* in the *appellations*, with stricter controls on yield and alcohol content.

With these controls, the maximum amount of effort is made to maintain quality in French wine. A certain laxity in terms of yield and alcohol content is now being balanced by the obligatory submission of samples for official tastings.

How and Where to Buy Fine Wines

More care should be taken in buying fine wines than in buying lesser wines simply because they are more expensive. While the pitfalls are perhaps fewer, since fine wines should have a built-in guarantee of quality and their names are more easily recognized and remembered, the disappointment in a poor bottle is correspondingly greater. Even if one knows all the wines of all the growers in all the vintages, one cannot always tell how they have been shipped and stored.

The traditional way of buying fine wines has usually been through a specialist wine merchant. The advantages are plain: the merchant knows his wines and tastes regularly enough to know their development and relative merits; his selection will represent a personal choice, and it is as important for the client to know the tastes of his wine merchant as it is for the merchant to know the tastes of his client; a delivery service is usual, and storage of wines and advice on when they should be drunk are all part of the service; finally, almost all wine merchants will take back wines which a client finds unsatisfactory and repurchase surplus wines. The disadvantage is that one pays for this knowledge and service, and the traditional merchant, despite the bargains and special offers, is seldom the cheapest place to buy wines.

This very personal service tends only to exist in owner-run establishments, so if it is impossible to call on the wine merchant, one must buy from his list. An alternative solution, common in Europe but forbidden in America, is the chain store. Here, a central office will have shops across the country, selling from a single list. The advantage is that the buying will have been done by somebody equally as knowledgeable as the specialist wine merchant and with a financial 'clout' that he does not possess. The price will be competitive, due largely to the emergence of the supermarkets, and the service efficient. However, the range may be less individual than that of the specialist and, from the point of view of volume, many fine wines that are in short supply cannot be handled by such stores.

The supermarkets themselves are the newest element in the fine-wine business, who, having only in the last few years changed the habits of the wine-buying public for lesser wines, are now turning their attention to fine wines. Their buying power, the high quality of their buyers and their wish to attract clients to this new aspect of the business will make them very competitive on price, particularly for well-known names. The disadvantage is that the range is small, usually limited to big-volume brands and, even with excellent storage conditions before sale, the heat and light of a supermarket is not good for wine.

One of the best ways to buy fine wine is by mail, either from the list of the specialist merchant, or from mail-order wine companies, usually called clubs. Here again, buying is of a high level of expertise, with a volume to get the best prices, the wine lists (the only selling tool they have) are interesting and informative and the range of wines very wide, possibly wider than the specialist can afford and than the chain store would want to stock. The advantage of buying by mail is that one can compare lists and reflect before placing the order. Most clubs will take back unsatisfactory wine and offer storage facilities. The disadvantage is the price, which in this case should not be the prime factor in buying fine wine.

Perhaps the most concentrated sales of very fine wine are at auction. In France, for instance, the volume of fine wine sold at auction has tripled in the last five years. The range of wines sold, particularly the spread of vintages, is quite extraordinary. Very few of these wines are offered for tasting, but their origin is indicated and the storage conditions and state of each bottle will have been checked before sale. The advantage is that it is an opportunity to purchase wines that have disappeared from wine merchants' lists, or purchase (in quantity) surplus trade stock. The disadvantage is that, apart from the rarest items, the wines are sold in case lots. This fact, along with the growing interest in old and rare fine wines or those which are hard to get, has spawned a new breed of wine shop, specializing in just these wines. The stock is bought at auction or from private cellars, and the personal quality of the shop acts as a further guarantee.

The final, or the first, solution is to go direct to the producer. The advantage is in the price (taking into account the expense of getting yourself to the wines, or the wines to you), but many top producers do not sell direct. Moreover, you must rely on your own knowledge and taste, and it is also very difficult to return a wine to a grower once it has left his cellars.

The Vintages of the Last Ten Years

The decade of the 1970s was recognized as being blessed with the best run of good vintages in memory, or at least the fewest poor ones. Much of this is due, of course, to the weather, but the unpredictability of the climate has been lessened in importance by enormous progress in fighting disease in the vineyards and cleaner, more confident vinification. The 'luck' of the 1970s has continued, quite without precedent, into the 1980s. While vintages are always compared to each other and 'look-alikes' are found from previous years, each vintage is different at the time of picking, during fermentation and in the way it ages. The following notes on the fine-wine-producing regions of France are intended to put some of these differences into perspective. The scale of rating is as follows: 0–9 bad, very poor, poor; 10–11 acceptable; 12–13 quite good; 14–15 good; 16–18 very good; 19–20 exceptional.

Bordeaux, white

(NB the figure for dry wines precedes that for *vins liquoreux*)

1973 Very elegant dry whites, now past their best and light, not very botrytised sweet whites, very good *en apéritif.* 13/12.

1974 Firm, rather acidic dry wines; almost all the sweet wines were declassified. 12/8.

1975 Well-balanced, long-lasting dry wines, still very good; sweet wines generally very good, with some exceptionally fine and long-lasting. 17/18.

1976 Very hot summer resulted in rich, heady dry wines and very rich sweet wines, but quicker maturing and less class than 1975. 15/16.

1977 Small production of lively, rather tart dry whites but only a few successes in Sauternes. 13/12.

1978 Quite firm, long-lasting dry wines with excellent balance; Sauternes very rich in sugar but very little botrytis and will age well. 15/14.

1979 Large crop of immediately attractive dry whites and very fine *vins liquoreux* with richness and finesse. 15/16.

1980 Small crop of dry whites lacking in character and a very difficult vintage for sweet wines, with some concentrated *cuvées.* 13/13.

1981 Average crop of well-balanced dry wines with excellent fruit and finesse; sweet wines are elegant, rich and concentrated. 17/17.

1982 Very large crop of supple, dry wines, lacking in acidity and ready to drink early; the first pickings of *vins liquoreux* were exceptional, the richest since 1959, but early rain ruined most of the vintage. 16/17.

1983 Good quantity of fine dry wines with balance, elegance and fruit; large (for the Sauternais) volume of exceptionally rich sweet wine, the most impressive for many years. 18/19+.

Bordeaux, red

1973 Huge crop, generally light, supple wines, more successful in Médoc. All but the best are starting to fade. 13.

1974 Large crop, whose quality was spoiled by a cold, wet vintage. Rather charmless wines, needing a rigorous selection. Some good Graves. 13.

1975 Average volume of very firm concentrated wines, high in acidity and tannin. The minor wines are now ready, the finer wines beginning to show, but need 5-10 years to be at their best. 18.

1976 Large crop of wines high in sugar but low in acidity, good, but slightly hollow and maturing quite quickly and mostly ready to drink. 15.

1977 Small crop from a cold, late vintage. The Merlot was not successful and the better wines are from the Graves and southern Médoc. Highish acidity but some finesse, mostly ready to drink. 12.

1978 Average volume from a very late harvest in perfect conditions. Classic, well-balanced wines, less long-term than the 1975s. Better on the left bank. 18.

1979 Very large crop from another late harvest producing wines with excellent colour, fruit and depth from Saint-Emilion, Pomerol and Graves, a little lighter in the Médoc. Good from 1985. 17.

1980 Average crop from a difficult vintage producing light, attractive wines in the 1973 style. Less good in Saint-Emilion and Pomerol, best in the Graves. Very attractive for the next 3-4 years. 13.

1981 Good volume of fine, well-balanced wines that have the finesse but not quite the fruit of 1978-9. Excellent Graves. Start in 1986. 16.

1982 Very large crop of dark-coloured, plummy wines with very great richness and depth of fruit. An extraordinarily impressive vintage, particularly in the Libournais. In very many cases, the best since 1961, with softer tannins. Begin the better wines in 1990. 19+.

1983 Large crops of firm, tannic wines, leaner than the 1982s, more irregular in Saint-Emilion/Pomerol than in the Médoc/Graves, which are generally excellent. 17+.

Burgundy, white

1973 Very large crop of well-made wines with finesse and distinction. Only the Grands Crux have still kept their freshness. 16.

1974 Average yield, of rather hard Chablis and quicker-maturing Meursaults and Pulignys, now past their best. 13.

1975 Exceptional in Chablis, where the wines are still holding well, quite poor in the Côte d'Or due to rot. 18-10.

1976 Very hot summer that caused problems of vinification. Chablis has better balance, with some very successful, rather weighty *cuvées*, but there were also some impressive wines from the Côte d'Or. Should be drunk. 16.

1977 Small and late vintage, high in acidity. Better than at first thought, but very few real successes. 11.

1978 Very successful vintage from Chablis to Mâcon; admirable, perfectly balanced wines with fruit, firmness and length. The 1er and Grands Crus are still improving. 18.

1979 Large crop and another generally successful vintage, but less depth than the 1978s and may now be drunk with pleasure. 16.

1980 Small crop of uneven wines. Some of the Chablis were clean and stylish, but the wines from the Côte d'Or lacked stuffing and balance. 12.

1981 Small crop, with varying quality of Chablis, where the best resemble 1978, but very successful further south, with excellent concentration, acidity and fruit. 18.

1982 Large crop of rich, bouqueted, quite full-bodied wines, a richer version of the 1979s. Very impressive wines for relatively quick drinking due to low acidity. 17.

1983 Wines remarkably high in glycerine and grape sugar, difficult to vinify, but the successful *cuvées* will make very great bottles. 10-18.

Burgundy, red

1973 Very large crop of lightish, fruity wines, now past their best. 12.

1974 Largish crop of slightly firmer wines, but lacking colour and charm. Should have been drunk. 11.

1975 Very great problems of grey rot. To be avoided. 5.

1976 Small crop of wines highly concentrated due to a hot, dry summer. Some of the wines have too much tannin for the fruit and are drying out, but the best will make magnificent bottles in the old-fashioned style. Do not start before 1986. 18.

1977 Small crop from a cool vintage of wines light in colour with acidic edge but the better *cuvées* in the Côte de Beaune have more charm than the 1974s. Should be drunk. 11.

1978 Small crop from a late (miracle) vintage with excellent colour, fruit and balance. Have proved to have more structure than at first thought, and still need 2 years to show their full quality, but should be drunk before the 1976s. 19.

1979 Large crops of supple, fruity, quick-maturing wines, very attractive and may be drunk now. Better in the Côte de Beaune. 15.

1980 Smallish crop and not an over-all success, with some of the Côte de Beaune wines lacking colour and fruit, but much better in the Côte de Nuits. Drink before the 1978s. 13-16.

1981 Small crop of uneven wines, but passable in the southern Côte de Nuits and the northern Côte de Beaune. Drink from 1985. 12.

1982 Very large crop of wines often lacking colour and balance. Only those *vignerons* who did not overproduce and carefully selected their vats for bottling made a wine of quality, midway between 1978 and 1979. 12–16.

1983 Very variable quality due to extraordinarily high sugars and some rot. The successful *cuvées* have a dark colour, with a vigorous fruit and tannin, wines for keeping. Careful selection is needed. 13–17.

Alsace

1973 Very big crop making round, fruity wines now mostly too old. 15.

1974 Average volume, rather hard, charmless wines that have lasted. 13.

1975 Average crop, very aromatic with good acidity, especially the Riesling. 15.

1976 Average crop, the hot, dry summer bringing very high natural sugars and a mouth-filling fruit. Despite low acidity, they are holding well, especially the *vendange tardive* Tokay and Gewürztraminer. 18.

1977 Average crop of wines high in acidity and not well balanced. The Rieslings are the most successful in this poor vintage. 12.

1978 Small crop of well-balanced wine with style but not much definition. 14.

1979 Very large crop of fruity, aromatic wines, some a little too soft. The best wines will still improve. 15.

1980 Very small crop and uneven across the *appellation*. Should be drunk now, except for the Grands Crus and *vendange tardive* selections. 12–15.

1981 Largish crop, successful throughout the *appellation* and in all grape styles. Well-balanced wines with good fruit, acidity, elegant and will keep. A fine vintage. 17.

1982 Enormous crop, with many wines too soft and washed out, but some very well-made wines from good vineyards and serious *vignerons*. Less fine than 1981 and should be drunk earlier. 14–15.

1983 Average volume of quite exceptional wines, with high sugars and perfect balance. The finest *vendange tardive* wines (and even *sélection des grains nobles*) since 1921, and the best vintage in Alsace since 1959. 19+.

Anjou/Touraine, white

1973 Well balanced and fruity, the dry wines slightly too old, *moelleux* at their best. 13.

1974 Mediocre and hard, lacking fruit. 11.

1975 Well-made wines, high in acidity, now quite ready. 14.

1976 Very hot year, with the finest *moelleux* since 1959, but lacking a little concentration. 16–17.

1977 Cool summer and cold vintage, producing wines that were thin and acid. 10.

1978 Well-balanced wines with good fruit and great finesse, with some very fine *demi-secs*. A delightful vintage. 15–16.

1979 Larger crop, similar to 1978 but a little less class. 14.

1980 Average quantity and quality, light, quick maturing. 12.

1981 Very fine vintage, especially in Vouvray and Montlouis, wines with excellent fruit and balance and more length than the 1978s. 16.

1982 Very large crop, with some very good *moelleux* but slight lack of concentration and acidity in the dry wines. 15.

1983 Large crop of well-balanced wines with very good fruit and more structure and acidity than 1982. 16

Anjou/Touraine, red

1973 Light, pleasant and fruity, should have been drunk. 13.

1974 Light, but lacking in fruit and charm. 12.

1975 Firmer and with more fruit, especially at Chinon. 14.

1976 Very hot summer and dry vintage time produced exceptionally dark-coloured wines with great depth of fruit and character. The best since 1947. 19.

1977 Light and thin. 10.

1978 Well-balanced wines, very drinkable young but fading quicker than expected. 14.

1979 Very large crop of pleasant, fruity wines, now drying out a little. 13.

1980 A cool summer did not bring enough fruit, but better than 1977. 11.

1981 Well-balanced wines with good style, colour and fruit, drinkable young with the better *cuvées* still improving. 14.

1982 Very large crop, the better wines have the best fruit and colour since 1976, but are not in the same class. Fruity, plummy wines now reaching their best. 15.

1983 Crop reduced by hail, leaving a deep-coloured, intense wine high in tannin and acidity. Will make some impressive bottles for laying down. 16.

Champagne

1973 Large crop but with good acidity and excellent balance, perhaps now just past its best. 16.

1974 Hard and lacking in charm. 10.

1975 Very fine wines, particularly from the Côte des Blancs, with much finesse, now at their best. 16.

1976 A contrast to 1975, with much bigger, riper wines in the style of 1959 and 1964. Some are very impressive. 16.

1977 Hard and high in acidity. 10.

1978 Excellent wine, firm and well balanced, the most classic since 1970. 18.

1979 Large crop of elegant wines, especially successful in the Côte des Blancs. This vintage was put on sale in 1984. 15.

1980 Very small crop of average quality. Probably will not be sold as a vintage wine. 11.

1981 Very small crop of excellent quality. 17.

1982 Very large crop of pleasant wine but lacking in acidity and depth. Will be very good in the non-vintage blends. 14.

1983 Very large crop, better in the Côtes des Blancs, but less good than 1982. 13.

Northern Rhône Valley, white

1973 Large crop of well-balanced wines that are still very good. 14.

1974 Firmer wines, with more structure. 15.

1975 Too much rot at vintage time. 8.

1976 Hot, dry summer producing magnificent, full-bodied wine that is now at its best. 17.

1977 Firm wines, high in acidity which are softening out. 14.

1978 Less successful than the reds, big wines, but sometimes lacking in acidity. 15.

1979 Fine, classic wines with bouquet, flavour, weight but perfect balance. Will last well, but are now ready. 18.

1980 Very good vintage, with a rich, sweet fruit, but less complete than 1979. 17.

1981 Firm, aromatic wines, more lively but with less roundness than 1980. 16.

1982 Big vintage of extremely rich, aromatic wines (extraordinary Condrieu), as rich as the 1976s, but more expressive. Very fine and will last well. 18

1983 Very successful, not quite so aromatic as 1982. 17.

Northern Rhône Valley, red

1973 Very large crop, now losing its fruit, except at Cornas. 13.

1974 Firmer and with more colour. Côte-Rôtie better than Hermitage. 14.

1975 Too much rot, not very successful in any *appellation*. 9.

1976 Very hot summer gave some wines too much tannin and extract, but others a magnificent dark colour and rich velvety texture (Côte-Rôtie), now very fine. 15–18.

1977 High acidity gave this year a poor reputation at first, which the wines have finally proved wrong. 14.

1978 Perfectly balanced wines of great colour, fruit, power and elegance. The finest since 1961. Should not be drunk yet. 19+.

1979 Well-made wines with good plummy fruit, overshadowed by the 1978, the Hermitage being the most successful. 17.

1980 Fine, elegant wines, with Côte-Rôtie and Cornas the most successful. Crozes-Hermitage, Saint-Joseph and Hermitage are fruity and can be drunk now. 15–16.

1981 A difficult year, with much rot, but the best *cuvées* are firmer and have more potential than the 1980s. 8–15.

1982 Very hot weather during the vintage made vinification difficult but produced some very deep-coloured, aromatic wines between 1976 and 1978. 10–18.

1983 Very great promise from wines that are more tannic and less fruity than 1978, but even more concentrated. 18–19.

Southern Rhône Valley, red

1973 Large harvest, now past its best. 14.

1974 Smaller crop of firmer, more structured wines. At their best. 15.

1975 Prevalence of rot at vintage time. 9.

1976 Very dark-coloured and rich in alcohol and tannin, with a tendency towards massiveness, can be drunk or kept. 16.

1977 A light vintage, quite elegant and supple, now mature. 13.

1978 Very fine wines indeed from a healthy harvest, with intensity of colour, flavour and a firm acidity. The best year of the 1970s, by far. Can be drunk, but should be kept. 19.

1979 Large crop of smooth wines, full of fruit, less concentrated than 1978 but

elegant. Can be drunk or kept. 15.

1980 Average crop, with more body and balance than 1979, very good wines. 16.

1981 Very correct wines, but a little less fine than 1979 and 1980. Good colour and plummy fruit for drinking quite young. 14.

1982 The overripeness of the Grenache caused most of the wines to be unbalanced, too high in alcohol without enough colour and tannin. Difficult. 7–15.

1983 The *coulure* of the Grenache brought about a wine in complete contrast to 1982, dark-coloured, hard and tannic, very impressive but slow to mature. 17.

The white wines from the Côtes-du-Rhône Méridionales should be drunk young, with very, very few exceptions.

How to Use the Book

The book is divided into the seven major regions in France that produce fine wines: Champagne; Alsace, with reference also being given to the wines of Jura; Burgundy; the Loire Valley; the Rhône Valley; Provence, the Midi, Corsica; and Bordeaux. Each section is introduced with information on the soil, climate and grape varieties planted, which lead to the type of wine made. The various *appellations* are studied (although in Champagne and Alsace there is only one *appellation*), and within these *appellations* the *climats*, Premiers Crus and Grands Crus. In many instances the actual size and position of the vineyard is given, the encépagement and average production, since this information, particularly the exact situation and make-up of grape varieties, results in subtle differences in flavour. Individual growers and châteaux are singled out if their wines are the best and most typical of the *appellation*. Much of this selection is classic (one could hardly omit Château Latour or the Domaine de la Romanée-Conti) but much also was the result of my personal experience and that of my colleagues at l'Académie du Vin.

The quality rating of the wines is apparent in the text, either in its Cru status or through comparative comments. The price is based on that charged by the producer to *négociants*. In a book on fine wines, where differences in quality are generally related to financial investment or to voluntary limiting quantity, the range of price in each *appellation* is very marked. Further, the finer wines, particularly those of Bordeaux, tend to be handled by more middlemen than the *petits vins*, so that the producer controls to a lesser extent the price on the retailer's shelves. Finally, the variance in price from vintage to vintage and the speculative element in the fine wine market may cause an unforeseen change in the price charged by the producer, which may have no effect at all on that already in the shops.

	FF per bottle export	FF retail	£ retail	$ retail
A	up to 20	up to 40	up to 4.50	up to 6.00
B	20–30	40–60	4.50–6.25	6.00–8.00
C	30–50	60–100	6.25–9.00	8.00–12.00
D	50–75	100–150	9.00–12.50	12.00–18.00
E	75–100	150–200	12.50–15.00	18.00–24.00
F	100 and over	200 and over	15.00 and over	24.00 and over

Champagne

The ancient province of Champagne produces wines of the same name from the most northerly vineyards in France. The vines are spread across 5 *départements* – the Marne, the Aube, the Seine-et-Marne, the Aisne and the Haute-Marne – with a possible 34,000 hectares accepted as suitable for vineyards by the INAO, of which almost 25,000 hectares are actually planted. Four-fifths of the land under vines is in the Marne, 15% in the Aube and the rest extend over the other three *départements*. The Champagne vineyards can be divided into three regions of production: the centre of production, around the towns of Reims and Epernay, comprising the Montagne de Reims, the Vallée de la Marne and the Côte des Blancs; the vineyards of the Aube, 75 kilometres to the south-west; and the 'marginal' vineyards on the edge of the Champagne region that are in the process of being replanted. While the last two regions possess no Grands Crus or Premiers Crus, and do not, on their own, produce the finest bottles of Champagne, their wines are found in some of the finest blends.

Only three grape varieties may be planted in Champagne: Pinot Noir, Pinot Meunier and Chardonnay. The Pinot Noir represents 28% of the vineyard area and is concentrated on the Montagne de Reims, where it ripens well on the easy south-south-east-facing slopes and gives wines of depth and finesse from the chalky-sandy soil. The Pinot Meunier, covering 12,000 hectares, 48% of the area under vines, is a more sturdy varietal that ripens later than the Pinot Noir and is particularly suited to the more fertile soils of the Vallée de la Marne and the Aube. Pinot Meunier is not admitted in the Grands and Premiers Crus vineyards, but its reliability and high yield make it the most planted grape in Champagne. The Chardonnay is at its best on the very chalky soil of the Côte des Blancs, where it is the only grape permitted. It flowers later than the Pinot Noir and is therefore less exposed to the risk of spring frosts, and has a higher yield. Its qualities of lightness and finesse are essential for balancing the richness and weight of the Pinot Noir, and are very desirable on their own as a Champagne Blanc de Blancs.

The Champagne vineyards are made up of flatlands and easy slopes at a height of 100-150 metres above sea-level. The soil is a chalk base with a thin layer of top-soil. The chalkiness and poverty of this soil are

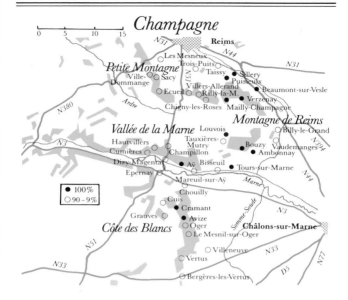

Champagne

responsible for the special quality and elegance found in the wines produced in Champagne by the Pinot Noir and Chardonnay grapes, which give a more intense wine in their native Burgundy. The climate is cool and, at an average of 10°C over the year, it is at the limit for the survival of the vine. Apart from providing at the same time excellent drainage and useful water retention, the chalk soil absorbs and reflects the sun's rays to give much needed extra warmth to the vine. The cool spring nights carry a high risk of frost, especially in the Vallée de la Marne, where for this reason the more resistant Pinot Meunier is planted. The most desirable exposition is full south (Bouzy), but there are some north-facing slopes on which the vines manage to ripen, and the slopes on the Côte des Blancs mostly face east.

Champagne AOC

To have the right to the *appellation* Champagne, the wines must be made from the Pinot Noir, Pinot Meunier or Chardonnay grapes grown in the *départements* of the Marne, Aube, Aisne, Seine-et-Marne and Haute-Marne. The still wines must be made sparkling by the process of secondary fermentation in bottle, known as *méthode champenoise*, and no stage of this process may be undertaken outside the Champagne region. Maximum yield is in terms of kilograms of grapes per hectare, and is limited to 13,000 kilograms and may in no case exceed one hectolitre per 150 kilograms of grapes, a maximum yield of 85 hl/ha. Non-vintage wines must spend at least one year in bottle before *dégorgement*, and vintage wines (which must have a minimum of 11° natural alcohol and of which no less than 80% of the *cuvée* must be from the stated vintage) has to remain in bottle three years. Finally, all corks must be marked with the word 'Champagne' and the name of the vintage if there is one. With such strict controls, Champagne is the only *appellation* in France that may, and does, omit *appellation contrôlée* from its label. Production is very variable, with an average of 200 million bottles a year, of which 5% are produced as Champagne Rosé. Price C–D–E–F.

Champagne Rosé

Champagne Rosé is the only wine in France in the making of which red and white wine (not grapes) may be blended. This will happen at the time of the *assemblage* (page 24), when a tiny quantity of still red wine (obligatorily from Champagne) will be added to the still white wine to achieve the colour, character and 'weight' of rosé desired by the particular Champagne house. Champagne Rosé may also be made from red grapes left overnight in the press, so that the must is lightly coloured, or by the *saignée* process, whereby the red grapes begin to ferment in vat and the wine is drawn off when the desired colour has been attained. These last two are true *rosés de Noirs*. A shorter maceration period will result in the very rare *oeil de perdrix* Champagnes, where the colour is mid-way between a blanc and a rosé. Price D–E–F.

Coteaux Champenois AOC

Red, white or rosé wines from the same grapes as for Champagne from the same vineyard area. This still wine used to be called 'Vin Naturel de la Champagne', which was a simple vin de table, and the current *appellation* only dates from 1974. Wines from the Grand Cru and Premier Cru villages are often used unblended, and in this case the name of the village will appear on the label; the best known include Bouzy, Ambonnay and Avize. The whites are flowery, clean and fresh, with an appley acidity that is sometimes too pronounced. The finest, as well as the only regularly successful, wines are from the Grands or Premiers Crus vineyards on the Côte des Blancs (Chardonnay de Laurent Perrier, Moët & Chandon's Château de Saran). The rosés are very rare, the best coming from the red grape villages on the Montagne de Reims and not usually seen outside France. The reds are the most famous, led by the soft, elegantly fruity Bouzy Rouge (Georges Vesselle, Jean Vesselle, Paul Bara), and wines from Ambonnay, Ay (Bollinger, Le Côte aux Enfants), Mareuil (Philipponat) and Vertus. The whites should be drunk young, while the reds can age if kept in a cool cellar. Production varies with that of Champagne, being insignificant in years of low volume and never more than 1% of the total crop. Price C–D.

Rosé des Riceys AOC

Non-sparkling rosé made from the Pinot Noir planted in the commune of Les Riceys in the Aube *département*. The wine must have a minimum alcohol content of 10°, from a yield not exceeding that of Champagne. Only the grapes from the slopes facing due south ripen sufficiently to make a good rosé, the rest being destined for Champagne. Rosé des Riceys is a natural rosé that gains its colour from 2 to 4 days' maceration, and the moment that the wine is drawn off the skins is the key to the special *goût des Riceys:* if the wine is too pale, too dark or has not the required character, it is declassified. The wine should be an onion-skin rosé, with a delicate bouquet but a firm, slightly nutty flavour. It is very rare, with an average production totalling only 7,500 bottles (Alexandre Bonnet, Horiot Père & Fils). Price C.

The Crus in Champagne

The cru system in Champagne differs from that in Burgundy or Bordeaux since, while it is geographical, it is also an index to the price of grapes from a particular vineyard. In 1919 a scale of quality was imposed on the different communes, beginning at 100% for the finest (Grands Crus) and descending to 50%. Today, Premiers Crus are indexed at 90–9%, Deuxièmes Crus at 80–9%, with the least good grapes selling at 77%. The index refers to the price for one kilogram of grapes that is determined between the *négociants* and the growers before the vintage. Thus grapes from a Grand Cru vineyard will sell for 100% of the declared price, those from a Premier Cru for 90–9% of this price, and so on. A Grand Cru vineyard may often mention 'Grand Cru 100%' if the Champagne or Coteaux Champenois is the produce of that single commune. There are 12 Grands Crus: Ambonnay, Avize (white), Ay, Bouzy, Cramant (white), Louvois, Mailly, Puisieulx, Sillery, Tours-sur-Marne, Verzenay and Vesle. Well-known Premiers Crus are Chouilly (white), Chigny-lès-Roses, Cuis, Dizy, Ludes, Le Mesnil-sur-Oger (white), Oger, Rilly-la-Montagne and Verzy. The quality of a *negociant*'s or grower's Champagne will be closely related to the quality of grapes he uses. Virtually no Grandes Marques Champagnes have an average classification of under 90%, and many still maintain an average over 95%.

The Méthode Champenoise

The *méthode champenoise* is the process whereby still wine is made sparkling by undergoing a secondary fermentation in bottle. While this method is used in many other parts of France and throughout the world, the actual making of Champagne is more elaborate and disciplined than elsewhere. The system begins in the vineyards, where the grapes are sorted, poor-quality grapes discarded and particular attention paid to keeping the grapes unbroken before pressing, to avoid pigment from the skins of the black grapes colouring the must. For the same reason, the grapes are pressed as quickly as possible in large, low, vertical presses unique to the region (although horizontal presses have now been introduced), in units of 4,000 kilograms. From this unit (known as a *marc*) a maximum of 2,666 litres of juice may be extracted, obtained by three separate pressings: the first, *la cuvée*, produces 2,050 litres, the second, *la taille*, 410 litres and the third, *la deuxième taille*, 205 litres. The more the grapes are pressed, the darker in colour and the more tannic is the must, and many of the Champagne houses use only the *cuvée*, selling off the two *tailles* to houses whose standards are not so high. The impurities in the must are then allowed to settle (*débourbage*) before the alcoholic fermentation (now mostly carried out in stainless steel vats instead of in oak casks), and this is followed, in most houses, by the malolactic fermentation to lower the total acidity. At this point, the wine resembles most other still white wines, but this is changed by the making of the final blend (*assemblage*) and the *champagnisation* of this blend or *cuvée*.

The *assemblage*, along with the *terroir* of Champagne, is what sets Champagne apart from other sparkling wines. The aim of the blender, whose skill is a major influence on the future of his particular house, is to create each year a Champagne from the wines available to him from the current vintage, plus the reserve wines, that corresponds to the 'house' style. Vintage Champagnes must follow the house style (unless there is a decision to alter this), while reflecting the particular characteristics of the vintage. Once the blend is created, from as little as three or four and as many as sixty or seventy different wines, the wine is bottled (*le tirage*) with the addition of cane sugar dissolved in old wine and impregnated with selected yeasts (*liqueur de tirage*) and is taken to the cellars to undergo its second major fermentation *in the bottle*. This fermentation (*la prise de mousse*) should take place as slowly as possible over many months to result in a constant presence of many extremely small bubbles once the wine is in the glass. A poor *prise de mousse* will result in a reduced number of bigger bubbles that will quickly dissipate. The pressure of the gas or sparkle thus produced is normally between 5 and 6 atmospheres for a fully sparkling Champagne, and only 3 for a Champagne Crémant.

The secondary fermentation takes place with the bottles lying horizontally and, apart from creating the sparkle, leaves a deposit consisting mostly of dead yeasts along the side of the bottles. The process of eliminating this deposit begins with placing the bottles in specially designed racks (*pupitres*) at an almost horizontal level, where they are turned daily (*le remuage*) over a period of weeks to arrive at an almost vertical position with the deposit shaken down to rest on the cap or cork. (Much progress has been made in automatic *remuage* in large *gyropalettes*, replacing the individual *remueur* and doing the job more quickly and cheaply.) At this stage the bottles are removed from the *pupitres* or *gyropalettes* and placed nose-to-tail vertically (*mise sur pointe*) to mature slowly and await the operation known as *dégorgement*. For this, the bottles are taken from the cellar, still in their upside-down position, and placed in a conveyor machine that passes the neck of the bottle through a freezing ($-18°C$) liquid that captures the sediment or deposit in a tiny block of frozen wine. The *dégorgeur* then up-ends the bottle, removes the cap or cork, and allows the pressure of the gas to expel the pellet of ice, leaving the wine clear. The final operation (*le dosage*) follows immediately, whereby the loss of Champagne is compensated by an addition of still Champagne with a little sugar-cane solution, known as *le liqueur de dosage*.

Depending on the percentage of *liqueur* the wine will be more or less sweet. Some Champagnes, of only the finest provenance (otherwise they would taste too rough or acidic), receive no *liqueur*, just more of the same wine; these are bone dry and may be called Brut Zéro, Brut Intégral, Brut *non-dosé*, Brut 100%, etc. In general, a Champagne is considered brut if it has up to 1% liqueur added, extra-sec at 1-3%, sec at 3-5%, demi-sec at 5-8% and doux at 8-15%. The finer *cuvées* are always reserved for the Brut. Following *dégorgement* and *dosage* the bottle is corked with the classic Champagne cork, wired down to prevent explosion, and may be either returned to the cellar for further maturing, for the *dosage* to 'take', or labelled, capsuled (*habillage*) and cartoned up ready for sale. Throughout the whole process, it is vital that sufficient time is allowed for the various stages. The minimum period is one year, from bottling to sale: most responsible Champagne houses extend this to three years, and five years or more for their vintage wines.

The Champagne Label

The label will carry the name of the producer, or owner of the brand, the address where the Champagne was produced and a registration number preceded by two letters which represent the status of the producer. The letters are: RM (Récoltant-Manipulant), a grower who can only vinify and sell the produce from his own grapes, although in some cases the vinification is carried out by his Coopérative; NM (Négociant-Manipulant), a producer who makes the Champagne, but has to buy in some or all of the grapes; CM (Coopératives de Manipulation); Caves Coopératives who vinify the grapes of their members and sell under many different labels; and MA (Marque Auxiliaire or Marque Autorisée), the brand name belonging to a buyer who may purchase his Champagne from RMs, NMs or CMs. Since almost all Champagne is a blend of wine from different vineyards, it is very rare for the name of a single vineyard (Clos des Goisses from Philipponat, for example) to appear on a Champagne label.

The Grandes Marques

The 'Grandes Marques' houses, the oldest-established companies in Champagne, are the ambassadors for the region's wine throughout the entire world. They are generally the biggest and certainly the best known of the Négociants-Manipulants who, as a whole, own only 13% of the vines in Champagne, but commercialized (in 1981) two-thirds of the production. Eighty per cent of the wines are sold as non-vintage Brut, the balance being made up of vintage Champagne, Champagne Rosé, Cuvées Spéciales or de Luxe and a declining amount of Sec and Demi-sec. The non-vintage will follow as closely as possible the house style and it is the wine on which the reputation of the Grandes Marques is based. Vintage wines will certainly have more class and probably more body and may be kept for 10 to 12 years from the vintage date. The luxury *cuvées* are the best the house can do, both in terms of the wine's presentation and its quality, which in some cases is quite extraordinary, and well worth the high price. Listed below are the major Grandes Marques, with a comment on their house style and specialities.

Ayala (0.9 million bottles, Ay) possesses no vineyards of its own, but has contacts with many growers and sells a mature non-vintage from 2/3 black and 1/3 white grapes and a very fine Blanc de Blancs. **Besserat de Bellefon** (1.8 million bottles, Reims), best known for its light Crémant Blanc and the only Crémant Rosé made in Champagne. **Billecart-Salmon** (0.5 million bottles, Mareuil-sur-Ay) sells a delicately fruity non-vintage and an especially fine, pale rosé. **Bollinger** (1.2 million bottles, Ay), an immensely prestigious house, wth its own vineyards covering 70% of its needs. Even in the non-vintage, the average classification of the crus is 98%, with the Pinot Noir dominant. The whole range is classic, slightly old-fashioned Champagne that can age well. The luxury *cuvée*, the recently disgorged 'Tradition', that has spent 6–10 years *sur pointes*, is even more robust and complex than the vintage. Bollinger also owns 0.41 hectares of un-grafted French vines, which produce a 100% Pinot Noir of a biscuity colour and unforgettable flavour. **Canard-Duchêne** (2.5 million bottles, Ludes) makes a pleasant, if soft, non-vintage and a well-presented luxury *cuvée*, Charles VII. **De Castellane** (1.5 million bottles, Epernay) has a fine 75% black grape non-vintage, an excellent vintage Blanc de Blancs and a luxury *cuvée* Commodore from only Grand Cru vineyards. **A. Charbaut & Fils** (2 million bottles, Epernay), with vineyards on the Montagne de Reims, produces a rare vintage Blanc de Blancs from Grand Cru vines. **Veuve Clicquot** (6.7 million bottles, Reims) possesses one of the three largest holdings of vines in the region, well balanced between the 'noirs' Bouzy, Ambonnay, Verzenay and the 'blancs' Cramant and Avize: big, rich, recogniz-

able Champagnes, with a prestigious non-vintage, vintage Rosé and luxury *cuvée* La Grande Dame. **Deutz** (0.7 million bottles, Ay) produces well-aged Brut non-vintage wines with a high proportion of Pinot, an extraordinary vintage Blanc de Blancs from Avize and Le Mesnil and a very fine *cuvée* William Deutz with 60% Pinot Noir. **Gosset** (0.2 million bottles, Ay) is the oldest *maison de vin* of the region (celebrating its 400th anniversary in 1984) and has a good non-vintage, but makes a speciality of Rosé (in a clear bottle) and a very fine Grand Millésime luxury *cuvée*, where the elegance of the presentation is matched by the wine inside the bottle. **George Goulet** (0.35 million bottles, Reims) makes a fine, mature non-vintage and an excellent Crémant. **Heidsieck Monopole** (2 million bottles, Reims), produces a meaty, Pinot Noir-based non-vintage and vintage, mostly from its own vineyards, and a very fine Chardonnay-Pinot luxury *cuvée*, Diamant Bleu. **Charles Heidsieck** (3.5 million bottles, Reims) owns no vineyards and all its quite full-bodied and long-lasting wine is made at Henriot. **Henriot** (1.2 million bottles, Reims) has made a name for its very dry Blanc de Blancs and the Pinot Noir-based Réserve du Baron Philippe de Rothschild. **Krug** (0.5 million bottles, Reims) represents Champagne at its most luxurious and uncompromising: the non-vintage Grande Cuvée is 35% Chardonnay, 50% Pinot Noir and 15% Pinot Meunier, with an average classification of 97%, and is commercialized at 6 years as opposed to the normal 3. The vintage is less opulent than it used to be, but very fine, and the very small quantity of Rosé, launched in September 1983, is a work of art. **Lanson** (5.2 million bottles, Reims), with 210 hectares of vines, bases its reputation on the fruity, lively non-vintage Black Label, the Blanc de Blancs style vintage and the recently introduced luxury Noble Cuvée de Lanson, a non-vintage 80% Chardonnay, 20% Pinot Noir. **Laurent-Perrier** (6.5 million bottles, Tours-sur-Marne) relies on long-term contracts with 200 growers working 700 hectares of vines to provide the grapes for a well-made non-vintage, a *non-dosé* Ultra-Brut, the non-vintage but extraordinarily fine *cuvée* Grand Siècle and one of the best Coteaux Champenois Blanc de Blancs. **Abel Lepitre** (0.8 million bottles, Reims) specializes in Crémant Blanc de Blancs. **Ste-Marne et Champagne** (10 million bottles, Epernay), one of the newest houses, is now the second-largest producer of Champagne. Most of the wine is sold under *sous-marques* such as A. Rothschild and Georges Martel. **Mercier** (5.5 million bottles, Epernay) sells a non-vintage Brut Blanc de Noirs of average quality mostly on the French market. **Moët & Chandon** (18 million bottles, Epernay) is the largest Champagne house and has remained one of the most prestigious. The Brut Impérial, 90% Blanc de Noirs, is sometimes sold a little young, but improves in bottle as do all good Champagnes, while the finest Chardonnay and Pinot Noir grapes

are reserved for the impeccable *cuvée* Dom Perignon, always vintaged and sold 6–7 years after *tirage*. The *vin nature* Château de Saran from the company's vineyards at Cramant is one of the best Coteaux Champenois Blancs. **Mumm** (8 million bottles, Reims), one of the largest houses, is best known for the non-vintage Cordon Rouge with an average classification of 95% but rather heavily *dosé* at 1.5%, and the very fine half Chardonnay-half Pinot Noir *cuvée* René Lalou. The small production of Crémant de Cramant (non-vintage) is quite exceptional. **Joseph Perrier** (0.65 million bottles, Châlons-sur-Marne) produces an elegant, fairly light non-vintage (despite it being ⅔ Pinot Noir and Pinot Meunier), a very reliable vintage and a very good Coteaux Champenois rouge from their own vineyards at Cumières. **Perrier-Jouët** (2 million bottles, Epernay) makes very good, meaty non-vintage from grapes with an average classification of 95%, a fine vintage and two excellent luxury *cuvées*, Blason de France, with Pinot Noir dominant, and Belle Epoque (also Belle Epoque rosé) where Chardonnay from Avize and Cramant is blended with Pinot Noir from the Montagne de Reims. **Philipponat** (0.5 million bottles, Mareuil-sur-Ay), one of the smaller houses, now linked with Gosset, makes some correct non-vintage, an interesting Mareuil rouge Coteaux Champenois and a quite exceptional vintage Le Clos des Goisses, from their own 98% vineyard at Mareuil-sur-Ay. **Piper-Heidsieck** (5 million bottles, Reims) commercializes a lively non-vintage that is sold relatively young and rather over-*dosé*, and by contrast a fine *non-dosé* Brut Sauvage and the excellent luxury *cuvée* Florens-Louis (60% Chardonnay) in which the 12 crus that make up the *assemblage* are nearly identical to those in a *cuvée* elaborated for Marie-Antoinette. **Pol Roger** (1.3 million bottles, Epernay) is one of the finest houses in Champagne, making classic, elegant non-vintage, perfect vintage wines and a Rosé (Pinot Noir 100%), a Chardonnay (100%) and Réserve Spéciale PR (half Chardonnay 100%, half Pinot Noir 100%) of exceptional quality. **Pommery & Greno** (4 million bottles, Reims) possesses one of the largest vineyard holdings of the region concentrated on the Montagne de Reims, producing wines of great class, ⅔ Noir, ⅓ Blanc, elegant and dry from a light *dosage*. The vintage is from vineyards classified 100%, and the non-vintage Cuvée de Prestige de Pommery will be released in 1985. **Louis Roederer** (1.6 million bottles, Reims) produces big, creamy Champagnes of great class, an excellent vintage Blanc de Blancs and is especially known for the original *cuvée prestige* Cristal Roederer, a rich, long-lived wine, and the very pale Cristal Rosé. **Ruinart** (1.3 million bottles, Reims), the first house to sell Champagne as opposed to still wine, produces a good non-vintage and a superlative, pure Chardonnay *cuvée de luxe* Dom Ruinart, which is also available as a Rosé by the addition of some Pinot Noir. **Salon** (0.5 million bottles, Le

Mesnil-sur-Oger) only makes a vintage Blanc de Blancs from the 99% cru Le Mesnil-sur-Oger, a wine of great breed. **Taittinger** (3.5 million bottles, Reims), a very prestigious house, makes a lively, dry non-vintage, a well-balanced vintage and an exceptionally fine Blanc de Blancs Comte de Champagne. **De Venoge** (1 million bottles, Epernay) commercializes some good Blanc de Blancs.

The Growers

The Récoltant-Manipulant and the Caves Coopératives possess 87% of the vines in Champagne and commercialize one-third of the production. While the 1970s saw a rise in the number of growers making and selling Champagne under their own label, this seems to have stabilized in the 1980s, partly due to the high price for the grapes offered by the *négociants*. The best growers' wines come from the Grand Cru and Premier Cru vineyards, and although it is in the nature of Champagne to be a wine blended from different crus, the Récoltant-Manipulant Champagnes have the interest to be almost without exception *mono-crus*, the product of one single cru. Some notable wines are made by: Paul Bara, Alain Vesselle, George Vesselle, Jean Vesselle, Brice-Barancourt at **Bouzy**; Michel Gonnet, **Avize**; Albert Lassalle, **Chigny-lès-Roses**; Legras, **Chouilly**; Bonnaire, Guiborat, Pertuis, **Cramant**; Pierre Gimonnet, **Cuis**; Leclerc-Briant, **Cumières**; Yves Beautrait, **Louvois**.

Champagne Bottles

Champagne comes in many sizes, but only the half-bottle, bottle and magnum are always sold in the bottle in which they were *champagnisé*. Jereboam sometimes are, but it is more normal that this size, the even larger sizes and the quarter-bottles will be decanted under pressure from ordinary bottles. The different sizes with volume are listed here:

Quarter	18.7 cl
Half	37.5 cl
Bottle	75 cl
Magnum	2 btts
Jereboam	4 btts
Rehoboam	6 btts
Mathusalem	8 btts
Salmanazar	12 btts
Balthazar	16 btts
Nabuchodonosor	20 btts

Alsace

The vineyards of Alsace occupy the north-eastern corner of France between the Vosges Mountains and the Rhine Valley in the Haut-Rhin and Bas-Rhin *départements*. The mountains protect the 110-kilometre stretch of vines from the wind and rain emanating from the north-west, to the extent that Alsace has one of the driest climates in France, with sunny days lasting long into the autumn. The Bas-Rhin, to the north, is slightly less well protected than the Haut-Rhin, where the wines tend to be correspondingly richer and more intensely aromatic. The types of soil are most varied, with a mix of limestone, clay, silt, sandy-gravel, sandstone and granite running through the vineyards, suiting the Alsatian grape varieties to a greater or lesser degree. The vines are mostly planted on hillsides facing east and south, at an altitude of 200–450 metres above sea-level, with some magnificently accentuated slopes with due-south exposure that give extra ripeness to the grapes to produce *vendange tardive* or even *sélection des grains nobles* wines in good years. The grape varieties permitted in Alsace are the Chasselas (for everyday wines), Sylvaner, Pinot Blanc (also known as Klevner or Clevner), Pinot Noir, Muscat, Gewürztraminer, Tokay (Pinot Gris) and Riesling. In contrast to other wine regions in France, the wines of Alsace are recognized not by their geographical origin, but by their grape variety.

Gewürztraminer

The Gewürztraminer grape produces the most typical and popular of the range of Alsatian wines. The colour ranges from pale yellow for the lighter wines to full gold for the splendid *vendange tardive* bottlings, with a heavily perfumed, slightly spicy aroma and explosive, rather exotic fruit flavours. The lighter wines, with a soft, dry finish, may be drunk young, while the sweeter *cuvées* need 5-10 years to show their full complexity. They are generally quite full-bodied, but this should never spoil the impression of liveliness and fruit. The Gewürztraminer does well in the heavy limestone-clay soil that is common in Alsace and represents just under 20% of the vineyard area.

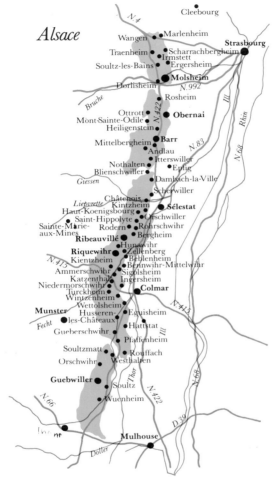

Alsace

Cleebourg

Marlenheim
Wangen •

Strasbourg

Traenheim • Scharrachbergheim
Irmstett
Soultz-les-Bains • Ergersheim

Molsheim
Dorlisheim • *N.992*

Rosheim

Ottrott
Mont-Sainte-Odile • Obernai
Heiligenstein

Mittelbergheim • Barr
Andlau
Nothalten • Itterswiller
Blienschwiller • Eplig
Giessen Dambach-la-Ville
Scherwiller

Liepvrette Châtenois
Haut-Koenigsbourg • Kintzheim • Sélestat
Saint-Hippolyte Orschwiller
Sainte-Marie- Rodern • Rohrschwihr
aux-Mines Bergheim

Ribeauvillé
Hunawihr
Riquewihr • Zellenberg
N.415 Kientzheim • Beblenheim
Ammerschwihr • Bennwihr-Mittelwihr
Katzenthal Sigolsheim
Niedermorschwihr Ingersheim
Turckheim
Wintzenheim • Colmar
Wettolsheim

Munster Husseren- • Eguisheim
Fecht les-Châteaux • Hattstat

Gueberschwihr • Pfaffenheim

Soultzmatt • Rouffach
Orschwihr • Westhalten

Guebwiller • Soultz
• Wuenheim

Mulhouse
Doller

Muscat

Muscat d'Alsace is usually a blend of wine from the Muscat à Petits Grains (the same grape as the Muscat de Frontignan) and the quicker ripening and less fragile Muscat d'Ottonel. Both are extremely aromatic and the richness and body of the former enhance the lightness

and elegance of the latter. The heady, slightly 'musky' aroma combines with the pure, grapy taste to make this wine the perfect aperitif. Muscat is a difficult wine to make and although it is much in demand in good years, colder vintages produce a rather thin wine. Production is a little under 4% of the total crop.

Pinot Blanc – Pinot Auxerrois

The Pinot Blanc now represents 16% of the production and is being more and more planted in Alsace, since it is a sturdy varietal and the wines are solid and fruity, mid-way in complexity between Sylvaner and Riesling. The Pinot Auxerrois can be known as Klevner or Clevner and has perhaps an edge of finesse over the Pinot Blanc which is straightforward and reliable. Much of the wine goes into Crémant d'Alsace.

Pinot Noir

The red grape from Burgundy is usually vinified as a rosé, as only in very sunny years (1976, 1983) is there enough colour in the skins to make a fully red wine. It is also used to make Crémant d'Alsace Rosé and may be vinified *en blanc* to be part of the blend of Crémant d'Alsace. The finer examples are from the north (Cleebourg, Marlenheim, Ottrott and Rodern) yet even at its best it is a fruity, straightforward wine with no great complexity.

Riesling

Clos Ste Hune
RIESLING 1976

Riesling is known as 'the king' of the wines of Alsace, although Gewürztraminer is called 'the emperor' and Tokay 'the sultan', and it is without doubt the most elegant of the three. In contrast to the heady richness of the Gewürztraminer and Tokay, and the clean grapeyness of the Muscat, Riesling is a wine of almost restrained fruit, with a markedly floral bouquet and a firm, clean flavour with a lemony acidity that only adds to its vitality and breed. Lighter *cuvées* are refreshing and can be drunk young, but the *réserve* or Grand Cru wines should be kept for 2 to 3 years, and may still be improving ten years after the vintage. Excellent *vendange tardive* wines are made and in great years some superlative *sélection des grains nobles* that show the full grandeur of the Riesling grape. The Riesling occupies the finest vineyard sites in Alsace and represents 18% of the vineyard area.

Sylvaner

Representing a little over 20% of the vines planted in Alsace, the Sylvaner makes a refreshing, light-coloured, crisp, fruity wine that is best drunk young. It is a high-yielding grape, which does well even in cool, wet vintages, as it is highly resistant to rot.

Tokay d'Alsace (Pinot Gris)

Although it is made with the Pinot Gris grape, the wine is still known by the old name of Tokay d'Alsace. It is the richest wine in Alsace, lacking perhaps the spicy exhuberance of Gewürztraminer or the firm elegance of Riesling, but with an impressive bouquet, mouth-filling, slightly honeyed fruit and luscious but dry finish. Tokay lends itself particularly well to the *vendange tardive* style and, despite its low acidity, will improve for several years in bottle. Tokay represents about 5% of the area under vines.

Alsace AOC

Red, rosé, dry and sweet white wines from 11,600 hectares of vines planted one-third in the northern Bas-Rhin *département* and two-thirds in the Haut-Rhin. The minimum alcohol content must be a natural 8.5° from a maximum yield of 100 hl/ha. Despite this yield being the highest in France, it is regularly exceeded and, with the exception of the *vendange tardive* and *sélection des grains nobles* bottlings, Alsace wines almost always need chaptalizing to bring them up to the expected 11°. The style varies according to the type of grape, region (soil, exposition, micro-climate) and vinification. Reds and rosés, obligatorily from the Pinot Noir, are fruity and unpretentious, while the whites have a flowery fruitiness, more or less *sec* according to the varietal and the vintage, but always fermented out to have a dry finish. Production of a *méthode champenoise* sparkling wine, Crémant d'Alsace AOC, is rising and is particularly good if the base wine comes from the Pinot Blanc. With few exceptions (see below) the wines are best drunk young. Production is nearly 120 million bottles. Price A–B.

Alsace Grand Cru AOC

This *appellation* is limited to white wines only produced from the Riesling, Gewürztraminer, Pinot Gris (Tokay) and Muscat grapes from specific vineyards. Minimum degree of alcohol before chaptalization is 10° for the Muscat and Riesling, 11° for the Gewürztraminer and Pinot Gris, from a yield of 70 hl/ha. The label must carry the name of the vineyard, the vintage date and the name of the grape (unblended). An Alsace Grand Cru should always have more structure, body and flavour than a simple Alsace, yet the final character is still determined by the grape variety, soil, siting of the vineyard and vinification. Many producers do not take advantage of the Grand Cru *appellation*, either because they find it too limiting or too confusing, and prefer to differentiate their better wines with such words as *cuvée spéciale, cuvée tradition, réserve particulière, réserve personnelle* and so on. The Grands Crus, with other vineyards under consideration, now number 26, varying in size from the 2.66-hectare Kantzlerberg to the 75.74-hectare Hengst.

They are listed here, from north to south. Altenberg de Bergbeiten, Kirchberg de Barr, Wibelsberg, Kastelberg, Moenchberg, Gloeckelberg, Kantzlerberg, Altenberg de Bergheim, Geisberg, Kirchberg de Ribeauvillé, Rosacker, Sonnenglantz, Fürstentum, Schlossberg, Sommerberg, Brand, Hengst, Eichberg, Hatschbourg, Goldert, Spiegel, Kessler, Saering, Kitterlé, Ollwiller. Rangen. Despite this list, certain well-situated vineyards such as Zotzenberg, Mambourg, Kaefferkopf, Wineck, Sporen, Schoenenbourg and Zinnkoepfle are not yet awarded Grand Cru status by reason of their *encépagement*. Price B–C.

Vendange Tardive

These late-picked wines where the grapes are allowed to over-ripen on the vines, often into December, may be made from any of the noble grapes, but are usually limited to the same as for the Grands Crus: Riesling, Muscat, Gewürztraminer and Tokay. No chaptalization is allowed and the minimum degree of alcohol plus residual sugar must be 12.6° for the Riesling and Muscat, 14° for the Tokay and Gewürztraminer. The naturally aromatic, floral bouquet of the Alsace style is thus intensified, leaving a slight residual sweetness. Only the most conscientious growers make these wines (which must be vintaged and subject to a severe tasting control), and only in good vintages and from the best vineyards. Price B–C.

Sélection des Grains Nobles

Wines resulting from extra-late picking of individual grapes affected by botrytis (*pourriture noble*), very much in the manner of the greatest Châteaux in Sauternes. The sugar in the grapes is concentrated beyond the point of *vendange tardive* by the *pourriture noble* to obtain a minimum of 14.6° potential alcohol for the Riesling and Muscat, 16° for the Gewürztraminer and Tokay. Such wines are made only in exceptional years (1971, 1976, 1983) in miniscule quantities. They possess extraordinary intensity and richness, great finesse and a fine acidity coupled with a huge, but totally uncloying, natural sweetness which permits the wine to improve over 20 years or more. The wines from Hugel are exceptional, often the only examples of this style, true works of art. Price E–F.

The Route du Vin

In Alsace the accepted grape varieties may be planted virtually at will, potentially eliminating geographical differentiation. However, certain villages and micro-climates *do* suit certain grape varieties.

The Route du Vin begins at Marlenheim, west of Strasbourg, but there is an enclave of vines at Cleebourg to the north, near the German border, where the Cave Coopérative makes some very good Tokay. The speciality at Marlenheim is Pinot Noir, usually vinified as a rosé (Michel Laugel). Another good Pinot Noir is the Rouge d'Ottrott, produced near Obernai. At Heiligenstein, the finest wine is Gewürztraminer (Louis Klipfel, Charles Wantz). Mittelbergheim is known for the Zotzenberg vineyard, with a magnificent southern exposure, where some Tokay and Gewürztraminer is planted (E. Boeckel), and more is being considered, while Sylvaner-Zotzenberg remains probably the finest example of this variety in Alsace (A. Seltz & Fils). Klevner (Clevner or Pinot Blanc) also does well at Mittelbergheim and particularly so at Dambach-la-Ville (Willy Gisselbrecht). The Gewürztraminer comes into prominence at Bergheim (Marcel Deiss, Gustave Lorentz), and at Rorschwihr Rolly-Gassmann makes full-bodied wines of an excellent quality. Ribeauvillé is particularly famous for its Riesling (Louis Sipp, Bott Frères and the crisp, long-lasting wines of Trimbach) as well as for some elegant, grapy Muscat.

Riquewihr, the most beautiful wine town in Alsace if not in France, has two spectacular vineyards, Schoenenbourg and Sporen, and two of Alsace's finest grower-*négociants:* Dopff & Irion and Hugel. All the grape varieties grow well on the easy slopes around Riquewihr, especially Riesling. Hugel has deservedly the best reputation possible for their firm, aromatic wines and their speciality of Riesling, Gewürztraminer and Tokay *vendange tardive*. To the south-east, Beblenheim and the neighbouring Mittelwihr are both particularly good for Gewürztraminer and some fine Muscat (Edgard Schaller). The large commune of Sigolsheim has an excellent Cave Coopérative, with vines in the two best sites, Mambourg (Gewürztraminer) and Altenbourg (Riesling), and some rich, spicy Tokay comes from Pierre Sparr. Kientzheim, the centre of the Confrérie Saint-Etienne, harbours the Fürstentum and part of the Schlossberg vineyard, with particularly fine wines from Paul Blanck, while neighbouring Kayserberg shares the Schlossberg vineyard which is planted almost entirely in Riesling (remarkable wines, with great purity of style from Madame Colette Faller of Domaine Weinbach). The famous Kaefferkopf vineyard at Ammerschwihr produces excellent Gewürztraminer and Riesling (Kuehn), distinctive Pinot Blanc and some fine Muscat. South of Colmar (the centre of the Alsace wine trade), Turckheim is a major wine commune with a good Coopérative and very fine wines from the four noble grapes planted in the Brand vineyard.

Further south, Wintzenheim is the home of two of the best family domaines in Alsace, Jos. Meyer and Zind-Humbrecht, who make superb Gewürztraminer from the Hengst vineyard; Wettolsheim produces some good Muscat from the Steingrubler vineyard; Eguisheim is known for its Coopérative, the largest in Alsace, and for the wines of Léon Beyer; the south-facing slopes at Husseren-les-Châteaux give very good Gewürztraminer and Riesling (Kuentz-Bas) and the Muscat comes into its own again at Voegtlinshoffen (Théo Cattin). At Pfaffenheim, the wines become more full-bodied, richer in style (fine Pinot Blanc and Gewürztraminer from Pierre Frick) and are very unctuous and aromatic at Rouffach (A. & O. Muré). The dry, limestony slopes at Westhalten are suitable for Muscat and Gewürztraminer (Alfred Heim), and the latter also thrives at Orschwihr (Lucien Albrecht, Paul Reinhart). In the very south, Schlumberger dominates at Guebwiller, with overpoweringly fruity Gewürztraminer (Cuvée Christine and Cuvée Anne), and Zind-Humbrecht makes some splendid Reisling from the newly reclaimed Rangen vineyard.

Jura

The vineyards of the Jura are among the oldest in France and its wines are perhaps the most distinctive. The *appellation* covers 1,100 hectares, all in the Jura *département*, and since the last decade has been in full expansion. The vines are planted on slopes with an incline of between 10% and 40%, at an altitude of 250–470 metres. Exposition is generally south-south-east and the soil is a heavy, multi-coloured clay on a limestone base. The climate is semi-continental, with hard winters, some risk of spring frosts, often heavy rain in summer but with dry, sunny autumns to allow the grapes to ripen. Local *cépages* are much in evidence, with the red and rosé wines coming from the Trousseau, making relatively deep-coloured, long-lasting wine; the Poulsard, seen only in the Jura, giving a light-coloured wine, often more rosé than red; and the Pinot Noir, lending a light Burgundy fruit. For the whites, the local grape is the Savagnin, which makes very particular full-bodied wines with a sherry-like bouquet, to which some Chardonnay or Pinot Blanc may be added, except in the case of Vin Jaune, which must be made from the Savagnin alone. There are four main *appellations* in the Jura: Arbois, Château-Chalon, Côtes du Jura and L'Etoile, with a total production of around 4.5 million bottles.

1 Côtes du Jura
2 Arbois
3 Château-Chalon
4 L'Etoile

Arbois AOC
Côtes du Jura AOC

Red, white, rosé, *gris* and sparkling wines from a recently increased yield of 45 hl/ha for the reds and rosés, and 50 hl/ha for the whites. The *méthode champenoise* Arbois Mousseux is usually light and fruity, especially if the too distinctive Savagnin grape is omitted. The more intense wines of Pupillin have their own *appellation*, **Arbois Pupillin**, as do the fine, elegant wines of **L'Etoile**, including a delicious **L'Etoile Mousseux**. Good growers include Jacques Forest, Jean Bourdy, Rolet Père & Fils, Jacques Tissot, Château d'Arlay and Château Grea. Price B.

Château-Chalon AOC

The only *appellation* attributed to the different Vins Jaunes produced in the Jura, covering only 25 hectares around Voiteur and Château-Chalon. Despite a legal maximum of 30 hl/ha at Château-Chalon (40 hl/ha for Vins Jaunes produced elsewhere) the actual production is often declassified due to insufficient ripeness, and the average yield is only 45,000 bottles. Only the Savagnin grape may be used, picked as late as possible, even into December. After fermentation, the wine is racked into oak barrels (*pièces* or *demi-muids*) where it will age with no topping-up for at least 6 years. As the level of wine in the barrel descends through evaporation, down to perhaps one-third empty, a *voile* or *flor* of yeast cells forms on the surface of the wine, transforming it, little by little, into a Vin Jaune, a wine of deep yellow colour with a heady, nutty bouquet of great complexity and the flavour of a concentrated fino sherry. After the minimum of six years, during which many casks may have to be discarded since they have not 'taken' the *flor* and have followed the rules of oenology to become vinegar, the wine is bottled in the squat high-necked 62 cl *clavelins* and may last indefinitely. It is best drunk on its own, or at the end of a meal, as the pungent flavour of all Vins Jaunes will destroy any subsequent wine. Good growers in Château-Chalon are Jean-Marie Courbet, Jean Macle and Marius Perron. Price E.

Vin de Paille

A dessert wine of great rarity, where, after picking, the bunches of grapes are placed on straw mats (*lits de paille*) or suspended from the rafters for a period of three months during which they become raisin-like and very highly concentrated in grape sugar. A very slow fermentation will produce an astoundingly rich, amber-coloured nectar, more like a liqueur than a wine. Vin de Paille may age for 3–4 years in wood before being bottled in special 37.5 cl *pots*, and can be kept almost indefinitely. It is usually drunk on its own and is even supposed to have therapeutic qualities. Price D (*le pot*).

Burgundy

The wine-producing region of Burgundy stretches across four *départements*: the Yonne, the Côte d'Or, the Saône-et-Loire and the Rhône. Within these *départements* are six major sub-regions: from north to south, Chablis, the Côte de Nuits, the Côte de Beaune, the Côte Chalonnaise, the Mâconnais and the Beaujolais. While fine wines are made throughout Burgundy, the greatest concentration is found in the Côte d'Or, harbouring both the Côte de Nuits and the Côte de Beaune.

In complete contrast to the age-old rival for fine wines, Bordeaux, where there are few major *appellations* and many large properties producing a unified wine, Burgundy has a large number of *appellations*, often smaller than a single Cru Classé château, each of them parcellated between several growers. Fine-quality wine in any region will result from a combination of the following factors: soil, exposition, age of the vines, yield, vinification, *élevage* and, above all, a special effort on behalf of the producer to make a fine wine. In Burgundy more than anywhere else, with scores of *appellations* split between thousands of growers, vinified, bottled and sold by either themselves, the Caves Coopératives or the *négociants*, it is the name of the bottler on the label that counts for as much, if not more, than the *appellation*. For this reason, the names of good growers or *négociants* are given, since their wines can be taken as classic examples of each *appellation*.

The idea of a classic wine has become more important with the recent (1982) increase of the permitted yields in Burgundy by between 10 and 25%. The INAO authorized these increases 'in the face of reality', but it is a moot point whether reality lies in modern viticulture being able to produce fine wine in larger quantities than before, or in the easy sale for these wines provided they carry the prestigious name. It is difficult to imagine that a Montrachet will have the same intensity of bouquet and concentration of flavour from vines allowed to produce 40 hl/ha (or considerably more: see page 11) as from the same vines limited to 30 hl/ha. The 'classic' wine is thus one that represents the best that the *appellation* can produce.

Chablis

1 Grand Cru **2 Premier Cru**

N77
Serein
Ligny-le-Châtel
Villy
Maligny
Lignorelles
Fontenay-
près-Chablis
La Chapelle-
Vaupelteigne
Collan
Poinchy
Fyé
Fleys
N65
Beine
1
Milly
Chablis
Viviers
Béru
Chichée
Courgis
Préhy
Chemilly-
sur-Saône
Poilly-sur-
Saône

Appellations de Grand Cru

Dijon

Chambertin
Chambertin Clos de Bèze
Latricières-Chambertin
Charmes-or Mazoyères-Chambertin
Mazis-Chambertin
Ruchottes-Chambertin
Chapelle-Chambertin
Griotte-Chambertin

1 Côte de Nuits
2 Côte de Beaune
3 Rully
4 Mercurey
5 Givry
6 Montagny

Fixin
Brochon
Gevrey-Chambertin
1
Morey-Saint-Denis
Chambolle-Musigny
Vougeot
Flagey-Echézeaux
Vosne-Romanée

Clos de la Roche
Clos Saint-Denis
Clos de Tart
Bonnes Mares

Musigny

Clos de Vougeot

Grands Echézeaux
Echézeaux

Burgundy

Nuits-Saint-Georges
Premeaux
Comblanchien
Prissey
Pernand-Vergelesses
Corgoloin
Aloxe-Corton
Serrigny-Ladoix
Savigny-lès-Beaune
Chorey-lès-Beaune
Beaune
2

Romanée-Conti
Richebourg
La Romanée
La Tâche
Romanée-Saint-Vivant

Corton

Charlemagne

Saint-Romain
Pommard
Volnay
Auxey-Duresses
Monthélie
Meursault
Saint-Aubin
La Rochepot
Puligny-Montrachet
Dezize-les-
Maranges
Chassagne-Montrachet
Santenay
Sampigny
Chagny
Cheilly
Rully
3
Mercurey
4

N6
N6
Saône

Corton
Corton-Charlemagne
Charlemagne

Montrachet
Chevalier-Montrachet
Bâtard-Montrachet
Bienvenues-Bâtard

Montrachet
Bâtard-Montrachet
Criots-Bâtard-Montrachet

N78

5 Givry

0 5 10 15
N78

Buxy
Montagny-lès-Buxy
6
N6

Côte de Nuits – Côte de Beaune

Mâconnais and Beaujolais

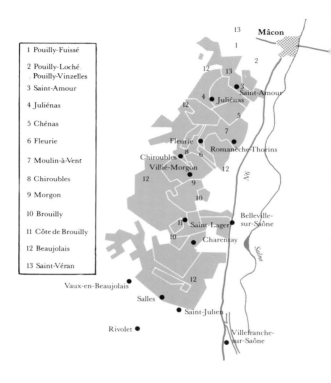

1 Pouilly-Fuissé

2 Pouilly-Loché,
  Pouilly-Vinzelles

3 Saint-Amour

4 Juliénas

5 Chénas

6 Fleurie

7 Moulin-à-Vent

8 Chiroubles

9 Morgon

10 Brouilly

11 Côte de Brouilly

12 Beaujolais

13 Saint-Véran

Regional or Generic Appellations

These represent the base of the pyramid of Burgundy wines, and may be used throughout the region, regardless of where the wine is made, provided that the accepted varietals are used. In ascending order of quality the *appellations* are: (red) Bourgogne Grand Ordinaire, Bourgogne Passe-Tout-Grains, Bourgogne; (white) Bourgogne Aligoté, Bourgogne; (rosé) Bourgogne Grand Ordinaire, Bourgogne Clairet, Bourgogne Rosé; (sparkling) Crémant de Bourgogne. With few exceptions, these should be pleasant country wines at reasonable prices, to be drunk young. There are, unfortunately, many poor-quality wines that are asked for (and sell) thanks to their Burgundy *appellation*, and there are some generic wines that are very good indeed. The important thing, applicable to the whole spectrum of Burgundy, is the name and address of the producer.

Chablis

The wines of Chablis are classified as Burgundy, even though they are an enclave of vineyards surrounded by arable land in the Yonne *département*, 100 kilometres (60 miles) north of the Côte de Nuits. The soil is the limestoney-chalk of the Bassin Parisien, also found in Champagne, on which the Chardonnay produces a complex, austere, long-lived wine, but less fleshy and rich than on the more clayey soil of the Côte de Beaune.

Chablis AOC

Chablis is a dry white wine which should be pale yellow with a greeny edge, and should never look too watery or too rich; the bouquet should be flowery, lively, fresh and mouthwatering, the taste crisp, fruity, with a certain structure and a firm finish. Over-production and/or poor vinification leave many of today's Chablis with little or no bouquet, a washed-out taste and a flat finish. It is often better to buy a Petit Chablis or Bourgogne Aligoté at a lower price, or a Chablis Premier Cru at a higher one, but good examples are distinctly delicious. Chablis should be drunk 1–5 years after the vintage. Good producers are Jean Durup, the Defaix family, Alain Geoffroy, Michel Laroche, and the Cave Coopérative 'La Chablisienne', while reliable local *négociants* are Pic/Remon/Regnard, Simmonet-Febvre, J. Moreau and Lamblin & Fils. Total production is now around 6 million bottles (from a maximum yield of 50 hl/ha, often exceeded) and is increasing as old vineyards are replanted and new sites cleared. Price A–B.

Chablis Premier Cru AOC

The Premier Cru vineyards surround the town of Chablis on both banks of the river Serein, but the best-exposed and generally the finer wines are from the right bank, to the north and east of the town, on either side of the Grands Crus. While there are officially 29 Premiers Crus, since 1967 the different *lieux-dits* have tended to group themselves behind the 12 most famous names. Some of the best known are: *Beugnons:* light, pretty wine that can be drunk early. *Les Forêts:* full-bodied, firm and needs time, with probably the best wine coming from René Dauvissat. *Fourchaume:* round and slightly honeyed, opening up quickly, with good wines from the *négociants* Drouhin, Regnard and Lamblin, and the Cave Coopérative. *Montée de Tonnerre:* lively and firm, with great finesse, almost the quality of a Grand Cru, and can keep well. Especially fine wines are from François and Jean-Marie Raveneau, Maurice Duplessis, Marcel Servin, William Fèvre, Louis Michel and the modern-style Domaine de l'Eglantière. *Montmains:* fruity and supple, quite quick maturing, with very good wine from Louis Pinson. *Monts de Mileu:* well balanced, not too had, but with the typical flinty Chablis edge; this cru is a speciality of Simmonet-Febvre. *Sechets:*

firm, elegant, lighter than Les Forêts and also very good from René Dauvissat.

Vaillons: fruity, straight-forward and lasts well; fine wines from the Defaix family and the good *négociants*. Depending on the *lieu-dit* or *climat* (which can be blended and sold simply as Premier Cru), but more on the vintage, vinification and ageing (in wood or in stainless steel), they are best drunk at 2–7 years. Production is about 3 million bottles. Price B.

Chablis Grand Cru AOC

Planted on the chalky-limestone slopes above the right bank of the river Serein, just to the north-east of the town of Chablis, a Grand Cru must have a higher alcohol content (11°) than a Premier Cru, from a lower yield (45 hl/ha). There are 7 Grands Crus, covering an area of 110 hectares now in full production, giving an average yearly yield of 500,000 bottles. They have the weight and structure of the best white Burgundies from the Côte de Beaune, but are always a little more reserved. Each of the Grands Crus has its own character and style, which is tempered by the different methods of vinification and ageing, as well as by the age of the grower's vines. The 7 Grands Crus are: *Blanchots:* supple, elegant wines with great persistence of flavour. The wines of François Raveneau, Marcel Servin and Robert Vocoret are particularly good, as well as the Domaine Laroche.

Bougros: vigorous, bouqueted wines that make up in ageing potential what they perhaps lack in finesse, the most northerly of the Grands Crus.

Les Clos: the largest of the Grands Crus and the most southern, apart from Blanchots, producing big wines, with a honey-like bouquet, great structure and great length of taste, not really at their best until 5 years old. The wines from Raveneau, Dauvissat, Maurice Duplessis and William Fèvre are exceptional. An enclave of Les Clos is the excellent vineyard called Le Clos des Hospices, now the monopole of J. Moreau & Fils.

Grenouilles: fine, but lightish wines with a pronounced floral bouquet, but not quite the quality of Valmur and Vaudésir, the crus on either side. 'La Chablisienne' is the largest owner. *Preuses:* lovely, almost feminine wines, with great finesse and charm, yet a firm finish. Very fine wines come from Dauvissat, and the *négociants* Drouhin, Simmonet-Febvre and Regnard. *Valmur:* highly perfumed wines, with more body than Preuses, but less than Les Clos: a very reputable Grand Cru, and quite quick to mature.

Vaudésir: generally considered to be the finest of the Grands Crus, Vaudésir may be drunk young, but really needs 4–5 years to develop its potential. Excellent wines come from the Domaine de la Maladière (William Fèvre), Paul Droin, Louis Michel and the better *négociants* of Chablis and Beaune. The vineyard called 'La Moutonne' (an honorary Grand Cru) is mostly in Vaudésir. A Grand Cru Chablis is an expensive wine, but one which is well worth it. Price C.

Côte de Nuits

The Côte de Nuits produces almost exclusively red wines from its 1,300 hectares of vines that run from the outskirts of Dijon to south of Nuits-Saint-Georges. There is a little rosé produced around the village of Marsannay-la-Côte, the most northern commune, while the very rare *cuvées* of white wine come from Morey-Saint-Denis, Musigny, Clos Vougeot and Nuits-Saint-Georges. Together, these account for a little over 1% of the production. The Aligoté and Gamay grapes are planted, particularly in the communes of Gevrey-Chambertin and Morey-Saint-Denis, to make Bourgogne Aligoté and Bourgogne Passe-Tout-Grains, attractive, fruity wines, but with no great character or ageing potential. The fine wines from the Côte de Nuits are made from the Pinot Noir, with a minimum alcohol content of 10.5° from a maximum basic yield of 40 ha/ha. The vines are planted on slopes facing south-south-east, the Côte de Nuits being an archetypal *vignoble de coteaux*, with the best wines coming from vineyards which are situated at between 250 and 300 metres above sea-level. Above, thinner soil and cooler weather do not always allow the grapes to ripen fully, while below the soil is too rich and the wines tend to lack finesse. The soil itself is a slightly stony marl on a base of hard limestone.

The Côte de Nuits is basically divided into *appellations communales* (Gevrey-Chambertin, Morey-Saint-Denis), Premiers Crus within these *appellations* (Gevrey-Chambertin Clos Saint-Jacques, Morey-Saint-Denis les Sorbés) and Grands Crus (Chambertin, Clos Saint-Denis) that have *appellations* of their own. Below this hierarchy come the *appellations régionales:* Bourgogne Hautes-Côtes-de-Nuits, Côte de Nuits-Villages. Due to the nature of their particular soil and exposition, each commune has its peculiar character and style, which become more defined among the wines from individual *climats*, and the names of these *climats* or *lieux-dits* may appear on the label, even if they are not Premiers Crus.

Vineyard holdings on the Côte de Nuits are extremely parcel-lated: with the exception of a few large estates, the small proprietors with less than 5 hectares dominate, and these holdings are more often than not across several *appellations*. The differences in the site of the actual vines of each grower, their age and the style of wine-making and ageing are such that as much attention should be paid to the name of the person who bottles the wine, whether grower or *négociant*, as to the *appellation* of the wine itself.

Côte de Nuits-Villages AOC

Red and dry white wines from vineyards at both extremes of the Côte de Nuits, covering the communes of Brochon and Fixin in the north and Comblanchien, Corgoloin and Prissey in the south. Most is now sold under its own *appellation*. Production of white is minute, while that of red is in excess of 1 million bottles from around 300 hectares of vines. The wines generally have a good colour and firm fruit and in good years are quite robust and can last ten years or more. The *appellation* is principally used by the Nuits-Saint-Georges *négociants* as a good-value example of wines from the northern Côte d'Or. The best grower's wines are in Brochon and Corgoloin. Price B.

Bourgogne Rosé de Marsannay AOC
Bourgogne Rouge de Marsannay AOC

Red and rosé wines from the communes of Marsannay-la-Côte and Couchey, whose vines are being progressively surrounded by the suburbs of Dijon. Only the Pinot Noir is permitted, with a minimum alcohol content of 10° from a maximum yield of 55 hl/ha. The better-known wine is the rosé, with its light salmon-pink colour from a very short maceration, and delicate strawberry-like bouquet backed up by the habitual firmness of wines from the Côte de Nuits. Along with Tavel, Palette and Bandol from the South, and the very rare Rosé des Riceys, Marsannay rosé is considered one of the best rosés in France, and one of the very few to stand up well to food more usually associated with red wines. It is best drunk young, at 1–3 years, before it loses its fruit. Average production is 250,000 bottles, including the Rouge de Marsannay, which is slowly gaining a reputation of its own. Previously made only in good years for red wine, owing to the commercial success of the rosé, Marsannay rouge is a firm, fruity wine in the style of the Côte de Nuits-Villages, sometimes a little hard-edged when young, but lasting well. The largest and best-known grower in Marsannay is the Domaine Clair-Daü (who invented the Rosé de Marsannay with the 1919 vintage); other good wines come from Charles Quillardet and Huguenot Père & Fils. The wines from Marsannay represent good value. Price A.

Fixin AOC

Red and a very little white wine from the most northern *appellation communale*. In the past, much of the wine was sold under the *appellation* Côte de Nuits-Villages, but Fixin has recently acquired a recognition of its own. A typical red Fixin is deep-coloured and full-bodied, not unlike its neighbour, Gevrey-Chambertin, but more rustic. In years of heavy production (1973, 1979) the wine can be light, pretty and fruity, but it generally needs 5 years to show well and can be very long-lived. In common with all wines from the Côte d'Or, the Premiers Crus are much finer than the *villages* wines, and well worth the extra money. The best Premiers Crus are the Clos de la Perrière (Philippe Joliet) and the Clos du Chapitre (Domaine Gelin et Molin), both *monopoles*. Les Hervelets makes fine, robust wine, while Le Clos Napoléon (Domaine Gelin et Molin, *monopole*) is softer and quicker maturing. Another good grower in Fixin is Guy Berthaut and the *négociant*'s wines are usually very sound. Fixin is one of the best values in Burgundy. Production varies between 150,000 and 200,000 bottles. Price low C.

Gevrey-Chambertin

Gevrey-Chambertin AOC

Red wine only from the largest commune in the Côte de Nuits, with a total of almost 500 hectares under vines, of which 70 hectares are Grands Crus. The diversity of the *terroir*, running from Brochon to Morey-Saint-Denis, with much of the *villages* wine coming from the plain on either side of the main Dijon–Beaune road, allied to the very different styles of vinification, makes it difficult to describe a typical Gevrey-Chambertin. They should be firm, powerful wines, with a good deep colour for a Pinot Noir, a bouquet of fruit and spice and a long, velvety finish. In good years, and from good growers or *négociants*, they are, but many wines are either too light, as a result of over-production and/or too short vinification, or too alcoholic, from over-chaptalization. All of the major domaines have holdings in Premier Cru vineyards, and while it is usually worth paying the extra money, the simple *villages* wines receive the same care from these producers as do their Premiers and Grands Crus wines. Among the growers that can be relied on are: Drouhin-Laroze, Clair-Daü, Pierre Damoy, Domaine des Varoilles, Henri Rebourseau, Alain Burget, Joseph Roty, Armand Rousseau and Louis Trapet. Production of plain Gevrey-Chambertin is very large at 1.2 million bottles a year, larger even than that of Beaune, whose vineyards cover more hectares, and there is more wine available for the *négociants* than in smaller *appellations* such as Vosne-Romanée or Volnay. J. H. Faiveley, with considerable vineyards in the *appellation*, produces fine, sturdy wines, and Leroy, Joseph Drouhin and Louis Jadot are also good. Gevrey-Chambertin is a popular name, and its price reflects this, so careful selection is most important. Price C–D.

Gevrey-Chambertin Premier Cru AOC

Gevrey-Chambertin possesses 25 Premiers Crus, from over 60 hectares, the best being on the slopes behind the village, and going north towards Brochon. Here, as at Gevrey-Chambertin, only red wine is produced and quality is much more evident than the plain *villages* wines, the 15–30% increase in price being definitely worth it. The most famous is the Clos Saint-Jacques, owned almost 50% by the Domaine Rousseau, which thinks so highly of the wine that it is priced higher than the Grands Crus with the exception of Chambertin and Chambertin Clos de Bèze. Les Lavaux-Saint-Jacques and Les Cazetiers are very fine, while Les Varoilles (*monopole* of the Domaine des

Varoilles) has great class, although not perhaps the lasting velvety elegance of the Clos Saint-Jacques. La Combe-aux-Moines is another well-known cru, with lovely pure wines from Fernand Pernot and solid, meaty ones from J. H. Faiveley, and down at the southern end of the *appellation*, on the edge of Morey-Saint-Denis, lies Les Combottes, especially fine from Domaine Dujac. A few proprietors and most *négociants* sell a Gevrey-Chambertin Premier Cru, usually a blend of more than one vineyard. The house of Leroy offers a particularly impressive range of wines which are intended for keeping. In light vintages, the Premiers Crus are attractive at 3–4 years, while the better vintages need 6–7 years to open up and are at their best at 10–15 years. Production averages 240,000 bottles. Price mostly D, some E.

The Grands Crus of Gevrey-Chambertin

Gevrey-Chambertin possesses 8 Grands Crus, more than any other commune in Burgundy. Minimum alcohol content must be 11.5°, as opposed to 11° for the Premiers Crus and 10.5° for the *villages* wines, from a yield of 35–7 hl/ha. All the Grands Crus are from vineyards south of the village, from the middle of the *coteaux*.

Chambertin AOC

One of the best-known wines of France and certainly the most famous red wine from Burgundy, Chambertin (and Chambertin Clos de Bèze) has all the qualities of a great wine: clarity and depth of colour, striking yet delicate bouquet, intensity of flavour, finesse and harmony in the lingering aftertaste. Chambertin is a big wine, yet should never be heavy in the way that a Corton may be and a Châteauneuf-du-Pape should be, which takes several years to develop the sought-after elegant, velvety character. Fifteen growers own the 13 hectares of Chambertin, to which must be added the very many *négociants* who have to have a Chambertin on their list. Of the growers, very fine wines come from Camus, Rebourseau, Rousseau, Tortochot and Trapet, while of the *négociants*, Drouhin, Jaboulet-Verchère, Jadot, Leroy and Latour are very good. Chambertin from a good vintage should be kept at least 6 years, is at its best at 12–20 years, while exceptional vintages can last half a century. Production at 35 hl/ha is no more than 60,000 bottles. Price F.

Chambertin Clos de Bèze AOC

Chambertin Clos de Bèze occupies 15 hectares on the same *coteaux* adjacent to Chambertin, going north towards the village. The wines may be sold as Chambertin, but the name of the Clos is usually added to distinguish it from Le Chambertin. While possessing the same blend of solidity and finesse, warmth of flavour and elegant finish, the Clos de Bèze is thought to have the edge for stylishness and length. (Charles Rousseau, who has vines in both crus, serves the Clos de Bèze before Chambertin at a tasting, as he thinks the former more 'lacy', the latter more powerful.) The largest holding is that of Damoy, and the wines of Clair-Daü, Drouhin-Laroze, Drouhin, Faiveley, Gelin and Rousseau are superb. The keeping qualities are as for Chambertin, while the quantity produced at 35 hl/ha is slightly less, despite the higher acreage. Price F.

Chapelle-Chambertin AOC

Extremely fine wine, although less vigorous than Chambertin, from a 5.4-hectare vineyard just south of the Clos de Bèze. What Chapelle-Chambertin lacks in weight, it makes up for in delicacy. The best-known producers are Damoy, Drouhin-Laroze and Trapet. Production is 20–25,000 bottles. Price E.

Charmes-Chambertin AOC

The largest of the Grands Crus, with 31.6 hectares of vines just south of Le Chambertin, producing a fine, supple red wine, generally very good, but occasionally not up to Grand Cru quality. The *appellation* includes 19 hectares previously (and still) classified as Mazoyères-Chambertin, a name which all growers except Monsieur Camus have forsaken in favour of the more attractive-sounding Charmes. Among the best domaines are Camus, Rebourseau, Roty, Rousseau, Taupenot and Tortochot, while the size of the *appellation* allows the *négociants* to produce some successful *cuvées*. Good vintages can be drunk at between 6 and 12 years of age. Production is about 120,000 bottles. Price E.

Griotte-Chambertin AOC

The third-smallest Grand Cru in size, after Ruchottes- and Chapelle-Chambertin, with 5.48 hectares, yet the smallest in production, averaging hardly 10,000 bottles from a permitted yield of 37 hl/ha. The wine has a beautiful deep velvety colour and seems to have more depth and personality than its neighbour Chapelle-Chambertin. Growers, all of them making superb wine, include Pernot, Roty and Thomas-Bassot (with 1.75 hectares), while among the *négociants*, Drouhin is one of the few to propose a Griotte-Chambertin. Price E–F.

Latricières-Chambertin AOC

The vineyard of Latricières covers 6.94 hectares, being the southern continuation of the Chambertin vineyard, above Mazoyères-Chambertin and north of the Premier Cru Les Combottes. In style, it is reckoned to be the nearest thing to Chambertin, yet lacking the grandeur and longevity of its neighbour. Latricières is certainly a more 'masculine' wine than Charmes, Chapelle or Mazis-Chambertin, at its best at 10–15 years. The domaines Camus and Remy produce a meaty, old-fashioned wine for keeping, while Drouhin-Laroze and Trapet make lighter wines with great finesse. Faiveley is a major proprietor (1.5 hectares). Average production, from 37 hl/ha, 30,000 bottles. Price E–F.

Mazis-Chambertin AOC

The 12.59-hectare Grand Cru is the continuation of the Chambertin Clos de Bèze vineyard north towards the village of Gevrey-Chambertin. Mazis, or Mazy, has the most finesse of the second group of Grands Crus, Chambertin and Clos de Bèze apart, and perfect balance. It matures relatively early and may be drunk at 6–12 years. Principal owners are Camus, Rebourseau, Roty, Rousseau, Thomas-Bassot (3 hectares), Tortochot and Faiveley. Production averages 40,000 bottles. Price E–F.

Mazoyères-Chambertin AOC

See Charmes-Chambertin, page 51.

Ruchottes-Chambertin AOC

The smallest of the Grands Crus with 3.10 hectares of vines situated higher up the slopes from Mazis-Chambertin. Ruchottes-Chambertin is rich and delicate at the same time, with a firmer edge than Mazis and longer-lasting. The principal owner is the Domaine Rousseau, with a one-hectare *monopole* – the Clos des Ruchottes – with Thomas-Bassot possessing ¾ hectare. Average production 14,000 bottles. Price E–F.

Morey-Saint-Denis

Morey-Saint-Denis AOC

Red and a very little white wine produced from 93 hectares of *villages* and Premier Cru and 40 hectares of Grand Cru vines. The commune of Morey-Saint-Denis is situated between those of Gevrey-Chambertin and Chambolle-Musigny, and it is only in the last ten years that the wines have made a name for themselves and sell at prices similar to other communes in the Côte de Nuits. In fact, the over-all quality of the *villages* wine at Morey-Saint-Denis is more reliable than at Gevrey-Chambertin and perhaps even at Vosne-Romanée. They have a good, full colour, an intense bouquet with a certain animal-like *rôti* overlaying the Pinot fruit, and a smooth but firm finish: perfect wines for laying down. In good vintages, they must not be drunk for at least 6 years. The white wine, mostly from the Premier Cru Les Monts Luisants planted with the same strain of Pinot Noir as discovered by Henri Gouges in Nuits-Saint-Georges, and owned by the Domaine Ponsot, is rich and full with certain Meursault characteristics. Production varies between 2 and 5,000 bottles. Good growers for red Morey-Saint-Denis *villages* include domaines Dujac, Bryczek, Taupenot, Tortochot and Truchot-Martin, while many other fine domaines make only Premier or Grand Cru wine. Average production, including Premiers Crus, 280,000 bottles. Price C.

Morey-Saint-Denis Premier Cru AOC

Although there are 25 Premiers Crus in Morey-Saint-Denis, they tend to be overshadowed by the five Grands Crus in the same commune. The high quality of the *villages* wine also means that it is not necessary to buy a Premier Cru, and the actual names of the crus themselves are less well known. Perhaps the best are Le Clos des Ormes (Georges Lignier), Les Sorbés (Truchot-Martin), Le Clos Sorbés (Bryczek), Les Sorbets (Bernard Serveau), Les Fremières (Louis Remy), Les Charmes (Pierre Amiot) and Le Clos de la Bussière, a *monopole* of the Domaine Georges Roumier. These robust, velvety wines are at their best at 8–12 years. Price D.

The Grands Crus of Morey-Saint-Denis

These are situated on the same latitude as the Grands Crus of Gevrey-Chambertin, perfectly exposed on the slopes back from the village. The maximum yield is 35 hl/ha, with a minimum alcohol content of 11.5°, while the actual content is nearer 13°. Since only the Clos Saint-Denis carries the name of the commune, the remaining four tend to be less closely associated with their village than are the Grands Crus from other communes in the Côte de Nuits, especially since two of them are *monopoles*.

Bonnes Mares AOC

Only 1.84 hectares of the 15.54-hectare Bonnes Mares vineyard are in Morey-Saint-Denis, the remainder coming from the commune of Chambolle-Musigny. Most of the vineyard is owned by the Domaine Clair-Daü, who make a fine, aromatic, powerful wine that requires long ageing in order to be at its best. Domaine Roumier has a few rows of vines here, but the vast majority of its holding is situated in Chambolle. Price F.

Clos des Lambrays AOC

Although the label always stated 'Grand Cru Classé', this was merely the opinion of the last owner, Mme Cosson, and the 9-hectare vineyard only obtained official Grand Cru status in 1981. This used to be one of the finest wines from the Côte d'Or, due partly to the superb exposition on the higher slopes above the village and partly to the great age of the vines, many of which were ungrafted. Erratic vinification led to some disappointments, and following the death of Mme Cosson the vineyard was sold in the late 1970s to the Saïer brothers, and considerable replanting has been instigated. Price F.

Clos de la Roche AOC

With 15.34 hectares, this is the largest Grand Cru of the commune, and is generally accepted to be the finest. Situated in the north of the *appellation*, with only the Premier Cru Les Combettes in Gevrey separating it from Latricières-Chambertin, Clos de la Roche is a powerful wine with great depth and elegance. The top-soil is poor and thinly laid over a solid bed of limestone, and the vines have to put down long roots to flourish. While the intense fruit of the bouquet shows quite early, the wine is really at its best from 8–15 years. Superlative wines come from Rousseau, Dujac, Ponsot, Lignier and Rémy. Production around 60,000 bottles. Price E.

Clos Saint-Denis *AOC*

Directly south of the Clos de la Roche, the 6.56-hectare Clos Saint-Denis has seen its name added to that of Morey in the way that Chambertin and Musigny have been added to Gevrey and Chambolle. The wine is lighter and perhaps more subtle than Clos de la Roche, but more reticent and less intense, almost untypical of the commune. Its elegance and harmony allow it to be drunk at 6–10 years. The domaines Dujac and Lignier are the largest proprietors and Domaine Bertagna has a half hectare. Production is now about 25,000 bottles. Always slightly less expensive than Clos de la Roche. Price E.

Clos de Tart *AOC*

A 7.22-hectare *monopole* of Ets. Mommessin of Mâcon, the Clos de Tart is a walled-in vineyard situated between the Clos des Lambrays and Les Bonnes Mares, on the edge of the village of Morey. It does not possess the richness of Clos de la Roche, but is perhaps more intense than Clos Saint-Denis, with all the velvety firmness of the best wines from the Côte de Nuits. The fact that the Clos de Tart is a *monopole* allows for more control from the vines to the bottling line, and the Morey-Chambolle character of the wine is confirmed with each successive vintage. It is a long-lasting wine, at its best at 8–15 years. Production varies, averaging 25,000 bottles. Price E.

Chambolle-Musigny

Chambolle-Musigny *AOC*

Red and a very little white wine only (from the Grand Cru Musigny), coming from 173 hectares of *villages* and Premier Cru vines. Maximum yield is now 40 hl/ha, in common with all other *appellations communales* of the Côte d'Or, with a minimum alcohol content of 10.5° (always exceeded). The soil is more chalky and less clayey than in other parts of the Côte de Nuits, and the wines of Chambolle are correspondingly more marked in finesse than weight. Their charm, elegance and 'femininity' mean they are often compared to wines from the Côte de Beaune, particularly Volnay. They should not, however, be too light, and the underlying firmness of the Côte de Nuits is there to back up the delicacy of bouquet and flavour, giving the wine a deliciously harmonious fruit and texture. These immediately attractive wines are at their best between 5 and 10 years. Domaines making fine, stylish wines include Jean Brunet, Jean Grivot, Alain Hudelot, Daniel Moine, Drouhin-Laroze, Ponsot, Marchard de Gramont and Roumier. Some other grower's and *négociant*'s wines are often too heavy or alcoholic. Total production, including the Premiers Crus, averages around 650,000 bottles. Price C, mostly D.

Chambolle-Musigny Premier Cru AOC

Of the 19 Premiers Crus in Chambolle-Musigny, the best are Les Amoureuses and Les Charmes. Les Amoureuses, situated just below Le Musigny and next to Les Petits Vougeots, is one of the most sought-after wines in Burgundy. The colour is much deeper than a Chambolle *villages*, the fruit more concentrated on the bouquet (raspberries, cherries, violets), and the taste more forceful and striking. The finest examples come from the Domaine de Vogüé (whose *régisseur*, Alain Roumier, produces an excellent Amoureuses from his family Domaine), Daniel Moine and Robert Groffier. Les Charmes, situated in the middle of the *appellation* below the village, is very fine but lacks the reputation of Les Amoureuses. Excellent wines from domaines Clerget, Grivelet (also in Amoureuses), Paul Hudelot and Servelle-Tachot. The *appellation* Chambolle-Musigny is in such demand that, Les Amoureuses and Les Charmes excepted, most growers do not put the name of the *climat* on the label, nor do the *négociants*, whose wine is generally a blend of more than one Premier Cru. These wines are at their best at 6–12 years, much more for great vintages. Price D–F.

Bonnes Mares AOC

Of a total 15.54 hectares of this Grand Cru, 13.7 are in the northern part of the commune of Chambolle-Musigny. While Bonnes Mares has the charm and femininity that is typical of the wines of Chambolle, they have a richness, depth and power that surpass even Les Amoureuses. Compared to the velvety finesse of Le Musigny, Bonnes Mares is almost tannic, and certainly has a greater capacity for ageing. A great Bonnes Mares is Burgundy at its best, on a par with the wines of Chambertin, Musigny and Corton, and will be perfect at 15–20 years but can last longer. The wines from de Vogüé, Drouhin-Laroze, Dujac, Groffier and Roumier are superlative, as are the *cuvées* from Bouchard Père & Fils, Drouhin and Jadot. Average production, including the 1.84 hectares in the commune of Morey-Saint-Denis, totals 60,000 bottles. Price F.

Musigny AOC

The Musigny vineyards cover 10.65 hectares, of which 0.30 hectares are planted in Chardonnay and constitute the *monopole* of Musigny blanc, owned by the Domaine de Vogüé. Permitted yield is 5 hl/ha higher, at 40 hl/ha (similar to the Grands Crus Blancs of the Côte de Beaune), than for Le Musigny or Bonnes Mares, but the actual production is rarely more than 100 cases of 12 bottles. While it is not in the same class as the finer Grands Crus of Puligny and Chassagne-Montrachet, Le Musigny blanc, with its lovely greeny-gold colour, firm texture and exquisite aftertaste of almonds, is respected for more than just its rarity. Red Musigny is almost without equal in Burgundy. Its perfect colour and delicate, silky, velvety flavour allow it to be compared to Château Margaux, as Chambertin might be compared to Château Latour. It is elegance personnified: almost impossible to imagine a wine more fine. The Domaine de Vogüé possesses 7 hectares, and with a combination of old vines, low yields, skilful vinification and rigorous selection at the time of bottling, produces the finest wine of the commune. Faiveley, Joseph Drouhin and the Domaine Jacques Prieur are important growers, while impeccable wines come from Roumier, Jadot and Leroy. A Musigny from a fine vintage needs 10–12 years to develop and can last more than 20. Production is about 40,000 bottles. Price F+.

Vougeot

Vougeot AOC

Red and white wines from the commune of Vougeot, of which the Grand Cru Clos de Vougeot are the most prestigious. The *villages* and Premier Cru vines cover only slightly more than 12 hectares, producing an average of 60,000 bottles of red and 9,000 bottles of white wine. The white (with a high permitted yield of 45 hl/ha) comes from the Clos Blanc de Vougeot, a *monopole* of L'Héritier Guyot, making a fine, well-balanced wine which, despite a firm acidity, is slightly reminiscent of a Meursault. The red, mostly seen under the Premier Cru *climats* of Clos de la Perrière (*monopole* of Les Ets. Bertagna), Les Petits Vougeots and Les Cras, is a middle-of-the-road Côte de Nuits but without great personality or finesse. Price C–D.

Clos de Vougeot AOC

The walled-in Clos de Vougeot comprises the same amount of land under vines as it did when the Clos was created in the late-19th century: 50.22 hectares, now divided between 77 proprietors, of whom about one-third only make between 2 and 3 *pièces* (215 litres) a year. This is an insufficient volume to vinify a red wine with great success, with the result that the grapes from these tiny parcels of vines tend to be vinified with other *appellations* and separated after fermentation, or simply do not have the depth and personality of a Grand Cru. Of the larger holdings, those from the top of the slope provide unquestionably the finest wines, while those from the more clayey, less well-drained soil at the bottom of the slope next to the *route nationale* give wines that are generally disappointing. The middle section provides fine-quality wines and, throughout the Clos, vinification counts for almost as much as – and sometimes more than – situation (this is true throughout the Burgundy region). A well-made Clos de Vougeot should have a fine ruby colour, a slightly reticent, floral bouquet with firmness and length of flavour. It is good between 7 and 15 years. Most *négociants* offer a Clos de Vougeot for prestige reasons, while only Champy Père & Fils of Beaune and J. H. Faiveley have large holdings. Grower's names to look out for: Drouhin-Laroze, Confuron, Jayer, Engel, Grivot, Rebourseau, Gros Lamarche and Mugneret. Average production, from a permitted yield of 35 hl/ha, nearly 200,000 bottles. Price E–F.

Château du Clos de Vougeot Les Chevaliers de Tastevin

The Confrérie des Chevaliers de Tastevin are owners of the Château du Clos de Vougeot, where they hold their banquets and receptions as well as the tastings to discern which Burgundy wines shall be *tasteviné*, and therefore have the right to be sold with the label of the Confrérie. The Chevaliers de Tastevin organization is known the world over, and is an excellent example of a successful propaganda machine born out of the necessity (in the 1930s) to sell Burgundy wines.

Vosne-Romanée

Vosne-Romanée AOC

Red wines only from the commune south of Vougeot and north of Nuits-Saint-Georges. Vineyards surrounding the villages of Flagey-Echézeaux and Vosne-Romanée cover an area of 240 hectares, of which 48 are in Premier Cru and 66 in Grand Cru. It is the concentration of 7 Grands Crus, harbouring the two most illustrious and expensive wines in Burgundy – La Romanée-Conti and La Tâche – that has given Vosne-Romanée the reputation of being *la perle du milieu* of the Côte de Nuits. In style, the wines of Vosne are lighter than those of Gevrey-Chambertin, firmer than Chambolle-Musigny, less concentrated but more elegant than Nuits-Saint-Georges. They should combine all the desirable qualities of a fine Burgundy, with a delicate but well-defined bouquet, a stylish, velvety depth of flavour and lingering but firm finish. Such wines, however, are more easily found in the Premiers and Grands Crus than in Vosne-Romanée *tout court*. Notable exceptions are from domaines Jean Gros, Gros Frère et Soeur, Mugneret-Gibourg and the *négociants* Faiveley and Leroy. Racy, elegant wines, at their best at 7–12 years. Average production is 650,000 bottles, including Premiers Crus. Price mostly C–D.

Vosne-Romanée Premier Cru AOC

Vosne-Romanée possesses 10 Premiers Crus, all admirably situated on either side of or above the Grands Crus. The finest is La Grande Rue, a 1.5-hectare strip of vines sandwiched between La Romanée-Conti and La Tâche, the *monopole* of Domaine Lamarche. While it does not have the satiny concentration of these two super-Grands Crus, it is a wine of great class and justifiably the most expensive of Vosne's Premiers Crus. In the north of the commune, lying between Echézeaux, Richebourg and Romanée-Saint-Vivant, are Les Beaumonts, Les Brulées and Les Suchots. In the hands of good *vigneron*-vinifiers, these wines can be exceptional, and fine examples are Les Brulées (René Engel and Henri Jayer), Les Beaumonts (Jean Grivot and Charles Noëllat) and Les Suchots (Henri Lamarche, René Mugneret, Mongeard-Mugneret, Manière-Noirot, Confuron and Jayer). To the south lie the rather richer, less fiery Les Malconsorts (excellent wines from Lamarche, Moillard-Grivot and the Clos Frantin) and the beautifully made Clos des Réas, the *monopole* of Jean and François Gros. Of the four remaining, Les Gaudichots has been largely absorbed by La Tâche, and Les Chaumes, Les Reignots and Les Petits Monts are seldom seen under their own name. A Premier Cru should be drunk at 8–15 years, depending on the vintage. Price D–E.

The Grands Crus of Vosne-Romanée

There are 7 Grand Crus, of which 2 – Echézeaux and Grands Echézeaux – belong in the commune of Flagey-Echézeaux, but as this village does not have an *appellation*, perhaps because it is on the 'wrong' (east) side of the *route nationale*, they come under the auspices of Vosne-Romanée. Minimum alcohol content is 11.5°, but is usually around 13°, from a maximum yield of 35 hl/ha. The 5 Grands Crus above the village of Vosne – La Tâche, Richebourg, La Romanée, La Romanée-Conti and La Romanée-Saint-Vivant – are dominated, La Romanée excepted, by holdings of the Domaine de La Romanée-Conti.

Echézeaux AOC

Wines from this large vineyard (30.08 ha) are often sold under the declassification Vosne-Romanée Premier Cru, which, lacking some concentration and length, they are nearer to in quality than the other Grands Crus. They do not, however, fetch Grand Cru prices. Good wines are made by the domaines Lamarche, Engel, Mongeard-Mugneret, René Mugneret, Louis Gouroux, Faiveley and the Domaine de la Romanée-Conti. Average production 120,000 bottles. Price mostly D–E.

Grands Echézeaux AOC

A 9-hectare vineyard adjoining the best parts of the Clos de Vougeot, producing wines with a rich ruby colour and fine bouquet. They are firm and velvety on the palate, in flavour not unlike a good Pomerol. The wines from the Domaine de la Romanée-Conti are outstanding, those of Lamarche, Engel and Mongeard-Mugneret very good. They need 10 years to show well, and age superbly. Production some 37,000 bottles. Price E–F (Domaine de la Romanée-Conti).

Richebourg AOC

An 8-hectare vineyard producing the richest, most voluptuous and overpowering wine of all the Grands Crus, with deep colour, an explosive floral-spicy bouquet, great warmth and generous concentration of flavour and a sturdy, velvet finish. Young, it is a little massive, and should be drunk at 12–20 years, more for great vintages. The two Gros families, Charles Noëllat, Henri Jayer, Liger-Belair & Fils from Nuits-Saint-Georges and Charles Viénot from the commune of Prémeaux, all make excellent wine; that of the Domaine de la Romanée-Conti is exceptional. Production around 30,000 bottles. Price F.

La Romanée AOC

La Romanée is the smallest *appellation contrôlée* in France, covering only 0.84 hectares just above La Romanée-Conti. It is the *monopole* of the Liger-Belair family and the wine is currently distributed by Bouchard Père & Fils of Beaune. In spite of its name and exceptional situation, it has not shown the extraordinary class of La Tâche or La Romanée-Conti, being rather hard and inelegant in comparison. Bouchard are determined to restore its reputation. Production is under 4,000 bottles. Price F.

La Romanée-Conti AOC

This 1.8-hectare *monopole* of the Domaine de la Romanée-Conti (DRC) is without doubt the most prestigious red Burgundy and probably the most sought-after red wine in the world. The vines are perfectly sited above the village of Vosne-Romanée, flanked by Romanée-Saint-Vivant and Richebourg to the north and La Grande Rue and La Tâche to the south, but even this does not explain the extraordinary elegance, purity of tone, complexity and sheer class of the wine. Pre-war, and even wartime, vintages from ungrafted vines are unforgettable, and the recent vintages, with grapes from vines over 30 years old and impeccable vinification, have again proved the uniqueness of La Romanée-Conti. It is always the last wine in comparative tastings of DRC wines, and follows the rich splendour of Le Richebourg and the satiny finesse of La Tâche with confidence. Ten years after the vintage is the earliest one should open a bottle of Romanée-Conti; it is better at 15 and may last twice as long. Average production 7,500 bottles. Price FFF.

La Romanée-Saint-Vivant AOC

A 9.54-hectare vineyard just above the village of Vosne and below the vines of Richebourg. Over half is owned by the Domaine Marey-Monge, but the vineyards are looked after by and the wine made at the Domaine de la Romanée-Conti. Charles Noëllat possesses almost 2 hectares and has recently made fine wine. Louis Latour owns the 1-hectare Les Quatre Journaux and Moillard has a small parcel. The wines should have perfect balance: initial lightness with great finesse, breeding and length. Should be drunk from 8–15 years. Production is usually 30,000 bottles. Price F.

La Tâche AOC

Separated from La Romanée-Conti by the narrow strip of vines known as La Grande Rue, La Tâche covers 6.06 hectares and is a *monopole* of the Domaine de la Romanée-Conti. Some tasters, fortunate enough to have drunk them both, prefer La Tâche to La Romanée-Conti. The colour is always beautiful, the bouquet subtle and entrancing, the taste silky and seductive with a totally satisfying finish. La Tâche shows itself earlier than La Romanée-Conti, and in light years may well be more attractive. It is perfection at 10–20 years, but will last longer. Production is around 24,000 bottles. Price FF.

Nuits-Saint-Georges

Nuits-Saint-Georges AOC

Nuits-Saint-Georges is the most southern *appellation* in the Côte de Nuits, covering 375 hectares in the communes of Nuits-Saint-Georges and Prémeaux, producing red and a very limited amount of white wine. Despite this world-wide reputation, the wines of Nuits-Saint-Georges are often a disappointment. This is partly due to the popularity of the name, which allows the poorer *cuvées* to sell at high prices, but also to the slow-maturing nature of the wine, which makes it hard and ungracious if drunk too young. A good Nuits-Saint-Georges is a sturdy, serious wine, lacking the finesse and charm of Chambolle-Musigny, the stylishness of Vosne-Romanée and the vibrancy of Morey-Saint-Denis, which needs 10 years to begin to show well. Many other fine burgundies with the fruity (blackcurrants, strawberries, raspberries, cherries), youthful Pinot Noir aroma are agreeable when young, but not Nuits-Saint-Georges, and in this respect they are like a Saint-Estèphe or Pauillac in comparison to the lighter Médocs. Once mature, however, their deep mahogany-red colour reveals a concentrated, complex bouquet of dried fruits with great warmth and length of flavour. Nuits-Saint-Georges possesses no Grands Crus, but has the largest number (38) of Premiers Crus in Burgundy, situated right cross the *appellation*. As the vines leave the commune of Prémeaux, they lose the right to the *appellation* Nuits-Saint-Georges, and the villages of Prissey, Comblanchien (more famous for its marble quarries) and Corgoloin produce Côte de Nuits-Villages (page 47). All the good domaines in Nuits-Saint-Georges own vines in one or more of the Premiers Crus, and it is generally worth paying the extra money for these. Average production is 120,000 bottles of red, not more than 4,000 of white. Price mostly C–D.

Nuits-Saint-Georges Premier Cru AOC

The Premiers Crus of Nuits-Saint-Georges cover the whole length of the *appellation*, from 6 kilometres south of Vosne-Romanée to just past Prémeaux, in a narrow stretch of vines planted right up to the tree-line. Those vineyards nearer to Vosne-Romanée have some of the finesse and style of this commune, while the most typical wines are from the south of the town to just north of Prémeaux. The commune of Prémeaux itself produces only Premier Cru wines, slightly softer than their neighbours, but with great finesse. From north of Nuits-Saint Georges comes Les Boudots, the next-door vineyard to Les Malconsorts in Vosne, with fine, elegant wines from Jean Grivot and Mongeard-Mugneret; Les Chaignots produces excellent wine from the middle of the slope (Maurice Chevillon and Alain Michelot), Les Cras and Les Argillats are well thought of. From south of the town come the finest wines, some up to Grand Cru standard. Les Saint-Georges is generally recognized to produce the most intensely flavoured, long-lived wines from its 7.5 hectares, with exemplary bottles from the domaines Robert and Maurice Chevillon, Auguste and Lucien Chicotot, Henri Remoriquet, Henri Gouges, L. Audidier and P. Missery. Just above Les Saint-Georges, Les Vaucrains (6 ha) produces deep-coloured, mouth-filling wines with great class, especially from the domaines Gouges and Audidier, and from Jean Chauvenet, Jean Confuron and Alain Michelot. As the vineyards move north towards Nuits, Les Cailles, largely owned by Morin Père & Fils, produces rich, smooth wines; Les Perrières robust, long-lived reds as well as the exceptional La Perrière white from the Domaine Gouges, an unctuous, splendidly fruity greeny-gold-coloured wine from an albino clone of the Pinot Noir; Les Porrets (including the *monopole* Clos des Porrets-Saint-Georges of Henri Gouges), Les Pruliers (Gouges and Chevillon) and Les Hauts Pruliers (Machard de Gramont) are typically Nuits in needing 10 years at least to show the complexity and fruit behind their hard exterior. It is a great pity that too many of the Premiers Crus are drunk long before they are at their best. One of the specialities of the *négociant* Leroy is bottling the Premiers Crus, each with the character of their particular *climat* intact, and releasing them only when they are fully mature. They are expensive, but a revelation. From the commune of Prémeaux come some very fine wines, many of them well known owing to their being *monopoles* of the local *négociants:* Clos de la Maréchale (9.5 ha, Faiveley), Clos des Forêts-Saint-Georges and Clos de l'Arlot (7 ha and 4 ha, Jules Belin), the latter producing a little white wine, Clos des Corvées (5 ha, Domaine Général Gouachon), Clos des Corvées-Paget (Charles Vienot) and Aux Perdrix (Bernard Mugneret-Gouachon). These wines may be drunk at 10–15 years, while those from nearer to Nuits (not forgetting the 4-ha Château Gris of Lupé-Cholet) may last a further 10 years or more. Price high D–E.

Les Hospices de Nuits

The foundation of the Hospices de Nuits dates from 1692, but the first public auction of wine was not held until 1962. The date is the Sunday before Palm Sunday, and the wines certainly show better after spending the winter in barrel than they would on the third Sunday in November, the date on which the Hospices de Beaune auction takes place. All the wines, a total of about 10 hectares of vines, are first growths. Price E.

The Côte de Beaune

The Côte de Beaune vineyards, the natural continuation of the Côte de Nuits, commence at Ladoix and end 21 kilometres further south at Chagny, covering over 2,800 hectares, an area more than twice that of the Côte de Nuits. Vines are planted on the right (west) side of the RN 74 right up to a height of 400 metres, with the accompanying risks of spring frost, while, with some few exceptions, wines from the left of the main road may only take the *appellation* Bourgogne. The rocky, limestone-based terrain is covered in part with a deep layer of dark-coloured soil, suitable for full-bodied red wines, and in other parts with a lightish marl, best for fine white wines. A higher proportion of chalk gives wines of more finesse than body, such as the lighter crus of Beaune and Savigny, while a more stony, clayey soil is found at Pommard and Volnay. The exposition of the vineyards is from north-east to south-west, and it is this diversity of exposition allied to the nuances of soil and elevation tht give the wines of each commune their different character. In contrast to the Côte de Nuits, a high proportion of the wines produced on the Côte de Beaune are white, and these are in several cases superior to the red wines from communes where both are produced. Some communes (Pommard, Volnay) produce exclusively red wines and some *appellations* (Corton-Charlemagne, Montrachet) exclusively white wine. Apart from the Aligoté and Gamay grapes, for the minor but pleasant wines Bourgogne-Aligoté and Bourgogne Passe-Tout-Grains, Pinot Noir is planted for red wines, and Chardonnay and a very little Pinot Blanc for the whites.

Côte de Beaune-Villages AOC

Red wine only from Pinot Noir grapes planted in 17 communes in the Côte d'Or and parts of the Saône-et-Loire, with a minimum alcohol content of 10.5° (almost always exceeded) from a maximum yield of 40 hl/ha. The following *appellations* may, and often do, sell their wine under the Côte de Beaune-Villages label, and this is obligatory if wines from two or more *appellations* are blended: Auxey-Duresses, Blagny, Chassagne-Montrachet, Cheilly-lès-Maranges, Chorey-lès-Beaune, Dezize-lès-Maranges, Ladoix, Meursault, Monthélie, Pernand-Vergelesses, Puligny-Montrachet, Saint-Aubin, Saint-Romain, Sampigny-lès-Maranges, Santenay, Savigny-lès-Beaune. The wine should naturally have all the qualities of a fine *villages:* an attractive ruby colour and distinctively Pinot bouquet and flavour. Depending on the vintage, they are at their best between 3 and 8 years. Many *négociants* show a reliable Côte de Beaune-Villages, while if the wine is domaine-bottled from a grower, the address on the label will indicate the origin. Production varies not only with the size of the vintage, but also according to the decision of the grower or *négociant* to use the individual *appellation* or not. Average production is around 1 million bottles. Price B.

Auxey-Duresses AOC

Red and white wine from 150 hectares north-west of Meursault, next door to Monthélie. The whites resemble a minor Meursault, lively and stylish, and are best drunk young before they maderize. The reds are rougher and harder than Monthélie and often lack fruit in poor years. There are two Premiers Crus of note: Le Val, with fine wines from Jean Prunier, Gérard Creusefond and Bernard Roy; and Les Duresses, again good from Bernard Roy and especially so from Jean-Pierre Diconne and Ropiteau-Mignon. The white Auxey from the Duc de Magenta is crisp and elegant and many growers from Meursault (Ampeau, Roulot) have vines here. The local *négociant*, La Maison Leroy, makes a Meursault-style white and a Pommard-style red of very high quality. Much of the wine of Auxey is still bought by the Beaune *négociants* to make up their *cuvées* of Bourgogne blanc or Côte de Beaune-Villages. Production is around 500,000 bottles of red, 160,000 of white. Price B.

Chorey-lès-Beaune AOC

Red wine (although the *appellation* does allow for white, only a few barrels are made each year) from an 121-hectare *appellation* almost entirely planted on the plain to the east of the RN 74. While most of the wine is sold under the Côte de Beaune-Villages label, the efforts of local growers including the domaines Jacques Germain, Goud de Beaupuis, Maurice Martin and especially Tollot-Beaut, have produced consistently fine wines to have given Chorey-lès-Beaune its own reputation. They have an attractive, lively fruit with a firm, slightly rustic finish. Of the *négociants*, Drouhin has a particularly good Chorey. Best at 4–8 years. Average production 500,000 bottles. Price B–low C.

Ladoix *AOC*

Mostly red, with a very little white wine, from Ladoix-Serrigny, the most northern commune of the Côte de Beaune. In the past, the wines were sold as Aloxe-Corton, and are now mostly seen under the Côte de Beaune-Villages label. The Premiers Crus, of which the best are Les Maréchaudes, La Toppe au Vert and Les Lolières, still carry the *appellation* Aloxe-Corton, while the best part of the vineyard, Le Rognet and Les Vergennes, are classified Grand Cru Corton. This leaves around 300,000 bottles of red and 15,000 of white *villages* wine, with some excellent *cuvées* from domaines Cachat, Capitain, Chevalier and Nudant. The red Ladoix is firm, fruity, rather acidic when young and long-lasting, while the white is deliciously clean yet also quite firm. Price low C.

Monthélie *AOC*

Mostly red, with a little white wine, produced from 100 hectares west of Volnay and north of Meursault. The reds are said to have the finesse of a Volnay and the power of a Pommard, which is generally true, albeit in a minor key. The finest wine in the *appellation* comes from the Château de Monthélie, where le Comte Robert de Suremain makes a deep-coloured, long-lasting wine (especially his *tête-de-cuvée*) from very old vines. The Premier Cru Les Champs-Fulliots, a continuation of Les Caillerets from the commune of Volnay, makes a rounded, fruity, harmonious wine (domaines Boussey, Ropiteau-Mignon), while that of Les Duresses, from the other side of the commune, above Auxey-Duresses, is elegant but lighter. The white wine is fruity and agreeable and should be drunk young. Other good domaines with vines in Monthélie are Thévenin-Monthélie, Deschamps, Maurice Bourgeois, Monthélie-Douhairet and Potinet-Ampeau, Parent and Roulot, and reliable *négociants* are Chanson, Leroy and Ropiteau. Monthélie can be drunk at 3–6 years, but the better *cuvées* age well. Average production 350,000 bottles of red, 7,000 of white. Price high B–low C.

Saint-Aubin *AOC*

Red and white wines from 120 hectares of vines planted entirely *en coteaux* up behind Chassagne- and Saligny-Montrachet. The white has great finesse, with a refreshing acidity and slightly nutty finish. It can be drunk very young, but is best at 3–4 years. The Premiers Crus Les Frionnes and Les Murgers-des-Dents-de-Chien are particularly fine. The reds have a lovely cherry-ruby colour and good fruit, and may be drunk at 3–5 years. The most important producer is grower-*négociant* Raoul Clerget, and other excellent wines come from domaines Jean Lamy, Thomas, Roux and Colin. Average production 250,000 bottles of red, 120,000 of white. Price B.

Saint-Romain AOC

Red and white wine from 140 hectares in the hills above Meursault and Auxey-Duresses. Although geographically in the Hautes-Côtes de Beaune, it is classified as a Côte de Beaune, yet is the only commune to have no Premiers Crus. The whites are fine, with good, sometimes too much, acidity, which allows them to improve with age. The reds have a good colour, are rather rustic and perhaps lack charm, but age well. Good domaines are Fernand Bazenet, Henri Buisson and René Thévenin-Monthélie. Production is around 200,000 bottles of red, 160,000 of white. Price B.

Aloxe-Corton

Aloxe-Corton AOC

Almost entirely red wine (with 2,000 or so bottles of white wine) from the commune of Aloxe-Corton. Although situated in the Côte de Beaune, the wines of Aloxe have much in common with those of the Côte de Nuits, with a deep colour and a solid, even rough, fruit that needs some years to soften.

They are well known through the local *négociants*, Latour and La Reine Pedauque, while particularly fine examples come from the domaines Antonin Guyon, Daniel Senard, Tollot-Beaut and Michel Voarick. They are at their best at 6–12 years after the vintage. Production, including the Premiers Crus, around 650,000 bottles. Price low D.

Aloxe-Corton Premier Cru AOC

Whether from the commune of Ladoix-Serrigny or Aloxe-Corton, the Premiers Crus are situated at the beginning of the slope, between the *villages* wines nearer the plain and the Grands Crus higher up. The wines, particularly those from Les Vazolières, Les Fournières, Les Maréchaudes and Les Paulands, are more intense yet with more finesse than Aloxe-Corton *simple*, and last longer. Price D.

Corton AOC

The Grand Cru of Corton covers nearly 120 hectares in the communes of Ladoix-Serrigny and Aloxe-Corton. If the wine comes from one of the *climats* with Grand Cru status (Bressandes, Clos du Roi, etc.), the name of the *climat* is generally added after Corton. The hillside vineyards of Corton are perhaps the most impressive of the Côte de Beaune. At the top, just under the Corton woods, is Le Corton, which gives severe, straightforward wines, finally maturing with great style, and the high incidence of limestone suits the Chardonnay grape, which produces an elegant, firm white wine, with a little less richness than Corton-Charlemagne. The major proprietors in Le Corton are Bouchard Père & Fils. Directly below Le Corton are the three best-known Grands Crus: Le Clos du Roi, producing deep-coloured, richly textured wines, especially fine from the domaines Chandon de Briailles, Dubreuil-Fontaine, Prince de Mérode, Baron Thénard, Michel Voarick and Daniel Senard; Les Renardes, perhaps (as the name suggests) rather more animal and aggressive, with superb long-lasting wines from the late Michel Gaunoux; and Les Bressandes, beautifully balanced wines of great finesse but still with the power of Corton, with excellent *cuvées* from Chandon de Briailles, Tollot-Beaut, Laleure-Piot, Pierre Poisot and Max Quenot. Of the other Grands Crus, Les Pougets is lighter, almost a feminine Corton (Louis Jadot owns 2.5 hectares here), Le Prince de Mérode (Domaine

de Serrigny) makes a splendidly meaty wine from the upper part of Les Maréchaudes, and Les Languettes (Domaine Voarick), Les Grèves (Tollot-Beaut), La Vigne au Saint (Domaine Belland, Louis Latour), Les Perrières, and the *monopole* Clos des Meix of Daniel Senard all combine the richness and style of a typical Corton. The largest owner in Corton is the Domaine Louis Latour, with 16 hectares of various *climats*, as well as the 2.75-hectare *monopole* Clos de la Vigne au Saint. The wine is vinified at Château de Grancey and sold as Château de Corton-Grancey, an honorary Grand Cru. Special mention should be made of the Cortons sold by La Maison Leroy, that carry the individual names of the Grand Cru *climats*, and are rarely surpassed in quality and ageing potential by any other wines throughout the Côte d'Or. The red wines of Corton seem to combine the splendid structure of the Côte de Nuits with the supple elegance of the Côte de Beaune. They should on no account be drunk young, being at their best only after being allowed to age for 10 or many more years. Average production, from a maximum yield of 35 hl/ha, totals 350,000 bottles of red wine, 5,000 of white. Price E–F.

Corton blanc AOC

Very small amount of white wine from the communes of Ladoix-Serrigny and Aloxe-Corton, not to be confused with Corton-Charlemagne. The finest wine is the Corton-Vergennes, bequeathed to the Hospices de Beaune by Paul

Chanson in 1975, which is planted in Pinot Blanc, not Chardonnay. The Domaine Chandon de Briailles makes a very fine Corton blanc from the Bressandes vineyard, planted half in Chardonnay, half in Pinot Blanc. Price E.

Corton-Charlemagne AOC

White wines only from vines planted on the higher, south-west-facing slopes of the communes of Aloxe-Corton and Pernand-Vergelesses. Corton-Charlemagne is sometimes placed alongside Le Montrachet as the finest expression of white Burgundy. While its rich, nutty wines have perhaps more in common with those of Meursault than with the floral wines of the Montrachet family, the grandiose structure and extraordinarily long life places the best in the category of works of art. It should never be drunk young, since the colour (changing from a butter-coloured yellow to a rich greeny-gold), the bouquet (a mixture of Chardonnay fruit, almonds, cinnamon, honey and oak) and the flavour (high in natural acidity despite being also, at 13–14°, quite rich in alcohol) need at least 2 years in bottle to harmonize, and may improve for 10 years or more. Quite spectacular wines are from Louis Latour and Louis Jadot, Bonneau du Martray and Dubreuil-Fontaine. Those from Bouchard Père & Fils, the domaines Roland Rapet, André Thiély and Laleure-Piot are very fine, and the Hospices de Beaune possesses a highly prized parcel of ¼ ha, the Cuvée François de Salins. (Many proprietors in Corton-Charlemagne make an excellent Bourgogne Aligoté.) Production rarely exceeds 150,000 bottles. Price F.

Pernand-Vergelesses AOC

Red and white wines from a 143-hectare commune between Aloxe-Corton and Savigny-lès Beaune. The reds, most of which are now sold under the *appellation* Pernand-Vergelesses rather than Côte de Beaune-Villages, are a little hard and rough when young, but age well, and the simple *villages* wine is one of the best values on the Côte d'Or. The Premier Cru Ile de Vergelesses produces without doubt wines with the most finesse, length and harmony of the commune, with excellent examples coming from the domaines Chandon de Briailles, Dubreuil-Fontaine and Laleure-Piot, while Les Vergelesses and Les Fichots (domaines Thiély and Doudet-Naudin) produce full-bodied, long-lasting wines. The *villages* wines need 4–5 years and the Premiers Crus 5–6. Les Caradeaux, just below the Corton-Charlemagne vines from the commune, produces a fine, none-too-soft white wine, a speciality of Chanson Père & Fils and Louis Jadot of Beaune. In general, the whites are firm, with a mouth-watering acidity, excellent mid-way in a meal between the fine Aligoté made in the village and the exceptional Corton-Charlemagne. Production is around 275,000 bottles of red wine, 50,000 of white. Price C.

Savigny-lès-Beaune AOC

Red and a little white wine from nearly 400 hectares in the commune of Savigny, surrounded by the vines of Pernand-Vergelesses, Aloxe-Corton and Beaune. The *villages* wines are generally attractive but rather light, and while they have the advantage of being able to be enjoyed young, they do not have the quality and intensity of the Premiers Crus. The finer wines of Savigny are of two different styles: the slopes on the Pernand-Vergelesses side of the *appellation* produce wines with a firm backbone that develop a silky texture and floral bouquet with age. The best *climats* are Les Clous, Les Serpentières (domaines Louis Ecard-Guyot and Pierre Guillemont), Les Guettes (domaines Pavelot, rather heavy wines from Doudet-Naudin, and Henri de Villamont), Les Lavières (deep-coloured, fleshy wines, especially from Pierre Bitouzet, Chandon de Briailles and Tollot-Beaut) and Aux Vergelesses (the most delicate and bouqueted, with lovely wines from Simon Bize & Fils); the slopes to the south, near to Beaune, with a more gravelly, less clayey soil, produce wines that are rounder and more complete and open up earlier than those from the other side. The best known are Les Marconnets, almost Beaune in style, Les Dominodes (solid, meaty wines, especially from Clair Daü), Les Jarrons (Ecard-Guyot, Valentin-Bouchotte), and the more delicate Les Rouvrettes. With its proximity to Beaune, it is not surprising that the local *négociants* have considerable holdings in Savigny, and the light, old-fashioned wines of Chanson (Les Marconnets, Les Dominodes), the richer Les Lavières from Bouchard Père & Fils, and the long-lasting *cuvées* from Leroy are good examples. A fine red Premier Cru from Savigny is sheer elegance and is sometimes likened to wines from Vosne-Romanée. They begin to be at their best after 6 years. The white Savigny-lès-Beaune is stylish and elegant, with a little less depth than the Pernand blanc, one of the finest examples coming from the Vergelesses vineyard of the Domaine Louis Jacob. Production of red Savigny is the third largest on the Côte de Beaune after Beaune and Pommard, averaging approximately 1.2 million bottles, with only about 45,000 bottles of white. They both represent good value for money. Price C.

Beaune

Beaune AOC

Mostly red wine, with about 5% of the total in white, produced from 538 hectares of vines running for 2 kilometres to the north and south of Beaune. Beaune is thus the largest commune in the Côte d'Or, although the quantity of wine produced is far exceeded by Gevrey-Chambertin from much smaller acreage. Although the town of Beaune is the centre of the Burgundy wine trade and despite the undisputed quality of wines produced from its vineyards, Beaune sells for less than Volnay or Pommard. Perhaps the size of the vineyards, however well exposed, which are owned largely by the town's *négociants*, offers such a range of Premiers Crus and different 'house styles' as to lead to confusion. Yet even the *villages* wine generally has a good colour and body, a clean fruit aroma and harmonious finish. Most of the vines in the commune are classified Premier Cru, so the simple *appellation* Beaune is not common, but good wines are to be had from the domaines Bernard Delagrange, Michel Gaunoux and Thévenin-Monthélie as well as some *négociants*. This *appellation* must not be confused with Côte de Beaune, originally a parallel *appellation* to Beaune, but one which is now dying out and has recently been limited to a few thousand bottles of red and white wine (domaines Marchard de Gramont and Voiret), nor with Côte de Beaune-Villages (page 64). May be drunk from 4–8 years after the vintage. Price C.

Beaune Premier Cru AOC

The style of the many Premiers Crus of Beaune are (allowing for the variations in the 'house styles' of the *négociants*), like those of Savigny, different between the north and the south of the vineyard. To the north they are firm and complete, with a velvety finish, wines of great breed and distinction that are excellent at 10 years and may last 20. The best known, from the borders with Savigny to the RN 470, are: Les Marconnets (classically light wines from Chanson, classically robust wines from Bouchard Père); Le Clos du Roi (perhaps the finest of all, from Tollot-Beaut, Robert Ampeau, Chanson, Louis Jadot, Louis Latour); the robust Les Perrières (Louis Latour); the lighter Clos des Fèves (Chanson); Les Cent Vignes (fleshy, fruity wines from domaines Duchet, Albert Morot and Besancenot-Mathouillet); Les Bressandes (velvety-soft, harmonious wines from Duchet, Albert Morot, Jaffelin, Louis Jadot); the extremely fine Les Grèves (Tollot-Beaut, Jean Darviot, Besancenot-Mathouillet, not forgetting the 4-hectare *monopole* of Bouchard Père, La Vigne de l'Enfant Jésus); Les Teurons (harmonious and aromatic, lovely elegant wines from Jacques Germain, more full-bodied from Bouchard Père and Louis Jadot); and Les Cras (including the *monopole* Le Clos de la Féguine of Domaine Jacques Prieur). South of the RN 470, going towards Pommard and Volnay, the wines are just as elegant, but softer and quicker maturing. The well-known crus include: La Montée Rouge (firm, lightish, Gaston Boisseaux, Léon Violland); Le Clos de la Mousse, *monopole* of Bouchard Père; Les Champimonts (Chanson, Coron Père & Fils); Les Avaux (Champy, Jaffelin, Patriarche); Les Aigrots; Les Vignes Franches (Louis Latour, and the very fine Clos des Ursules, *monopole* of Louis Jadot); Le Clos des Mouches, best known for the exceptionally stylish wines, both red and white, from Joseph Drouhin; Les Boucherottes (Louis Jadot) and, just on the edge of Pommard, Les Epenottes (domaines Parent, Mussy). Mention should also be made of Bouchard Père's red and white Beaune du Château, a blend of several Premiers Crus, and many fine wines from Leroy and Remoissenet. Total production, including the *villages* wines averages around 1.5 million bottles of red, 70,000 of white. Price high C–D.

Les Hospices de Beaune

The Hôtel-Dieu in Beaune was founded in the middle of the 15th century by Nicolas Rolin, chancellor to the Duchy of Burgundy, and his wife, Guigone de Salins. Since its inception, Les Hospices de Beaune, as it is more popularly known, has received legacies of all kinds, the most famous and profitable being the parcels of vines bequeathed to the Hospices, the produce of which is sold on the third Sunday in November at the largest (in financial terms) charity sale in the world. Today, Les Hospices possesses 55 hectares of Premier and Grand Cru vines, of which 1.5 are in the Côte de Nuits. They comprise 25 *cuvées* of red and 9 *cuvées* of white wine, sold under the following *appellations*, followed by the names of the benefactors:

Red wines

Mazis-Chambertin, Cuvée Madeleine Collingnon.
Corton, Cuvée Charlotte Dumay.
Corton, Cuvée Docteur Peste.
Pernand-Vergelesses, Cuvée Rameau-Lamarosse.
Savigny-lès-Beaune, Cuvée Forneret.
Savigny-lès-Beaune, Cuvée Fouquerand.
Savigny-lès-Beaune, Cuvée Arthur Girard.
Beaune, Cuvée Nicolas Rolin.
Beaune, Cuvée Guigone de Salins.
Beaune, Cuvée Clos des Avaux.

Beaune, Cuvée Brunet.
Beaune, Cuvée Maurice
Drouhin.
Beaune, Cuvée Hugues et
Louis Bétault.
Beaune, Cuvée Rousseau-
Deslandes.
Beaune, Cuvée Dames
Hospitalières.
Beaune, Cuvée Cyrot
Chaudron.
Pommard, Cuvée Cyrot
Chaudron.
Pommard, Cuvée Dames de
la Charité.
Pommard, Cuvée Billardet.
Volnay, Cuvée Blondeau.
Volnay, Cuvée Général
Muteau.
Volnay-Santenots, Cuvée
Jehan de Massol.
Volnay, Cuvée Gauvain.
Monthélie, Cuvée Lebelin.
Auxey-Duresses, Cuvée
Boillot.

White wines

Corton-Charlemagne,
Cuvée François de Salins.
Corton-Vergennes, Cuvée
Paul Chanson.
Meursault-Genevrières,
Cuvée Baudot.

Meursault-Genevrières,
Cuvée Philippe le Bon.
Meursault-Charmes, Cuvée
de Bahèzre de Lanlay.
Meursault-Charmes, Cuvée
Albert Grivault.
Meursault, Cuvée Jehan
Humblot.
Meursault, Cuvée Loppin.
Meursault, Cuvée Goureau.

Following much criticism for
unreliable wine-making and
great variation in the quality
even between different barrels
of the same *cuvée*, a modern
cuverie has been installed at
the back of the Hôtel-Dieu.
All the wines are lodged in
new oak barrels, and in
plentiful years like 1982 and
1983, a pre-selection is made
so that the least successful
barrels are not presented at
auction. The Hospices de
Beaune delivers its own
distinctive labels to each
purchaser, carrying with
them the prestige that
partially justifies the high
price of these wines. Price
E–F.

Pommard

Pommard AOC

Red wine from 340 hectares of
vines situated between
Beaune in the north and
Volnay in the south.
Pommard has a reputation for
being full-bodied to the point
of heaviness, the old-
fashioned idea of a typical
Burgundy, but the vines being
where they are, between
Beaune and Volnay, it is
nothing of the sort. The wines
from the bottom of the slopes,
between the RN 73 and RN
74, do tend to be full and
tannic, but those higher up
have a firmness and elegance

that is never heavy. The
popularity of the name has
made Pommard a fixture on
the wine lists of most
négociants, and many of these
are lacking in fruit, over-
chaptalized, or plain dull and,
as such, over-priced. As is
usual in Burgundy, while
there are some good *villages*
wines, the real quality and
value are to be found in the
Premiers Crus. Production of
Pommard, Premiers Crus
included, is the second largest
on the Côte de Beaune and
the total averages around
1.4 million bottles.
Price high C–low D.

Pommard Premier Cru AOC

There are no Grands Crus in Pommard, but Les Rugiens (and particularly Les Rugiens-Bas) and Les Epenots are certainly of Grand Cru quality. They are very different in style: Les Rugiens, with its reddish, ferruginous soil, produces sumptuous, deep-coloured wines with the weight of a Corton and the elegance of a Volnay. The domaines Mme de Courcel and Jules Guillemard are very fine, but are eclipsed by the Rugiens of Michel Gaunoux and Hubert de Montille which represent Burgundy at its best. Les Epenots is softer, with a rich, heady bouquet and velvet finish that is sometimes compared to a Musigny. Les Grands Epenots of Michel Gaunoux is exceptional, and excellent wines come from domaines Parent, Mme de Courcel, Jean Monnier and Pothier-Rieusset. On the

Beaune border lies the Clos des Epeneaux, *monopole* of le Comte Armand, not in fact a Premier Cru, but making rich, velvety wines of excellent quality from a high proportion of old vines. On the other side of the road is the 20-hectare *monopole* (Le Château de Pommard, whose wines are finer than the exposition of the vines (all planted on the plain) would suggest. Other fine Premiers Crus are Les Pézerolles (de Montille), Les Chaponnières (Parent), Les Arvelets (Gaunoux), Les Jarollères (light, elegant, Domaine de la Pousse d'Or), Le Clos de la Commaraine (*monopole* of Jaboulet-Vercherre), Le Clos Blanc (Roger Clerget), Le Clos du Verger (Pothier-Rieusset) and Le Clos Saint-Jean (Domaine Lahaye). Of the *négociants*, Louis Latour has a *cuverie* in the village, Drouhin of Beaune and Ropiteau of Meursault have some fine *cuvées*, and the firmness, intensity and ageing potential of the better Premiers Crus are very well seen in the wines of Leroy. A good Pommard needs 10 years to open up and is better at 15 or more. Price high D–low E.

Volnay

Volnay AOC

Red wine from 215 hectares of vines on easy slopes overlooking the Saône valley. They are considered the most lissom, bouqueted, expressive wines of the Côte de Beaune and are often compared with Chambolle-Musigny. The style is more homogenous than in any other commune in

Burgundy, with the words 'graceful, elegant, smooth, harmonious' applying to both *villages* and Premiers Crus. A Volnay *tout court* may be drunk at 4–5 years, when its violetty bouquet begins to expand and will improve for a few years more. Production, including Premiers Crus, around 1 million bottles. Price high C–low D.

Volnay Premier Cru AOC

The Premiers Crus in Volnay are neatly arranged on either side of the RN 73, with the woods above and the *villages* wines below. The vineyards above the road, with a higher proportion of limestone in the soil, tend to produce lighter, quicker maturing wines than those from the more iron-based soil below. Of the higher vineyards, the largest is Le Clos des Chênes, with firm, elegant wines from Michel Larfage and Louis Glantenay; continuing north, Les Taille Pieds (domaines d'Angerville, de Montille), produces wines that are more complete; around the village of Volnay, there are four *monopoles* in Premier Cru: Le Clos du Verseuil (Domaine Clerget), the delicious Clos d'Audignac, the spectacularly stylish and elegant Clos de la Bousse d'Or (both Domaine de la Pousse d'Or) and the fiery, even tannic Clos des Ducs (Domaine d'Angerville); after these last two, Les Angles (Henri Boillot) and Les Fremiets (Bouchard Père) tend to suffer by comparison. Below the road, descending towards Meursault, the most famous vineyard is Les Caillerets, perhaps the most typical Volnay, allying a certain firmness to lacy elegance: Le Clos des 60 Ouvrées (*monopole* Domaine de la Pousse d'Or) is sometimes the best wine in Volnay and may last 20 years, the simple Caillerets from the same Domaine has a fine bouquet of violets, while wines from d'Angerville, Jean Clerget and Bouchard Père are excellent. Actually in the commune of Meursault lies Les Santenots which, if planted with Pinot Noir, has the right to the *appellation* Volnay-Santenots (Domaine Potinet-Ampeau and superb Santenots-du-Mileu from le Comte Lafon). Les Champans is well situated, with classic, harmonious wines from d'Angerville, de Montille and Lafon (some of the finest Volnays currently made), while the other Premiers Crus planted towards Pommard – La Carelle sous la Chapelle, En l'Ormeau, Les Mitans and Les Brouillards – are less complex. There are many *vignerons* in Volnay with the same surname (Rossignol, Clerget, Glantenay), all making good wine. Volnay Premier Cru is excellent at 6–12 years after the vintage. Price D.

Meursault

Meursault AOC

Mainly white, with a very little red wine from 417 hectares of vines grouped around the town of Meursault, between Volnay and Puligny-Montrachet. The red wines are, naturally, found on the borders of Volnay, and the Premier Cru Les Santenots, if planted in Pinot Noir, is sold under the *appellation* Volnay-Santenots (page 75). There is also some excellent red wine from high up on the Puligny border at Blagny, and this also has its own *appellation* (page 77). Meursault rouge is full with good soft fruit, but has none of the qualities of the better-known Côtes de Beaune. The best wines are from the Clos de Mazeray of Domaine Jacques Prieur, and those of Ropiteau Frères. The make-up of the soil and sub-soil, however, is perfect for the

Chardonnay, and Meursault is white Burgundy at its most characteristic. Colour can vary from a pale, sometimes greeny, yellow to a full gold, the bouquet is rich, fruity, with buttery, nutty, spicy overtones leading into a full, complex flavour and dry finish. The finest wines, as usual, come from the Premier Cru vineyards, but the *villages* wines of Meursault are generally typical of the *appellation* and of good quality. Some of the *climats* around the town are often of Premier Cru quality, notably Le Clos de la Barre, Les Casse-Têtes, Les Narvaux, Les Tillets, Les Luchets and Les Tessons, these last three quite excellent from Guy Roulot. Wines like these are at their best 3–5 years after the vintage. Production is around 2.5 million bottles of white, including Premiers Crus, 100,000 of red. Price high C.

Meursault Premier Cru AOC

The finest Premiers Crus come from a band of vineyards running south from the town towards Puligny-Montrachet. North, on the Volnay borders, lie Les Santenots, where the Marquis d'Angerville makes a full-bodied Meursault-Santenots, Les Cras and Les Petures. On the Puligny border at Blagny, the wines are firmer and

tougher and sell under the *appellation* Meursault-Blagny (page 77). Of the six Premiers Crus south of the town, Les Perrières is reckoned to have the most distinction, both in its subtle bouquet and great length of flavour. The style of even a single cru varies according to the age of the vines, vinification and ageing, but there are few disappointing Perrières, and superb wines are to be found from the domaines Robert Ampeau, Comte Lafon, Michelot-Buisson, Guy Roulot, Coche-Dury and Pierre Morey. Les Genevrières is perhaps more intense than Les Perrières, and is often preferred by the local *vignerons* for its typical Meursault aroma of hazelnuts. Excellent wines from Lafon, Michelot-Buisson, François Jobard, Pierre Morey and Ropiteau-Mignon. Les Charmes is the largest of the Premiers Crus, with the higher part of the vineyard – Les Charmes Dessus as opposed to Les Charmes Dessous – making the finer wine. Charmes is richer than Les Perrières or Les Genevrières, but with a little less style and keeps less well. Excellent wines again from Lafon, Michelot-Buisson and François Jobard, as well as André Brunet, Pierre Matrot and René Monnier. Les Poruzots, the smallest of the Premiers Crus with only 4 hectares, is more lively than Les Charmes, less rich, but with great finesse. Fine wines from Ropiteau-Mignon and domaines Roux

and René Manuel. Les Bouchères resembles Les Poruzots but is a little less subtle, more straightforward, with good examples from Charles Alexant, Ropiteau-Mignon and Domaine René Manuel. Finally, La Goutte d'Or, just above the town, is round and full-bodied, a mouth-filling wine that sometimes lacks acidity, but is particularly good from Lafon, Ropiteau-Mignon and François Gaunoux. The size of the commune permits the *négociants* to choose some fine *cuvées*, and a selection of very good wines, both *villages* and Premiers Crus, can be had from Drouhin, Jadot, Latour and Leroy. Premiers Crus need 3 years in order to begin to show themselves at their best, and are splendid drunk between 5 and 8 years after the vintage. Price D.

Blagny AOC

White and red wine from vineyards just above the Premier Cru Les Perrières in the commune of Meursault, with vines both in Meursault and Puligny-Montrachet. The white wine is sold as Meursault-Blagny, and actually more resembles a Puligny than a Meursault, with a lively acidity and firm, elegant fruit, especially fine

from Domaine Matrot. The red has a good colour and, particularly if it comes from the Premier Cru La Pièce sous le Bois (Domaine Matrot, Robert Ampeau), has a certain harshness and *goût de terroir* that becomes very marked in more tannic vintages like 1976. In lighter vintages (1979, 1980), or if the vines are planted in the commune of Puligny-Montrachet (lovely, lightish wines from Domaine Leflaive), Blagny rouge may be drunk at 3–4 years, otherwise it needs twice this length of time to soften up. The wines of Blagny are not well known and are generally reliable and good value. Price high C.

Puligny-Montrachet

Puligny-Montrachet AOC

White and a very small quantity of red wine from 234 hectares of vines to the south of Meursault and to the north of Chassagne-Montrachet. The red wine can be sold as Côte de Beaune-Villages, but owing to its relative scarcity and the renown of the Puligny name, it is more often seen under the Puligny-Montrachet-Côte de Beaune *appellation*. It is fruity and quite soft, and may be drunk at 3–6 years (Domaine Henri Clerc). The white wine represents over 95% of the production and 100% of the reputation. It is paler in colour and lighter in style than Meursault, less rich, being both more flowery and more steely at the same time. It is perhaps more elegant than Meursault, more diffident or less aggressive, but some poorer examples lack concentration and flavour. The commune of Puligny harbours 4 Grands Crus and 11 Premiers Crus, all on beautifully exposed slopes above the village, which produce some of the finest white wine in Burgundy. A simple *villages* wine should be drunk 2–4 years after the vintage, but in good years from careful producers they may last longer. Total production is now around 1.2 million bottles of white, 50,000 of red. Price high C (red)–low D.

Puligny-Montrachet Premier Cru AOC

The Premier Cru vineyards of Puligny continue from those of Meursault (Les Charmes and Les Perrières) and run into the Grands Crus of Le Montrachet, Bâtard- and Chevalier-Montrachet on the border of the commune of Chassagne. Up near Blagny, Le Hameau de Blagny (Comtesse de Montlivault) and Les Chalumeaux (domaines Matrot, Pascal) are fresh, lively and firm, with a certain *goût de terroir*; below Les Chalumeaux, Le Champ-Canet (Domaine Etienne Sauzet) and La Garenne (extremely fine Clos de la Garenne, *monopole* of the Duc de Magenta) produce lightish, perfectly balanced wines with an aroma of hazelnuts; Les Combettes (the continuation of Les Charmes Dessus in Meursault) makes a bigger wine, stylish and complex with a certain richness (domaines Leflaive, Sauzet, Henri Clerc, Robert Carillon); Les Referts is similar to Les Combettes, with less intensity (domaines Carillon, Sauzet); Les Folatières produces wines combining body and finesse, with some of the length of a Grand Cru (Henri Clerc, René Monnier, Joseph Drouhin); just below Les Folatières, Les Clavoillons has a lovely bouquet of dog-roses, great breeding and a firm finish (quite superb wines from Leflaive, the principal owner in this cru); Les Pucelles is known for its suppleness and elegance, classic Puligny at its best (domaines Leflaive and Chartron); Le Cailleret, whose vines are separated by a footpath from Le Montrachet, produces wines which, with Les Pucelles, are the finest in the village, firm, perfectly balanced, requiring 4–5 years to show well (Pierre Amiot and Domaine Dupard Aîné, whose *monopole* Le Clos du Cailleret is sold by Drouhin). Puligny-Montrachet Premier Cru is much sought after by Burgundy's *négociants*, and fine examples can be found from Drouhin, Latour, Jadot, Antonin Rodet and Leroy. They may be drunk young, to appreciate the flowery aroma and purity of style, but can be kept 7–8 years. Price D– low E.

The Grands Crus of Puligny-Montrachet

Bâtard-Montrachet AOC

In common with Le Montrachet, the 11.83-hectare vineyard of Bâtard-Montrachet is situated in both the communes of Puligny and Chassagne. The vines are planted directly below those of Le Montrachet, and the wine has great richness and intensity of flavour, without perhaps the unique elegant concentration and suavity of Montrachet. A Bâtard-Montrachet is generally a wine of some weight (over 13° alcohol), and can in some cases lack acidity, but good examples have a fine golden colour, an assertive, nutty, toasty bouquet, mouth-filling fruit and the complexity and harmony of a *grand vin*. Excellent wines come from Leflaive, Pierre Morey, Etienne Sauzet, Domaine Poirier, Michel Niellon, Claude Ramonet, Ramonet-Prudhon, Bachelet-Ramonet and Delagrange-Bachelet. Drink 4–5 years after the vintage. Production around 50,000 bottles. Price high E.

Bienvenues-Bâtard-Montrachet AOC

Extemely fine wine from a vineyard of only 2.3 hectares situated entirely in Puligny below Le Montrachet, between Bâtard-Montrachet and Puligny-Montrachet Les Pucelles. It is lighter than Bâtard-Montrachet, but supremely elegant, and thanks to the superb vinification of the two best-known growers – domaines Leflaive and Ramonet-Prudhon – is seldom disappointing. At its best at 4–7 years. Average production about 12,000 bottles. Price E.

Chevalier-Montrachet AOC

A 7.14-hectare parcel of vines directly above Le Montrachet, entirely in the commune of Puligny, producing wines second only to Le Montrachet itself. Chevalier-Montrachet is a wine of great finesse and distinction, so finely structured, despite 13–14° of alcohol, and with such persistence of flavour that it is not easily forgotten. Quite superb wines come from the Domaine Leflaive, Bouchard Père & Fils, Louis Latour and Louis Jadot, who share between them the Demoiselles vineyard. These wines are magnificent at 5–10 years. Production, which is low for the size of the cru, is less than 25,000 bottles. Price high E–low F.

Le Montrachet AOC

The wine made from this 7.49-hectare vineyard (4 hectares on Puligny, 3.49 in Chassagne) is generally accepted to be the finest dry white wine in France. The soil, poor and stony with a high limestone content, is particularly well suited to the Chardonnay grape; the exposition is exceptional, on gently sloping south-facing *coteaux*, the drainage perfect. Many vineyards benefit from almost perfect growing conditions, yet do not produce wines with the almost mythical reputation of Le Montrachet. It combines the richness of a Bâtard with the finesse of a Chevalier and has an intense, floral aroma with a mixture of honey and almonds on the palate. It is a wine with a great concentration and richness of fruit that nevertheless finishes dry. The largest parcel of vines (2 hectares in Puligny) belongs to the Marquis de Laguiche, whose impressive but sometimes over-rich wine is made and commercialized by Joseph Drouhin; Baron Thénard has 1.89 hectares on the Chassagne side, producing a meaty, greeny-gold-coloured wine. The Montrachet of Bouchard Père & Fils, just over one hectare in Puligny, is spectacular, and that of the Domaine de la Romanée-Conti extraordinarily suave and complex. The domaines Jacques Prieur, Comte Lafon, Pierre Morey and René Fleurot have possessed vines in Le Montrachet for many years, while relatively new owners, making only 300 bottles or so, include Ramonet-Prudhon and Delagrange-Bachelet. Since Montrachet costs more than twice as much as Chevalier-Montrachet, its value for money is often questioned. The best wines need at least 5 years in bottle to show the complexity behind the power. Production is seldom more than 30,000 bottles. Price FF.

Chassagne-Montrachet

Chassagne-Montrachet AOC

Red and white wines from the second most southern commune on the Côte de Beaune, situated south of Puligny and north of Santenay. Chassagne is a large commune, with 356 hectares permitted for the *appellation*, but some of the land is still planted in Gamay and Aligoté. Even though the name Montrachet suggests that the finest wines from the commune are white, red is still produced in more volume, and the quality of Chassagne-Montrachet rouge is often very high. Even the simple *villages* wines have a good colour and firm, generous fruit, with more in common with wines from Aloxe-Corton or Nuits-Saint-Georges than with their neighbours Volnay or Santenay. The whites have a lovely greeny-gold colour, are a little less stylish than those from Puligny, but have a good natural fruit and acidity and are seldom disappointing. Chassagne harbours some very important domaines, most of which have been parcellated and re-formed through inheritance or marriage, and the following names are much in evidence on the wine labels: Ramonet, Bachelet, Delagrange, Gagnard, Deléger and Morey. Chassagne possesses 3 Grands Crus for white wine only, and many Premiers Crus for both red and white. Total production is 1 million bottles of red and 800,000 of white. Price low C (reds)–C.

Chassagne-Montrachet Premier Cru AOC

The white wines vary in style according to the situation of the vineyards. At the highest elevation, La Grande Montane, Le Virondot and La Romanée give lightish but firm wines with a certain flintiness (domaines Bachelet-Ramonet, Marc Morey); a little lower, Les Caillerets has great length and finesse (especially good chez Blain-Gagnard, a domaine that has inherited over half of the vines of Edmond Delagrange, and fine wines from Pierre Amiot, Albert Morey); Les Ruchottes and Les Grandes Ruchottes are extremely elegant, even delicate for a Chassagne, with superb wines from Marcel Moreau, Ramonet-Prudhon, Bachelet-Ramonet and André Ramonet; wines from Le Morgeot are more complete, with a more intense bouquet and great depth and complexity (Ramonet-Prudhon, André Ramonet, Claude Ramonet, Delagrange-Bachelet/Blain-Gagnard, Marquis de Laguiche, and the Abbaye de Morgeot of the Duc de Magenta); Les Chevenottes, turning towards Saint-Aubin, gives a very aromatic, honeyed, softer wine (Raoul Clerget, Marcel Moreau). A fine Chassagne Premier Cru blanc is at its best from 4–8 years after the vintage. The reds, which constitute the biggest wines of the southern part of the Côte de Beaune, have a good deep colour, a spicy aroma and a plummy, rather rough flavour that needs time in which to soften up. The best wines come from Le Clos de la Boudriotte (Ramonet-Prudhon, Claude Ramonet, Bachelet-Ramonet) and the Clos Saint-Jean (Ramonet, Bachelet, Paul Pillot). The Clos de la Chapelle of the Duc de Magenta and Le Clos Pitois of Joseph Belland are very fine, with definite Chassagne character, and good red wines come from the Morgeot vineyards of Blain-Gagnard, Alphonse Pillot, Marquis de Laguiche, Fleurot-Larose and Prieur-Brunet. These wines are best at 8–12 years after the vintage. Price D.

The Grands Crus of Chassagne-Montrachet

Bâtard-Montrachet

See page 79.

Criots-Bâtard-Montrachet AOC

The smallest (1.6 hectares) of the white Grands Crus of the Côte de Beaune lies entirely in Chassagne. The only domaine concentrating on Criots is Blain-Gagnard, who have inherited the vines of Edmond Delagrange. The wines are less fat than Bâtard-Montrachet with a more discreet elegance and the firm, persistent flavour of a *grand vin*. Very fine. 7,000 bottles are produced. Price F.

Le Montrachet

See page 80.

Santenay AOC

Almost entirely red wine from the most southern commune in the Côte de Beaune, covering 380 hectares, not all in production. The white wines are quite sturdy with a certain acidity, more resembling a Pernand-Vergelesses than, say, a Meursault. The reds, particularly those near to Chassagne-Montrachet, have a good colour, lively, fruity bouquet and firm, robust, even austere flavour. They have none of the soft charm of the wines of Volnay or Beaune and are more in the style of Pommard, needing several years to open up. The finest wines of the commune come from the Premiers Crus near to Chassagne-Montrachet: Les Gravières combines sturdiness and elegance (Domaine de la Pousse d'Or, Domaine des Hautes Cornières, Domaine Jessiaume, Philippe Mestre, Louis Clair) and the enclave

Clos de Tavannes is still more complete and satisfying (Domaine de la Pousse d'Or, Louis Clair); La Comme is generally lighter, with a more expressive, floral bouquet (Philippe Mestre, Louis Clair), with more vigorous, meaty wines from Joseph Belland and the Domaine Lequin-Roussot; Le Beauregard is similarly fruity and firm (Joseph Belland); Le Passe-Temps, near the village, gives firm, straightforward wines (Domaine Lequin-Roussot, René Fleurot), and above the village, La Maladière is lighter, supple, quicker to mature (Domaine Prieur-Brunet). The wines of Santenay are still not well known, and the well-made grower's wines and carefully selected *négociant's cuvées* (in particular those from Santenay-based Prosper-Maufoux) are good value. Santenay in a light vintage may be drunk at 4–5 years, with the better wines needing twice the length of time. Production of red wine is large, totalling over 1.5 million bottles, with 25,000 bottles of white. Price B–C (for the Premiers Crus).

The Côte Chalonnaise

The Côte Chalonnaise sees the continuation of the vineyards of the Côte d'Or into the *département* of the Saône-et-Loire. The area covers 24 kilometres running along the RN 481 from Chagny in the north to Saint-Vallerin in the south, but vines are planted less regularly here than in the Côte de Nuits and Côte de Beaune, keeping to the best south-facing slopes and alternating with fruit-growing, grazing and other forms of culture. Wines benefiting from the *appellations communales* (Givry, Mercurey, Montagny, Rully) must be from the Pinot Noir for the reds and rosés, and the Chardonnay for the whites, although the Pinot Blanc is still permitted. The Gamay is heavily planted for Bourgogne Passe-Tout-Grains or Bourgogne Grand Ordinaire (now little seen), and the Aligoté succeeds so well around the village of Bouzeron that a new *appellation* has recently been created: Bourgogne Aligoté de Bouzeron. Although Montagny produces only white wines, the reds are dominant in the region, led by those of Mercurey, to the extent that the Côte Chalonnaise is sometimes known as 'la région de Mercurey'. With high demand for Burgundies from the Côte d'Or, causing a notable rise in price for these wines, more interest has been focused on the Côte Chalonnaise, and improved vinification techniques coupled with a dedication to quality by the *vignerons* have had very positive results. Red wines produced outside the *appellations communales* are sold as Bourgogne, and to distinguish these wines from others in the Burgundy region from Chablis to the Beaujolais, a demand has been submitted to the INAO for the creation of an *appellation* Bourgogne Côte Chalonnaise for Pinot Noir and Chardonnay wines of superior quality. The Côte Chalonnaise also produces some of the finest *cuvées* of Crémant de Bourgogne.

Givry AOC

Red and white wines from 120 hectares of vines in the middle of the Côte Chalonnaise. Historically, the wines of Givry were more renowned than those of Mercurey, but today this is no longer true. The white wine is attractive, with a fresh acidity and firm fruit, but quite light and should be drunk young. The reds are similar to those of Mercurey, being a little lighter, a little smoother, but lacking Mercurey's definition and depth. They are quite drinkable 2–3 years after the vintage and very good at 5–6. There are no Premiers Crus at Givry, but some well-known *climats*, including Le Clos Salomon (du Gardin), Le Cellier aux Moines (Baron Thénard, Domaine Joblot), and Le Clos Saint-Pierre (Baron Thénard). Reliable wines come also from Madame Steinmeyer, Domaine Ragot and Domaine Desvignes. Current production averages a little more than 500,000 bottles of red wine, 65,000 of white. Price B.

Mercurey AOC

Red and white wines from the most prestigious commune in the Côte Chalonnaise. Over 600 hectares are in production, 95% for red wines. The small quantity of white is interesting, but less successful than Rully, owing to a high acidity, but the wine goes well with the local cuisine (Château de Chamirey, Michel Juillot, Bouchard Aîné, Faiveley). The red, which used to be grouped with the wines of the Côte de Beaune before the laws of *appellation contrôlée*, is a rather old-fashioned wine, deep in colour, with fruity, briary aromas and a firm, sinewy impression on the palate, with none of the easy charm of some of the softer wines from the Pinot Noir. They are concentrated and rather rough and tannic when young, and are at their best at 5–10 years. In light years, or as a result of over-production, the wines can be disappointingly pale and thin. Growers making excellent wine include Hugues de Suremain, Michel Juillot, Yves de Launay, Roland Brintet, Chanzy Frères, Domaine Jeannin-Naltet and Emile Voarick, while wines from François Protheau, Faiveley and Rodet are reliable. There are five Premiers Crus of which the best is Le Clos du Roy. The *vignerons* in Mercurey have grouped together to form La Confrérie des Disciples de la Chante Flûte, which blind-tastes wines of the region, much in the manner of the Chevaliers de Tastevin and just as seriously, and awards a special label to the wines that have been *chante-flûtés*. Production of red wine is now over 3 million bottles and about 130,000 of white. Price B–low C.

Montagny AOC

White wine only from the most southerly *appellation* of the Côte Chalonnaise. Where the wines of Rully tend to resemble those of the Côte de Beaune, those of Montagny are more in the style of the Mâconnais. They are stylish and fruity, with a lovely Chardonnay flavour and finish. Most are delicious young, and the better wines improve for 3–4 years in bottle, acquiring complexity and a nutty character. Although there are some excellent *climats*, such as Les Monts Cuchots of Mme Steinmeyer, the *appellation* Premier Cru is awarded to all wines which have more than 11.5° alcohol, the only example of this sort of legislation in Burgundy. Fine wines come from Bernard Michel, Mme Steinmeyer, Domaine Martial de Laboulaye, the Cave Coopérative at Buxy and Louis Latour. Production is increasing as the vineyards are replanted and is now around 350,000 bottles. Price A–B.

Rully AOC

Red and white wines from the communes of Rully and Chagny. The white is better known, the limestone-based soil allowing the Chardonnay to produce a stylish wine with a fresh sappy fruit and great length of flavour, the equal of many more prestigious wines from the Côte de Beaune. The well-exposed Premiers Crus are very fine, and excellent wines come from Robert de Suremain, René Brelière, Paul and Henri Jacqueson, Armand Monassier, Domaine de la Renarde, Domaine Ninot-Rigaud and Domaine de la Folie. Some Rully whites are full in style, resembling a Meursault (de Suremain), while others are lighter, with more acidity and panache (Domaine de la Folie). The reds tend to be lighter than those of the Côte de Beaune (Delorme, Monassier), but in good years have a striking ruby colour, a strawberry-blackcurranty aroma and a firm, fruity finish (Jacqueson, Chanzy Frères, Domaine de la Folie). The whites may be drunk as soon as they are in bottle, but a good natural acidity allows them to improve for 3–4 years more. The reds can be drunk 2–3 years after the vintage and improve with age. Production is increasing as new planting takes place, and currently averages 400,000 bottles of each red and white wine. Price B.

The Mâconnais

The vineyards of the Mâconnais continue Burgundy's descent through the Saône-et-Loire *département* towards Lyon. Six thousand hectares are in production, with 60% in Chardonnay including a little Pinot Blanc and Aligoté, the rest being planted in Gamay (30%) and Pinot Noir (10%). The white wines are unquestionably finer than the reds, for the Chardonnay thrives on the high limestone content of the granite-based soil. The most widely produced are Mâcon blanc and Mâcon-Villages, fruity, pure Chardonnay wines with some body and a refreshing acidity. The finest come from the villages mid-way between Tournus and Mâcon (all the vines are on the right bank of the river Saône): Clessé, Lugny and Viré. Further south, opposite and below Mâcon, are the vineyards of Saint-Véran and Pouilly-Fuissé. The reds – Bourgogne rouge, Bourgogne Passe-Tout-Grains and Mâcon rouge – are pleasant, fruity, everyday wines, completely outclassed by the Burgundies in the north and the Beaujolais in the south. The Mâconnais Caves Coopératives also produce some of the best Crémant de Bourgogne in Burgundy.

Pouilly-Fuissé AOC

White wines grown in the five communes of Fuissé, Pouilly, Solutré, Chaintré and Vergisson to the west of Mâcon. Wines made at Loché should be called Pouilly-Loché, but may take the name of the next-door village, Vinzelles, whose own wines are usually better, but not as full-bodied as Pouilly-Fuissé itself. Pouilly-Fuissé is without doubt the finest wine of the Mâconnais: when young, it has a straw-yellow colour, sometimes with greeny tints, a heady, floral bouquet and all the sappy fruit of the Chardonnay grape; if left to mature, its class is underlined by a richness and complexity of taste, while keeping its youthful freshness, that recalls some fine wines from the Côte de Beaune. Château de Fuissé (Domaine Vincent) is the most remarkable wine of the *appellation*, extraordinarily rich and long-lived, the result of a combination of old vines, late picking, long fermentation in a high proportion of new oak barrels and severe selection before bottling. Other very fine wines come from Mme Féret, André Forest, Maurice Luquet and Joseph Corsin. There are many other fine *vignerons* in the *appellation*, but international demand is such that a very high proportion of the crop is bought and bottled by *négociants* (Mommessin, Loron, Dubœuf, Rodet, Latour). While Mâcon blanc and Saint-Véran may be drunk young, at 1–2 years, Pouilly-Fuissé needs 3–5 years to show at its best. Despite a production of 4.5 million bottles, demand outstrips supply. Price C.

Saint-Véran AOC

White wines made from the Chardonnay grape planted in 8 communes surrounding Fuissé: Saint-Véran, Chanes, Chasselas, Davayé, Leynes, Prissé, Saint-Amour and Solutré. Before receiving its own *appellation* in 1971, these wines were sold as either Beaujolais blanc or Mâcon-Villages. They have a lovely pale yellow colour, more vivacity and fruit than a Mâcon blanc, without the richness and depth of a Pouilly-Fuissé. The finest wines come from Leynes (domaines Duperron, Chagny) and Davayé (Grégoire, Corsin and the Lycée Agricole). Georges Dubœuf is one of the most reliable *négociants*. The permitted yield has recently been increased from 45 to 55 hl/ha, more than Pouilly-Fuissé, less than Mâcon-Villages, but quality is still high. About 2 million bottles are produced. Price high A–B.

The Beaujolais

The Beaujolais is the most southerly vineyard area in Burgundy, running for over 70 kilometres down the right-hand side of the RN 6, from just below Mâcon to just above Lyon. The area covers 15,000 hectares, mostly in the Rhône *département*, producing nearly 150 million bottles of wine, and may be divided qualitatively into the Haut-Beaujolais in the north, with a clayey-sandy top-soil on a schistous-granite base, from which come all the Beaujolais crus and Beaujolais-Villages, and the Bas-Beaujolais (or Beaujolais-Bâtard) to the south, with a more limestone-clayey soil, producing Beaujolais *simple* and most of the Beaujolais Primeur. The only grape variety permitted for Beaujolais rouge and rosé is the Gamay, already seen in other parts of Burgundy as an element (⅔ maximum, with ⅓ minimum Pinot Noir) in Bourgogne Passe-Tout-Grains. The Gamay is particularly successful, due in part to its predilection for a granite-based soil, but also to the local style of *macération carbonique* vinification, whereby the bunches of grapes arrive in the fermentation vats uncrushed and whole, and the usually short fermentation takes place inside the grape itself. The light, fruity Primeur, released on 15 November, is a quaffing wine, to be drunk very young. Beaujolais *tout court* should be drunk in the year following the vintage, and Beaujolais-Villages at 1–2 years. While there are some very good Beaujolais-Villages from individual growers or conscientious *négociants*, they can hardly be considered fine wines. In the very north of the region some excellent Beaujolais blanc is still made (despite the introduction of the *appellation* Saint-Véran) from the Chardonnay, producing a fresh, mouth-wateringly fruity wine, with more verve than a Mâcon blanc. Only the nine Beaujolais crus are capable of producing wines of distinction, and in some cases with a potential for ageing, and even here differences in style can be lost in the interests of quick commercialization. They have a maximum permitted yield of 48 hl/ha (as against 55 hl/ha for Beaujolais *simple* and 50 hl/ha for Beaujolais-Villages), but this is almost always exceeded, and, thanks to the PLC (see page 11), an average of 20% more is permitted each year. The minimum alcohol content is 10°, 11° if a vineyard or *climat* is specified, but in practice the natural degree of alcohol is raised by chaptalization to 12.5–14°.

Brouilly AOC

The most southern, and largest of the nine crus, with 1,075 hectares on the lower slopes of Le Mont Brouilly. The wine has a violetty-red colour and soft grapy charm. Except in tannic vintages (1976) it should be drunk young. The best come from the communes of Odenas and Saint-Lager. Production over 8 million bottles. Price A.

Chénas AOC

The second-smallest cru, with 260 hectares between Moulin-à-Vent and Saint-Amour. The wine is dark-coloured, full-bodied, without perhaps the fruit of Juliénas or the class of Moulin-à-Vent, but very satisfying. It has a generous texture and a distinctively floral aroma (peonies), and can be drunk the year after the vintage, but keeps remarkably well. Production averages 1.5 million bottles. Price A.

Chiroubles AOC

The third-smallest cru, with 280 hectares on high slopes situated north-west of Morgon and south-west of Fleurie, producing lightish, racy wines with a very flowery bouquet and firm finish. Chiroubles is the most *primeur* of the crus, and should be drunk young to capture the charm. Production 2.3 million bottles. Price high A–low B.

Côte-de-Brouilly AOC

As the name implies, Côte-de-Brouilly occupies 200 hectares on the higher slopes of Le Mont Brouilly, surrounded by the *appellation* Brouilly. The schistous soil and the higher elevation result in a wine with a deeper colour than Brouilly, more vigorous and slower to open up. It has a distinctive aroma of violets and acquires great finesse after 2–3 years. The smallest production of the crus, with just under 2 million bottles. Good value. Price A.

Fleurie AOC

Producing perhaps the best-balanced and most sophisticated wines of the nine Beaujolais crus, the *appellation* Fleurie covers 710 hectares. With its fine, deep colour, floral bouquet of roses and irises, silky texture and harmonious finish, Fleurie is known as 'the Queen of the Beaujolais'. The wines are quite firm, but are best drunk 1–3 years after the vintage. The best *climats* are La Chapelle des Bois, Les Garands, Le Point du Jour, Les Viviers and Les Quatre Vents. The nearer the vines get to Moulin-à-Vent, the more assertive the wine produced becomes. Production averages 5.5 million bottles. Price high A–low B.

Juliénas AOC

The vines of Juliénas cover 500 hectares to the north-west of Chénas and Saint-Amour, producing deep, purple-coloured, exciting wines with a striking bouquet of raspberries and peaches. Juliénas may be supple and fruity or big and chewy, with a depth of fruit that makes them attractive the summer after the vintage, but that should keep them improving for 2–4 years more. The best wines come from the slopes around the village, where there is a very good Cave Coopérative. Production almost 4 million bottles. Price high A.

Morgon AOC

The second largest of the crus, with 950 hectares in the commune of Villié-Morgon, Morgon is also the most generous, meaty and robust. It has a deep garnet colour and an aroma of wild cherries when young that develops into a kirsch-like bouquet with age. Morgon ages well – the *vignerons* say 'il morgonne', as they say of a good Mâcon-Villages 'il pouillotte' – acquiring a rather Pouilly *goût de terroir* after 3–4 years in bottle. The wines coming from vineyards situated around the village of Villié-Morgon, particularly the *climat* Le Py, are the finest. Production 6.5 million bottles. Price high A.

Moulin-à-Vent AOC

The most prestigious of the crus, Moulin-à-Vent covers nearly 700 hectares of vines in the communes of Romanèche-Thorins and Chénas. The granite-based soil has a high magnesium content which imparts to the wines an intensity of bouquet (violets) and depth of flavour that seems to combine the best elements of the finer crus with an added touch of class. They are so stylish that they can be drunk young, for the rich, velvety fruit, but their real fame comes from bottles which are 5–10 years old and even more. If Moulin-à-Vent is known as 'the Burgundy of the Beaujolais', it is not through copying the wines which come from the Côte d'Or, but through the intrinsic quality that, in ageing, begins to resemble the *grandes appellations* from further north. The finest wines come from Romanèche-Thorins, in particular the *climats* Les Thorins and Le Moulin-à-Vent. Production averages around 4.5 million bottles. Price B.

Saint-Amour AOC

Saint-Amour is the most northerly of the crus, with 230 hectares of vines situated entirely in the Saône-et-Loire *département*. The wine is fruity and straightforward, softer than next-door Juliénas, much less intense than Moulin-à-Vent, with a lively peach-aroma flavour that should be appreciated quite young. The name is popular and it is one of the more expensive crus. Production nearly 2 million bottles. Price high A–low B.

The Loire Valley

The Loire is the longest river in France, with vineyards planted along both banks and those of its tributaries, offering a wide range of delightful wines. The gentle climate and pure luminosity of the region are reflected in the appealing liveliness of the wines produced. Most of these – the dry whites from the Sauvignon or the Melon de Bourgogne (Muscadet), the fruity reds and rosés from the Gamay and Cabernet Franc – are uncomplicated, refreshing wines for early drinking. While the Cabernet Franc produces some fine red wines in Touraine, the only really great wines come from the Chenin Blanc, whose ability to attain very high degrees of natural sugar (usually through *pourriture noble*), while retaining a natural acidity, can result in some of the finest sweet white wines.

The Loire rises in the Auvergne, where the Gamay, Pinot Noir, Sauvignon and Chardonnay produce pleasant, fruity, 'country' wines. In the Nivernais, at Sancerre and Pouilly-sur-Loire, the Sauvignon comes into its own and can be appreciated in its purest form, while the Pinot Noir produces some interesting reds. Following the river to the sea, the Gamay and Sauvignon are much planted in Touraine, but the better *appellations* are limited to the Cabernet Franc and Chenin Blanc. In Anjou, these two varieties are dominant, giving way, quite suddenly on approaching the Atlantic, to the Muscadet and the Gros Plant du Pays Nantais.

1 Muscadet	6 Bourgueil	11 Sancerre
2 Coteaux du Layon	7 Chinon	12 Pouilly-Fumé
3 Saumur	8 Vouvray	13 Bonnezeaux
4 Coteaux de l'Aubance	9 Montlouis	14 Savennières
5 Touraine	10 Coteaux du Loir	

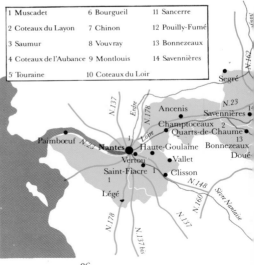

Vins du Centre

Pouilly-Fumé or Blanc Fumé de Pouilly AOC

Dry white wine made from the Sauvignon grape covering 600 hectares of vineyards around the town of Pouilly-sur-Loire in the Nièvre *département*. Throughout the *appellation* the Chasselas may be planted, to produce a minor, fruity *vin de carafe* that must be sold as Pouilly-sur-Loire, but this only represents 15% of the land under vines. A Blanc Fumé de Pouilly (the Sauvignon is known locally as *le Blanc Fumé*) must have over 11° of alcohol from a maximum yield of 45 hl/ha, and while the degree is usually exceeded in good years, production is often curtailed by spring frosts. The soil has a chalky-clay base, with a limestone element in the two best-known *climats*, Les Loges and Les Berthiers. The wine should be pale yellow, sometimes with green tints, with a fragrant red or blackcurranty aroma, slightly spicy, pleasantly tart, more subtle than a Sancerre, with a firm fruit flavour and elegant finish. An initial acidity and 'leanness' softens after one year and, contrary to the other Sauvignon-based wines from the Loire valley, good examples may improve for two or three years more. The most important person in the wine community is Patrick de Ladoucette, who commercializes over 60% of the production with two brands, Château de Nozet and the exceptional Le Baron de L. Other good growers, making flowery but firm wines, are Bailly Père & Fils, Jean-Claude Dagueneau, Paul Figeat, Jean-Claude Guyot, Landrat & Guyollot and Château de Tracy. Production is around 3 million bottles.
Price B–C.

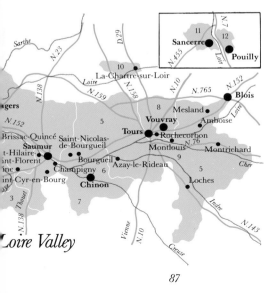

Quincy *AOC*
Reuilly *AOC*
Ménétou-Salon *AOC*

The fame that surrounds Sancerre and Pouilly-Fumé has not yet attached itself to these three *appellations* of the central Loire, that produce similar wines. The Sauvignon is the dominant grape (and the only one permitted at Quincy), producing wine similar in style to the better-known *appellations*, Ménétou-Salon and Quincy more resembling Sancerre, with a less intense flavour but a softer charm, and Reuilly tending towards the lean austerity of Pouilly-Fumé.

Ménétou-Salon produces some pleasant rosé and some very fine, fruity red from the Pinot Noir, and Reuilly a deliciously refreshing rosé, a *vin gris* in fact, from the Pinot Gris, which is more successful than the rather light red from the Pinot Noir. Good wines can always be found from the following growers: Ménétou-Salon: Henry Pellé, Georges Chavet, Bernard Clément, Jean-Paul Gilbert, Jean Tellier; Quincy: Claude Houssier, Pierre Mardon, Meunier-Lapha, Raymond Pipet; Reuilly: Henri Beurdin, Olivier Cromwell, Robert Cordier, Claude Lafond. Price A.

Sancerre *AOC*

Red, white and rosé wines from 14 communes around the town of Sancerre in the Cher *département*, with 1,500 hectares under vines and a further 500 in course of plantation. The grapes permitted are Sauvignon for the whites, Pinot Noir for the reds and rosés, the latter representing one-fifth of the production. The rosés have a lovely, pale, salmon-pink colour, a refreshing acidity (a little too marked in poor years) and, like most rosés, must be drunk young. The reds, particularly if the vines are south-facing, can have a good colour and pure Pinot Noir bouquet, a certain intensity of fruit with sometimes a slightly rustic

finish. In good years (1978, 1982) from good growers (Jean Vacheron, André Dezat), they can be very interesting. The most popular, and the best, wine in Sancerre is the white, a lively wine with a pale colour, a striking aroma of redcurrants, gooseberries, a certain grassiness or tart fruitiness that does not age elegantly, and a cheerful, fruity finish. Well made, they are exciting, satisfying and harmonious; poor examples, from over-production, over-chaptalization, over-sulphuring, are either thin and acidic or heavy and dull. The most important influence in Sancerre is the *terroir*, which is of three different types and produces three distinctive styles of wine. At Bué, the largest wine commune, the soil is stony on a heavy clay *tuffeau* base, producing round, immediately fruity wines, very stylish and quite *gras*. The best vineyards here are Le Clos de Chêne Marchand, Le Grand Chemarin and Le

Clos du Roy. Around Chavignol and Verdigny, the steeper slopes have a thin, pebbly top-soil on a base of chalky-clay, producing elegant, firm wines, with more reserve and often more finesse than those at Bué. The steepest slopes above the village, Le Clos de Beaujeu, Les Monts Damnés and Les Comtesses, produce the finest wines. Around Ménétréol and Saint-Satur and on the easy slopes leading up to the hill-village of Sancerre, the soil is a mixture of clay and flint, producing slightly austere, less obviously charming wines, with a fine steely finish. The first two types of soil represent 80% of the vineyard, and a Sancerre that is a blend of wines from two or three *terroirs* is the exception rather than the rule. Most wines are at their best in the 2 years following the vintage. As in neighbouring Burgundy, Sancerre is a region of small growers who have remained on their land throughout many generations, and the skill and dedication of the wine-maker is as important as the *appellation*. The many fine producers include Phillipe de Benoist, Paul Cotat, Lucien Crochet, Vincent Delaporte, Gitton Père & Fils, Roger Neveu, Lucien Picard, Bernard Reverdy, Jean Reverdy, Jean-Max Roger and Jean Vacheron. Production 6 million bottles of white, 1.5 million of red and rosé. Price A – B.

Vins de Touraine

Bourgueil AOC

Red and rosé wines principally from the Cabernet Franc (with the Cabernet Sauvignon tolerated to a maximum of 20%) covering 900 hectares on the right bank of the Loire between Tours and Saumur. The most important communes are Bourgueil, Restigné, Ingrandes and Benais, where the marked difference in the soil produces quite different styles of wine. The gravelly-alluvial soil on the plain produces quick-maturing wines with much bouquet and finesse; the *coteaux*, where the top-soil is gravel with a clay-limestone base (*le tuffeau*), produces deeper-coloured, meatier wines that need more time. A good Bourgueil (often a blend of the two styles) will have a lovely garnet-ruby colour, a bouquet reminiscent of raspberries, with a lively, sometimes rustic fruit and clean, dry finish. In poor years they tend to be rather thin, while in very sunny vintages (1976) they can have a huge colour and intensity of fruit that puts them in the category of fine wines. Red Bourgueil can be drunk (served cool) the year or two after the vintage, while the best wines last 10 years or more. The rosé has a delightfully pale, violetty-pink colour and is the perfect summer wine. Over-all quality is improving and very good growers include Georges Audebert, Caslot-Galbrun, Pierre-Jacques Drouët, Marc Mureau, Domaine de Raguenières and Lamé-Delille-Boucard. Production, from a maximum yield of 40 hl/ha, is around 4 million bottles. Price A (B for older vintages).

Chinon AOC

Red, rosé and white wines
from an *appellation* covering
1,200 hectares on the left
bank of the Loire and both
banks of its tributary the
Vienne, between Tours and
Saumur. The tiny production
of white wine is from the
Chenin Blanc (Pineau de la
Loire), with the typical floral
bouquet and lively character
of the grape, but is sometimes
a little tart. The reds (and
rosés) are made from the
Cabernet Franc, known
locally as 'le Breton', grown
on three different types of soil:
the sandy-gravelly soil along
the banks of the Vienne
produces light, fruity wines
for early drinking; the more
gravelly soil with some clay
on the plateaux produces a
wine with more body and
depth; while the heavier
tuffeau lends a further element
of intensity and flavour,
particularly if the vines are
planted *en coteaux*. These are
the finest wines of the
appellation, exemplified by the
Clos de l'Echo of Couly-
Dutheil and the Clos de la
Dioterie of Charles Joguet.
The best vineyards are at
Chinon itself, Cravant-lès-
Coteaux, Savigny-en-Véron
and Sazilly. A good Chinon
should have an entrancing
ruby colour, a pronounced
aroma of crushed flowers
(violets) and an impression of
soft fruit with a refreshing
finish, where the *terroir* is
matched by the elegant
smoothness of the Cabernet
Franc. The wines have great
charm and can usually be
drunk the year after the
vintage, while the better *cuvées*
and better vintages can
improve for 5–15 years. As at
Bourgueil, with which it is
often compared, the quality is
as much if not more
dependent on how the wine is
made than where it is grown:
it is the opinion of Charles
Joguet, the most innovative
wine-maker in Chinon, that if
the *appellation* has an image of
'rusticity', it is more the result
of poor wine-making than an
inherent *goût de terroir*. Quality
is improving, and excellent
wines can be found from
Couly-Dutheil, Charles
Joguet, Gérard Chauveau,
Gatien-Ferrand (including a
very fine white), René
Gouron and Jean Maurice,
Olga and Raymond Raffault.
Around 5 million bottles are
produced, under 1% of which
is white. Price A–B.

Montlouis AOC

White wines similar in style to
those grown across the river
at Vouvray, with the full
range from very dry to very
sweet still wines and a *méthode
champenoise*, all made from the
Chenin Blanc. The more
sandy soil at Montlouis
makes for a lighter, quicker-
maturing wine than Vouvray,
which none the less has a
similar honey-and-flowers
aroma and lemony-fruit
finish. Almost half the
average production of 1.3
million bottles is sold as
sparkling wine, for which
there is a steady local
demand. Two of the best
growers are Dominique
Moyer and Claude
Levasseur. Price A–B.

Saint-Nicolas-de-Bourgueil AOC

Red and rosé wines from a separate *appellation* within the Bourgueil region, covering not quite 500 hectares planted with the Cabernet Franc. The two specific types of soil – sandy-gravel and limestone-clay – exist in Saint-Nicolas, but there is more sand and the wine is correspondingly lighter than at Bourgueil and is usually drunk younger. Well-made wines come from Audebert Père & Fils, Pierre Jamet, Jean-Paul Mabileau and Daniel Moreau. Permitted yield is inexplicably lower than at Bourgueil, at 35 hl/ha, producing a total of 2 million bottles, including a little rosé. Price A.

Vouvray AOC

Vouvray produces a complete range of white wine from the Chenin Blanc, planted on 1,500 hectares of vineyards on the right bank of the Loire to the east of Tours. Depending on the weather throughout the vintage and the decision of the *vigneron*, Vouvray may be dry (*sec*), off-dry (*demi-sec*), sweet (*moelleux*) and very sweet (*liquoreux*), as well as semi-sparkling and sparkling. The soil is a heavy limestone-clay, the *tuffeau* of Touraine, with some chalk and a gravelly top-soil that is perfect for the Chenin Blanc. The minimum degree of alcohol is 11, which gives a firm backbone to the flowery, honeysuckle-scented wine, whose fruit is always balanced by a marked acidity. The maximum yield of 45 hl/ha is generally exceeded for the less good *cuvées* that are normally destined for the sparkling wine, but is very much lower, nearer 25 hl/ha, for the sweet, late-harvest wines. In poor years (1972, 1977) the still wines have an unacceptable amount of acidity when young, and even when mature never have the charm associated with wines from the Loire. In good or great years (1959, 1964, 1976, 1981) the dry wines will be perfectly balanced, with more style and length than even the best Sauvignons, and the late-picked bunches will produce wines with an intensely floral, fresh fruit aroma and honeyed richness of taste that can rival the finest Sauternes. While a dry Vouvray may be drunk young, but can improve over several years, the sweeter wines may last several decades, yet very few domaines are prepared to go to the trouble, expense and risk to produce these wines. Vouvray Pétillant, less sparkling than Vouvray Mousseux and less easy to make successfully, is quite delightful. First-class wines, many with the names of the individual Clos from which they are made, come from Domaine Huet, Prince Poniatowski, Domaine Allias, Jean Bertrand, Marc Brédif (now owned by Patrick de Ladoucette), André Freslier and A. Foreau. Production is now almost 10 million bottles. Price A–B (C for older vintages).

Vins d'Anjou et de Saumur

Bonnezeaux AOC

Sweet white wines produced from an enclave in the Coteaux du Layon *appellation*. The Chenin Blanc rarely attains the 25 hl/ha permitted, due to the obligatory late-picking of grapes affected by botrytis. Bonnezeaux is richer than even the best Coteaux du Layon, and has a more concentrated fruit, particularly on the nose, and a longer, more unctuous taste. It may be drunk the year after the vintage, to capture the explosive, flowery fruit, but is more interesting at 5–10 years, while the greatest vintages can last indefinitely. The best wines come from the Château de Fesle, which is owned by Jacques Boivin. Production is around 120,000 bottles. Price B (C for older vintages).

Coteaux du Layon AOC

Semi-sweet and sweet white wines produced by the Chenin Blanc from a possible 3,000 hectares on the banks of the Layon, a tributary of the Loire. The fall in demand and the economic risk of making sweet white wine has seen some of the *appellation* planted in Cabernet Franc to make a red or a rosé under the *appellation* Anjou, while much of the white wine is vinified dry and is sold as Anjou blanc. Coteaux du Layon is limited to 30 hl/ha as opposed to 50 hl/ha for Anjou, and must have at least 11° alcohol plus 1% residual sugar. This high degree is obtained by harvesting the grapes as ripe as possible, hopefully with the effects of *pourriture noble*. The result is a pale golden, sometimes greenish wine, with a summery, honeyed slightly spicy bouquet and sweet but not cloying finish. The high sugar allows the wine to age beautifully and the natural acidity of the Chenin provides a refreshing liveliness in even the richest years. The finest communes in the *appellation* – Beaulieu, Faye, Rablay, Rochefort, Saint-Aubin and Saint-Lambert – are now grouped as Coteaux du Layon-Villages, and may add their name to the label if the wine is richer and more intense in sugar and fruit. The commune of Chaume is considered superior to the others (Château de la Roulerie, Domaine de la Soucherie), but may only add its name if the yield does not exceed 25 hl/ha, the same as for Sauternes. Wine-making is improving and these delicious wines are coming back into fashion. Good domaines include the Domaine de la Motte, Château de la Guimonière, Château des Rochettes, Jean Baumard and Jean-Pierre Chéné. Production is large, around 5.5 million bottles. Price A–B.

Quarts de Chaume AOC

Sweet, perfumed, luscious wines from the Chenin Blanc grown on 40 hectares in a micro-climate of the Coteaux du Layon *appellation*. The permitted yield is the lowest in France, 22 hl/ha, with a minimum of 13° alcohol plus residual sugar. Quarts de Chaume, with Bonnezeaux, is the richest and most elegant of the sweet wines of Anjou. Harvesting is the result of successive *tris* to select only the most ripe bunches or those satisfactorily affected by noble rot, to produce a stunningly aromatic wine (peaches, apricots) with a fully sweet flavour and a fine, reserved finish. It can be drunk very young, or aged, but is best at 8–12 years. The Château de Belle Rive of the Lalanne family is once again making superb wines, and there are some lovely wines from Jean Baumard. Production is less than 100,000 bottles. Price C.

Saumur-Champigny AOC

Red wine from the Cabernet Franc planted on the most favourable limestone-chalk-based slopes on the left bank of the Loire to the east of Saumur. Champigny is the finest red wine in the Anjou-Saumur region, with a deep violetty-ruby colour, an immediate aroma of crushed fruit (raspberries), a generous, clean flavour and slightly rough finish. It is delicious when drunk young and cool, while the better vintages can last 5–10 years. Fine wines come from Denis Duveau, Domaine Filliatreau, Château de Chaintres, Alain Sanzay and René-Noël Legrand. Production 3.5 million bottles. Price A.

Savennières AOC

Dry and sometimes semi-sweet white wine from parcellated vineyards covering only 60 hectares on the right bank of the Loire to the south-west of Angers. The wine is made from the Chenin Blanc and has the highest minimum alcohol content (12°), and the lowest yield (30 hl/ha), for a dry white wine in Anjou. The soil contains a high proportion of slate, which gives the wine a flinty, rather austere acidity which needs a sunny vintage to provide the Chenin's floweriness and fruit. A good Savennières is less honeyed and direct than a Vouvray, but perhaps more refined. Many proprietors have planted Cabernet Franc, producing an attractive Anjou rouge, but recently demand has increased, particularly for the modern, softer and lightly aromatic wines. Fine wines come from Jean Baumard, Château d'Epiré, Château de Chamboureau and the Domaine du Closel. The two finest wines have their own *appellation*. **Savennières-Roche-aux Moines** produces a rounder, more concentrated and complex wine (Domaine de la Bizolière, Château de la Roche-aux-Moines), mid-way between the classic Savennières and the famous **Savennières-Coulée-de-Serrant**. This wine, owned as a *monopole* by Madame Joly, covers less than 7 hectares and produces no more than 20,000 bottles of slow to mature but satisfying wine. La Coulée-de-Serrant is tough and acidic when young and needs 5 years to open up, whereas the lighter, less '*grand cru*' Savennières can be drunk immediately. Price A–B (La Roche-aux-Moines), C (La Coulée-de-Serrant).

The Rhône Valley

The vineyards of the Rhône valley run from Vienne in the north to just below Avignon in the south, a distance of 200 kilometres. The region is divided into two main sections, the Côtes du Rhône Septentrionales (north) and the Côtes du Rhône Méridionales (south), the former dominated by the Syrah grape planted on granite-based terraces, the latter by the Grenache grape planted on the stony, arid plain. Nine bottles out of ten are red, deep-coloured and full-bodied, the better wines possessing an intensity of bouquet, elegance and ageing potential that can rival those from Bordeaux or Burgundy. The wines from the north tend to be firm and long lasting, those from the south heady and rich.

The Northern Côtes du Rhône

The vineyards of the Côtes du Rhône Septentrionales cover a 65-kilometre stretch running from Vienne to Valence, with the finest wines coming from well-exposed terraced vineyards overlooking the river. The latitude, close to the 45° parallel, offers a near-perfect climate for the vine. The soil is granite-based, exceptionally hard and costly to work, but allowing the *cépages* Syrah, Marsanne, Roussanne and Viognier to produce wines of an intensity of bouquet and flavour rarely rivalled elsewhere in France. Vines planted on the higher-yielding, more sandy soils of the plain produce wines of much less interest.

Château Grillet AOC

The smallest single *appellation contrôlée* (if one does not count the Burgundian Grand Cru *appellations* of La Romanée, La Romanée-Conti, Bienvenues- and Criots-Bâtard-Montrachet), covering 2.6 hectares in the communes of Vérin and Saint-Michel-sur-Rhône. It is the *monopole* of the Neyret-Gachet family, but now rumoured to have been sold to Lanson. The wine is white, from the same grape as Condrieu, the Viognier, planted on south-facing terraced slopes high above the right bank of the Rhône. Château Grillet spends 18 months in small oak casks before being bottled in the distinctive brown 70 cl *flûtes*, making a wine of similar aromatic intensity and richness to Condrieu, but perhaps closer-knit. It is best drunk at 3–6 years and does not improve past 10, even in very good vintages. Production is rarely more than 10,000 bottles. Price F.

1	Côtes du Rhône-Villages
2	Côte-Rôtie
3	Condrieu
4	Château Grillet
5	Hermitage
6	Crozes-Hermitage
7	Saint-Joseph
8	Cornas
9	Saint-Péray
10	Châteauneuf-du-Pape
11	Lirac
12	Tavel
13	Beaumes-de-Venise
14	Gigondas
15	Rasteau

Côtes du Rhône

Condrieu AOC

White wine, grown on the right bank of the Rhône in the communes of Condrieu, Vérin, Saint Michel-sur-Rhône and Limony. The *appellation* covers 200 hectares, yet only 17 are planted, with a further 5 to 6 coming into production in the next ten years. Fruit-growing, the proximity to Lyon for secondary homes and the unpredictability of the Viognier grape are the main reasons for the decline in production, which risked total extinction in the 1950s. The single grape planted, the Viognier, finds the perfect site in the rocky terraces with their fine, loose topsoil that have been carved out from the slopes above the Rhône, and, experimental planting apart, flourishes nowhere else in France. It is therefore the smallest produced *cépage noble* in the country, and Condrieu is one of France's rarest *appellations*. The wine is pale golden in colour, with an intense, floral, ripe-fruit aroma (violets and irises, dominated by the scent of peaches and apricots), spicy, glyceriny and quite full-bodied on the palate but with a dry finish. Some growers used to make a sweet Condrieu by stopping the fermentation, but this is no longer practised. Great years, such as 1978 and 1981, however, can produce wines with a little residual sugar. The wine is usually bottled early in the year following the vintage, and may be drunk immediately, but it is best at 1–3 years, before the extraordinary fruit fades, while good vintages can be kept for up to 10 years. The largest producer is Georges Vernay, with several *cuvées*, the most exceptional being his Coteaux de Vernon. Other good growers are Pierre Dumazet, Paul Multier (Château du Rozay), André Dezormeaux and Delas, who are replanting, while Marcel Guigal always vinifies a superb wine. The yield is limited to 30 hl/ha, but the Viognier is capricious, and actual yield, which used to average only 17 hl/ha, is now just above 20. Production is 50,000 bottles. Price D (worth it for the good wines).

Cornas AOC

Red wine only from 60 hectares of Syrah grapes planted on the right bank of the Rhône, opposite Valence. The wine of Cornas is Syrah personnified: very deep, nearly black in colour, with a rich, heady aroma of concentrated fruit (blackcurrants, raspberries, violets), finishing with a vigorous, mouthfilling flavour. The *appellation*'s unique micro-climate and exposition, sheltered from the Mistral, produces grapes of a more consistent ripeness than elsewhere in the northern Rhône, and the wine is correspondingly dark-coloured, full-bodied, rough at first, but never heavy. Lighter *cuvées* can be made from vines nearer the plain, from the more sandy soil near Saint-Péray, or from shorter vatting during fermentation, and may be drunk at 3–4 years. A classic Cornas should be drunk at 6–10 years and from a great year can last 15–20. The finest are made by Auguste Clape, with excellent wines from Guy de Barjac, Marcel Juge, Robert Michel, Alain Voge and the *négociants* Delas and Paul Jaboulet Aîné. Production, always below the permitted 40 hl/ha, about 250,000 bottles. Price B–C.

Côte-Rôtie AOC

The most northern *appellation* of the Rhône valley, with 120 hectares of vines planted on steeply terraced, south-west-facing slopes on the right bank of the river centred around Ampuis. Only red wine is made, principally from the Syrah, although up to 20% of Viognier grapes may be added during fermentation to produce a lighter, more aromatic wine. In fact, Viognier represents only 5% of the *appellation* and is to be found mostly in the Côte Blonde and above Condrieu. The Syrah, planted on the narrow terraces with inclines of more than 40%, has to be trained specially by the Guyot method, which allows the vine to climb up the support stakes to achieve maximum exposure. The stakes are cumbersome and the planting close together and disorganized, so no machinery can be used in these vineyards, which are the most labour-intensive in France. Vines are now planted on the plateau above the slopes, which is easier to work, but these tend to produce thinner wines, lacking the velvety intensity of a true Côte-Rôtie. A classic

Côte-Rôtie has a dark purple colour when young, ageing to a deep mahogany, a markedly floral, spicy bouquet and a rich, suave, complex flavour and a lingering finish. The finer wines undergo a slow fermentation to extract colour and body and spend 2, sometimes 3, years in cask, *pièces, demi-muids* or *foudres*, before bottling. Lighter vintages need 3–4 years more in bottle to open up fully, while bigger wines need 7–8, and can last up to 20 years. While most Côte-Rôties are a blend of grapes or wines from different parts of the *appellation*, the finest come from the middle, the Côte Brune and Côte Blonde. The heavier, clayey soil of the Côte Brune produces wines with immense colour, vigorous and concentrated, that require long ageing, the perfect example being Guigal's La Landonne. The lighter, more limestony soil of the Côte Blonde produces wines that are full-bodied but more gentle, with a scent of violets and a smooth finish, that are ready to drink earlier. The finest and most typical example is again from Guigal, La Mouline, which is a synthesis of richness, intensity and finesse: it is Musigny or Château Lafite to the Chambertin or Château Latour of La Landonne. Wines from the Coteau de Verenay in the north tend to be deep coloured and tannic, with excellent examples from Emile Champet and Albert

Dervieux, while those from the Coteau de Tupic, just above Condrieu in the south, are lighter, but fine and elegant, especially if some Viognier is used (Georges Vernay). Other fine producers are Georges and Robert Jasmin, Marius Gentax-Dervieux, René Rostaing, Pierre and Gilles Barge and Edmond Duclaux. Of the *négociants*, Vidal-Fleury at Ampuis have large holdings, especially in the Côte Blonde, and Jaboulet, Guigal and Chapoutier make excellent wine from the Côte Brune and Côte Blonde combined. Production is almost 500,000 bottles. Price high C.

Crozes-Hermitage AOC

Red and white wine from the largest *appellation* in northern Rhône, covering 800 hectares on the left bank of the Rhône, north and south of Tain-l'Hermitage. The style of wine, especially the red, which represents 90% of the crop, varies considerably. While production is expanding on the plain, where total mechanization is possible and the wines are pleasantly fruity but with no great depth, certain better-sited parts of the *appellation* provide wines of very high quality: the hillside vineyard and sandy soil at Mercurol is particularly suited to white grapes; at Gervans, the terraced, south-facing vineyards produce a wine of great solidity and character from a granite-based soil; at Les Sept Chemins, south of Tain, the stony, well-exposed vineyard produces firm, stylish wines, perhaps the best in the *appellation*. Made from the Marsanne (dominant) and Roussanne grapes, the white Crozes is a pale yellow, racily fruity wine with an acacia-like aroma. Many producers prefer it not to undergo malolactic fermentation, to preserve the acidity (Jaboulet, Jules Fayolle, Jean-Louis Pradelle), and these wines are best drunk young, while the wine of Albert Desmeure spends over a year in cask, and takes on the richness and complexity of an Hermitage. With few exceptions (Domaine de Thalabert from Jaboulet), a red Crozes-Hermitage cannot be compared to an Hermitage, although it comes from the same grape, the Syrah. The colour should be full, purple-red when young, with an aroma of raspberries and blackcurrants, a pleasantly fruity flavour and some Syrah firmness in the finish. Rather old-fashioned wines come from Albert Bégot and Raymond Rouré, more fruity *cuvées* from Tardy et Ange, Robert Michelas and the Cave Coopérative, and the *négociants* Chapoutier, Jaboulet and Revol are always reliable. The lesser vintages can be drunk at 2–3 years, while the more serious wines need 5–8 years to develop. Production, at 45 hl/ha, is 4.5 million bottles of red and 500,000 of white. Price high A.

Hermitage AOC

Red and white wines from 125 hectares of vines planted on the left bank of the Rhône around the town of Tain-l'Hermitage. The red is made from the Syrah, to which up to 15% Marsanne may be added during fermentation, although in practice the white grapes are rarely used and never exceed 5%. The white is made from the Marsanne and the Roussanne, the latter steadily declining owing to its low yield and fragility. The vines are planted on terraces, not quite so steep as at Côte-Rôtie, where the granite-based, flinty soil has the same heat-retaining qualities and is equally as hard to work. The slopes are less abrupt towards the east and the soil more sandy, producing a wine that is lighter and less intense. Throughout the Hermitage vineyards particular *lieux-dits* or *mas* are recognized as producing wines of different styles, although their names rarely appear on the label, most Hermitage wines being a blend of wines from several *mas*. White Hermitage is generally pale straw or golden in colour, with a pronounced aroma of apricots and dried fruit, a rich unctuosity on the palate, but a dry finish. Full-bodied wines, able to improve for 5–10 years, come from Gérard Chave, Chapoutier, Henri Sorrel, Guigal; a crisper style is that of Jaboulet's Le Chevalier de Sterimberg; and a very attractive elegant wine comes from Jean-Louis Grippat, Albert Desmeure and Domaine de l'Hermite. The red Hermitage should have a huge colour (deep purple, almost black when bottled, maturing to a rich mahogany with ruby glints), a pronounced aroma of blackcurrants and spices and an assured intensity of flavour. Vinification lasts two weeks or more to extract colour, fruit and tannin, followed by at least 12 months in *pièces* or *foudres* to produce one of the greatest wines in France. In good vintages it should be drunk at 10–20 years and even in lesser vintages between 5 and 10. The finest wines, delicately scented yet plummy and intense, come from the *mas* Le Méal, the heart of the *appellation* with superbly exposed vines (Henri Sorrel, Domaine de l'Hermite); Les Béssards produces tough, meaty wines, too hard when young, but with great structure; Le Greffieux produces rounder, more aromatic wines (B. Faurie), those from Le Beaume and Le Peléat are deep-coloured, less intense, with great finesse. It is rare to find an Hermitage from a single *mas*, and very successful *cuvées* come from Jaboulet (La Chapelle), Chapoutier (La Sizeranne), Guigal and especially from Gérard Chave of Mauves. Despite being a dark-coloured, 'manly' wine, red Hermitage should never be clumsy or heavy. The minimum alcohol content is 10°, but a fine Hermitage is usually between 12° and 13°. The allowed yield of 40 hl/ha is almost never attained from the Syrah. Production is now 400,000 bottles of red, 200,000 of white. Price high C.

Saint-Joseph AOC

Red and white wines from a very parcellated 65-kilometre stretch of vineyards running from just south of Condrieu to just north of Cornas on the right bank of the river Rhône in the Ardèche *département*. Grapes permitted are the Syrah for the reds and the Roussanne (now very seldom planted) and the Marsanne for the whites. The vines in the northern part of the *appellation* are mainly planted on the easier, lower part of the slopes, making a pleasant, fruity wine for relatively early drinking (2–3 years), most of it vinified at the Cave Coopérative at Saint-Désirat-Champagne. Much better wine comes from Saint-Jean-de-Muzols, where Raymond Trollot makes a fresh, lively white with an aroma of peaches and a sturdy, raspberry scent from vines facing those of Hermitage. At Tournon, the wines are bigger

and the acidity in the whites and the tannin in the reds allows them to keep well for 5–6 years. Excellent *cuvées* come from Jean-Louis Grippat (the best white of the *appellation*), Bernard Gripa and Chapoutier. Further south, around the village of Mauves, the heart of Saint-Joseph, the reds have a lovely purple colour and a striking raspberry-blackcurrant aroma when young, having more immediate fruit than Cornas or Hermitage, but maintaining the firm backbone from the Syrah. Very little white wine is made here, but superb reds come from domaines Chave, Coursodon, Gonon and Marsanne. Approaching Cornas, the wines are stronger and rougher and require long ageing. Production, from a maximum yield of 40 hl/ha, never achieved, is approaching 1,300,000 bottles, with 6–7% white. Price B.

Saint-Péray AOC

The last of the vineyards in the northern Côtes du Rhône, situated directly opposite Valence, the 60 hectares of Saint-Péray are planted with Marsanne and Roussanne (only 20%) grapes, to make a lively, aromatic white, most of which is sold as a *méthode champenoise* sparkling wine. The climate, the grape varieties and the sandy, stony, clay-based soil give a certain roundness to the wine, but it retains the high natural acidity that is essential for a successful sparkling wine. A fine Saint-Péray has more body but perhaps less finesse than Champagne, with a lovely pale gold colour, a bouquet of violets and a

lively, grapey taste. Its reputation is mostly local, where it is principally drunk as an aperitif. The still wine is usually made solely with the Marsanne, although Jean-François Chaboud makes a separate *cuvée* from the low-yielding and fragile Roussanne. The pale-straw-coloured, fruity, quite assertive wine should be drunk young, at 2–3 years, but can continue to develop for 7–8. Good producers are Jean-François Chaboud, Pierre Darona, René Milliand, Auguste Clape, Marcel Juge, Alain Voge, the local Cave Coopérative and the *négociants* Verilhac and Delas. Production, from 45 hl/ha, is 260,000 bottles, 80% *méthode champenoise*. Price B.

The Southern Côtes du Rhône

The vineyards cover a vast area of land on both sides of the Rhône between Pont-Saint-Esprit and Avignon, taking in the *départements* of the Drôme, Vaucluse and Gard. The dominant grape variety is the Grenache, although it is limited to 65% for the Côtes du Rhône-Villages *appellation*, and the Syrah, Cinsault, Mourvèdre play their part in varying degrees. Carignan, from the Midi, is progressively being limited to 10%, if not banned altogether, and white grapes (Bourboulenc, Clairette, Picpoul, Roussanne) may produce white wine, or be added to the red grapes during fermentation to make rosés and reds. The Caves Coopératives dominate the region, but the proportion of growers bottling their own wine is increasing as varietal selection and improved vinification have their effect. This change has been particularly evident in the search for elegance and fruit rather than alcohol in the red wines and rosés, and for freshness in the whites.

Côtes du Rhône-Villages AOC

Red, white and rosé wines from 17 vineyards in specific communes (soon to be increased) across the *départements* of the Drôme, Gard, Vaucluse and the Ardèche. To have the right to the *appellation 'villages'*, the wines must have a minimum alcohol content of 12.5° (12° for the white) from a yield of 35 hl/ha, in contrast to the *appellation* Côtes du Rhône *simple* which requires only 11° from a yield of 50 hl/ha. Further, the Grenache is limited to 65%, Carignan to 10% and Cinsault, Syrah and Mourvèdre must represent a minimum of 25%. In consequence, many growers choose the minor, but less restrictive *appellation*. The majority of Côtes du Rhône-Villages do not really fit into the category of 'fine wines', but special mention should be made of the dark-coloured, spicy wines from Vacqueyras, almost as fine in some cases as those from neighbouring Gigondas, the red wines from Cairanne, Sablet, Rasteau and Vinsobres, the rosés from Chusclan and the whites from Laudun. The excellent vins doux naturels produced at Beaumes-de-Venise and Rasteau are discussed on pages 114, 115. The current list of communes benefiting from the *appellation 'villages'* (in alphabetical order) is: Beaumes-de-Venise, Cairanne, Chusclan, Laudun, Rasteau, Roaix, Rochegude, Rousset, Sablet, Saint-Gervais, Saint-Maurice-sur-Eygues, Saint-Pantaléon-les-Vignes, Séguret, Vacqueyras, Valréas, Vinsobres and Visan. Price A.

Châteauneuf-du-Pape AOC

CHATEAU RAYAS
CHÂTEAUNEUF-DU-PAPE
APPELLATION CHÂTEAUNEUF-DU-PAPE CONTRÔLÉE

Red and white wines from the largest *appellation* in the Côtes du Rhône, covering 3,100 hectares north of Avignon, across the communes of Châteauneuf-du-Pape, Orange, Corthezon, Bedarrides and Sorgues. Although the wines of Châteauneuf are known the world over and are recognized as the foremost wines from the southern Rhône, quality has been variable, and only recently has a concerted effort been made by growers and *négociants* alike to ensure they reflect the quality of their reputation. Whereas many *appellations* in France are restricted to a single grape variety, the red wine of Châteauneuf-du-Pape may be made up of one or all of 13 grape varieties. This, combined with the differences in aspect of the vineyards – from the typical 'Châteauneuf' expanse of large, smooth stones, that cover completely the clayey soil beneath, to the gravelly, sandy soil of Château Rayas – gives widely varying styles of wine. In order of importance of planting, the 13 grape varieties are: Grenache (noir and blanc), Syrah, Mourvèdre, Cinsault, Clairette (blanc), Bourboulenc (blanc), Roussanne (blanc), Picpoul (blanc), Counoise, Terret Noir, Vaccarèse, Muscardin and Picardan (blanc). The Grenache is planted to over

80%, a proportion considered by the better growers to be quite excessive; nine-tenths of the 500 growers in the *appellation* have less than 6 varieties planted; and only two domaines, Château de Beaucastel and Domaine de Mont-Redon, have the full 13. While the Grenache dominates the *cuvées* of Châteauneuf, each *cépage* has particular characteristics that play their part: Grenache: body, fruitiness, high alcohol, glyceriny 'fat', good colour, but oxydizes rather quickly; Syrah: dark colour, spiciness, fruit and backbone; Mourvèdre: colour, depth, complexity and long-lasting firmness; Cinsault: leanness and lightness, tendency to be a little thin or 'mean'; Counoise: colour, firm backbone, spicy fruit (much favoured by Châteaux Fortia and Beaucastel); Vaccarèse: solidity, durability; the white grapes, fermented with the red, add freshness and delicacy of bouquet, but they are being used more and more on their own for the white Châteauneuf-du-Pape. The minimum alcohol content in a Châteauneuf is the highest in France at 12.5°, and many of the Grenache-dominated *cuvées* are nearer 14°. Chaptalization is forbidden, but would not be necessary in any case, since the stones covering most of the vineyards act as night-storage heaters to compound the effect of the naturally sunny climate to produce high grape sugars. Yield is limited to 35 hl/ha, which is low in itself, but considering the low density of plantation in the *appellation* (3,000 vines per hectare) the maximum yield per vine plant is relatively high, leading to further variation in quality. A particularity of Châteauneuf-du-Pape (and Gigondas) is that between 5 and 15% of the production must be declassified and may only be sold as *vin ordinaire*. This is known as *le rapé*, and is an effective incitement to maintaining quality.

A fine Châteauneuf-du-Pape rouge is a majestic wine, with a deep ruby colour, with floral, fruity, spicy, even herby aromas, and a rich, mouth-filling, warm flavour. It is a big, even massive wine, but one that should always have an edge of finesse and a well-balanced finish. They may be drunk earlier than wines from the northern Rhône, at 3–4 years, but wines from the better domaines benefit from longer ageing, and may still be good at 10–20 years. Vinification has changed much in recent years and some of the most modern equipment and sophisticated cellars are to be found in the area. Of the many fine domaines the following may be singled out: Château de Beaucastel (one of the most forward-looking growers, making complex wines for long ageing), Domaine du Vieux Télégraphe (superb vinification, big, plummy wines), Château Fortia, Château la Nerte (both classic wines), Château Rayas (now back on form after the death of Louis Reynaud in 1978), Clos de l'Oratoire des Papes, Clos des Papes, Domaine des Cabrières, Domaine de la Gardine, Les

Clefs d'Or, and the big properties Château de Fines-Roches and Domaine de Mont-Redon. Quicker-maturing wines, no less interesting, are made by the Domaine de Beaurenard, Domaine de Nalys, Domaine de la Solitude and Roger Sabon. In Châteauneuf itself, there are two *caveaux*, Caves Reflets and Prestige et Tradition, that group a number of smaller proprietors, all making reliable wine. Around 30% of the production is domaine-bottled, bearing the coat-of-arms of the Popes of Avignon embossed above the label. Of the *négociants*, Bérard, Brotte, Chapoutier, Guigal and Jaboulet regularly produce some fine *cuvées*.

There is growing interest in Châteauneuf-du-Pape blanc, which now represents 3% of the production. The Grenache Blanc and Clairette produce sunny, aromatic wines that do not go through malolactic fermentation, in order to preserve their acidity and freshness. The Bourboulenc and Roussanne have more character and body and may be aged. Stylish, racy white wines are the speciality of domaines Nalys, Mont-Redon, Père-Caboche, Font-de-Michelle and Bérard, while bigger wines come from Fortia, Beaucastel and Vieux Télégraphe. The whites are generally best drunk young, while the flowery freshness hides the basic high level of alcohol and lack of acidity. Production is around 14 million bottles. Price high B–low C.

Gigondas AOC

Red and rosé wines from 1,200 hectares planted at the foot of the Dentelles de Montmirail to the east of Orange in the Vaucluse *département*. A little white wine is produced which must take the *appellation* Côtes du Rhône, not Gigondas. The soil is made up of a heavy clay on the high ground just below the Dentelles, producing lightish wines for the *appellation*, a more stony, less clayey mix on the middle slopes, producing full-bodied, well-balanced wines, and the sandy, stony vineyards on the plain, producing rich, deep-coloured wines with a pronounced *goût de terroir*. Many growers believe that the most typical Gigondas is a judicious blend of wines from these three sectors. Grenache is planted to a maximum of 65%, with a minimum of 25% Syrah, Mourvèdre and Cinsault for firmness and finesse, the balance, if necessary, being made up with minor grape varieties such as the Clairette, now very little planted. A red

Gigondas is a big, sturdy wine, with a magnificent, deep, almost black colour, a powerful, briary, spicy bouquet and a rich, tannic taste. With a minimum of 12.5° alcohol from a yield of 35 hl/ha, it has the same weight as a Châteauneuf, and is even a little firmer. Gigondas may be drunk 3–4 years after the vintage, with its plummy, Christmas-pudding-like fruit matching the tannin, but really needs 5–8 years to develop complexity, and can last 15–20 years. The rosé, made from a maximum of 60% Grenache and a minimum of 15% Cinsault, is a very heady wine with the same weight as the red but not the richness of flavour, neither does it have the raciness and fruit of a Tavel. Gigondas is a village totally devoted to wine and there are many first-class domaines: Les Pallières, Domaine Saint-Gayan, Domaine Raspail, Domaine les Gouberts, Château de Montmirail, Domaine de Longue-Toque, Domaine de la Mavette, and Domaine l'Oustaou Fauquet. The Cave Coopérative is reliable, but not in the same class as the foregoing growers, and the local *négociants* Amadieu and Pascal produce some good wines as do Jaboulet and Guigal from the northern Rhône. Total production is 5 million bottles. Price B.

Lirac AOC

Red, rosé and a very small quantity of white wine from 660 hectares of vines planted just north of Tavel across the Rhône from Châteauneuf-du-Pape in the Gard *département*. The reds and rosés come from the main Rhône grapes, Grenache (minimum 40%), a high proportion of Cinsault, Syrah and Mourvèdre. Clairette is the principal grape for the whites, with Bourboulenc, Picpoul, the very rare Calitor and Maccabeo. Although the rosé is equally as fine as Tavel, though with less vinosity and depth, production is decreasing in favour of red and white (now only 3%), the last being the lightest, most aromatic white in the southern Rhône, rivalled only by the wines from just further north at Laudun. The red is lighter and more restrained than the other two major *appellations*, Châteauneuf-du-Pape and Gigondas, with a subdued ruby colour and a spicy elegance, and repays keeping for 4–5 years. The minimum alcohol content is 11.5° from a yield of 35 hl/ha, and with excellent wines being produced from the following domaines, Lirac is finally attaining recognition: Château Saint-Roch, Château de Ségriès, Domaine la Fermade, Domaine Duseigneur, Domaine de la Tour and the wines of Jean-Claude Assémat. Production is 2.5 million bottles. Price A.

Tavel AOC

Rosé wines from 750 hectares planted to the north-west of Avignon in the Gard *département*. Tavel is the major *appellation* in the Gard and the most important rosé in France. The major grape varieties are the Grenache, to a maximum of 60%, and the Cinsault, to a minimum of 15%. Ancillary white grapes are permitted, to add freshness (Bourboulenc, Picpoul, Clairette), as are red grapes (Syrah, Mourvèdre), to add depth and colour, but Tavel is basically a Grenache (fruitiness, body) – Cinsault (liveliness, acidity) wine. The soil is stony, with a clay base which gives the wine a robustness typical of the southern Côtes du Rhône. While some domaines still age their wine in wood to bring out an 'onion-skin' Tavel of some complexity but little freshness, the best wines have a pretty violetty-pink colour, a spicy, floral aroma and a fruity, firm finish. They should be drunk in the year following the vintage, and can hold for a year or two more but gain nothing. The Cave Coopérative produces 55% of the crop and is very reliable, while perhaps more individual wines come from the following domaines: Château de Trinquevedel, Domaine de la Génestière, Domaine du Vieux Moulin, Domaine la Forcadière, Château d'Aquéria and the wood-aged Château de Manissy. Production is almost 5 million bottles. Price A.

Provence, the Midi, Corsica

It used to be said that no fine wine could be found south of Avignon. The exceptions – little pockets at Bandol, Palette and Bellet – only served to confirm this. However, while the majority of wine produced continues to be without much interest, the recent emergence of a number of growers dedicated to producing wines of great individuality and high quality is one of the most encouraging aspects of the French wine scene. Slowly, the sea of vineyards from Nice to Perpignan is being revitalized by research into the make-up of the soil, the micro-climates and, concurrently, the planting of *cépages nobles*, voluntary reduction in yield and innovative wine-making and ageing (where suitable in new oak).

From east to west, the wines of Provence and the Midi cover six *départements*: the Var, Bouches-du-Rhône, Gard, Hérault, Aude and the Pyrénées-Orientales. The dominant grape varieties are still the Carignan and the Grenache, producing wine with good colour and body but little ageing potential or finesse, yet the interest shown in the local Mourvèdre, the Syrah from the northern Rhône, the Cabernet Sauvignon, Merlot and Sémillon from Bordeaux, the Sauvignon Blanc from the Loire and the Chardonnay from Burgundy is changing the accepted style of *les vins du Midi* for the better.

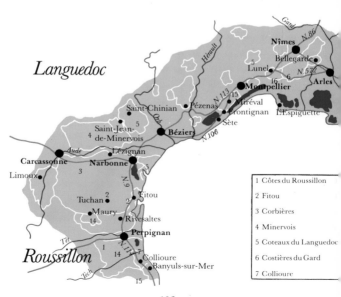

1	Côtes du Roussillon
2	Fitou
3	Corbières
4	Minervois
5	Coteaux du Languedoc
6	Costières du Gard
7	Collioure

Bandol AOC

Red, white and rosé wines from a possible 12,000 hectares of vines (although only one-third is planted) between Toulon and La Ciotat in the Var *département*. The white wine must come from a minimum of 60% local varietals (Bourboulenc, Clairette and Ugni Blanc), with a 40% maximum of Sauvignon. The local grapes impart a fruity floweriness while the Sauvignon adds an edge of acidity, and the wine should be drunk young. The rosé, which cannot be sold until 8 months after the vintage, has a lively colour, sometimes with a touch of orange, a spicy flavour from the Mourvèdre and Grenache, and a firm finish.

The red is the only style with real character and potential. It is made with a minimum of 50% Mourvèdre, with the balance of Grenache and Cinsault, and up to 20% of white grapes may be added during fermentation. The key to quality is the Mourvèdre, which completes the richness of the Grenache and the leanness of the Cinsault, giving a deep, velvety colour, a firm, vibrant fruit and great structure. By law, Bandol must spend 18 months in cask (usually in large *foudres*) before bottling, and needs the same amount of time to show its quality. Properly made, with a yield not exceeding 40 hl/ha, Bandol has none of the weightiness of a Châteauneuf-du-Pape or a Gigondas, and can age like a Médoc: good vintages from domaines like Tempier (the most fervent supporter of Mourvèdre), Ott and Pibarnon are at their best at 8–12 years. Production is 3 million bottles of red and rosé, 150,000 of white Price B.

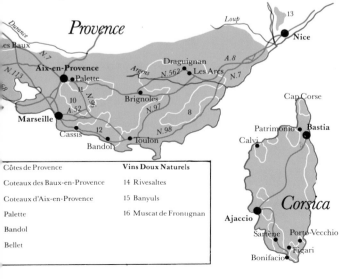

Côtes de Provence	Vins Doux Naturels
Coteaux des Baux-en-Provence	14 Rivesaltes
Coteaux d'Aix-en-Provence	15 Banyuls
Palette	16 Muscat de Frontignan
Bandol	
Bellet	

Bellet AOC

Red, white and rosé wines from a very small *appellation* whose vines are planted on terraces above the city of Nice in the Alpes-Maritimes. Due to the altitude of the vines at around 300 metres and the proximity of the Alps, the climate is cooler than on the plains of the Côte d'Azur, and the wine has a delicacy and finesse uncharacteristic of Provence. The *encépagement* is particular to Bellet: Braquet (Brachetto from Italy), Folle Noire (Fuella nera), Cinsault and a little Grenache for the reds and rosés, Rolle, Roussanne, Clairette, Bourboulenc and Chardonnay for the whites. The red has a fine deep colour, firm briary fruit and a touch of acidity that benefits from keeping; the rosés are delicate and firm at the same time and the whites, perhaps the most interesting of all, have a pale straw colour, a striking aroma of wild flowers and a firm, dry flavour with the weight of a white Burgundy. The two principal producers are the Château de Crémat and the Château de Bellet. Production is 100,000 bottles of red and rosé, only 40,000 of white. Price, as much for rarity as for quality, high C.

Côtes de Provence AOC

Red, white and rosé wines from 18,000 hectares across the Var *département*, which were granted AOC status in 1977. Fine wines are still the exception, as the move away from the Carignan grape and the dull rosés in their fancy bottles is in its infancy. Some of the original Grands Crus Classés of Provence are making excellent wine (Domaines Ott, Domaine de la Croix, Domaine de Rimauresq), while other growers are experimenting very successfully with *cépages nobles* from other parts of France (Domaine des Féraud, Domaine de Peissonnel, Domaine de la Bernarde). Price A.

Palette AOC

Red, white and rosé wines from a tiny *appellation* due south of Aix-en-Provence in the Bouches-du-Rhône. The particularity lies in the soil, derived from the geological formation known as the *calcaire de Langesse*, which is quite different from the neighbouring Côtes du Rhône and Côtes de Provence. The grapes, principally Clairette, Grenache Blanc and Ugni Blanc for the whites and Mourvèdre, Grenache and Cinsault for the reds and rosés, are all local, but acquire a firmness, even austerity, on the limestony soil that necessitates and repays ageing. As a result, the rosés sometimes lack the freshness of a Tavel, the reds have more the leanness of a Bordeaux than the 'fat' of a Côtes du Rhône and the whites have a sublety and vigour that is reminiscent of a Graves. The principal producer is Château Simone. Total production is about 60,000 bottles of red and rosé, 25,000 bottles of white. Price high B.

Vins du Midi et de Provence

Provence and the Midi are in a constant state of flux and while there are many excellent wines among the AOCs, VDQSs and Vins de Pays, they are too numerous to mention and the *appellations* as a whole do not qualify for inclusion in this book. The progress in the last ten years, however, has been so marked, that it is worth citing certain domaines that stand out in each region, representing the best of their respective *appellations:* Clos Sainte-Magdelaine and Le Mas Calendal (Cassis blanc AOC); Domaine de Trevallon and Mas de Gourgonnier (Côteaux des Baux-en-Provence VDQS); Château Vignelaure, wth a heavy proportion of Cabernet Sauvignon (Coteaux d'Aix-en-Provence VDQS); Mas des Tourelles (Costières du Gard VDQS); Domaine Gilbert Alquier (Faugères AOC); Château de Gourgazaud (Minervois VDQS); Domaine de Rivière le Haut (La Clape VDQS); Domaine de Daumas Gassac, Domaine de Saint-Jean de Bébian (Vins de Pays de l'Hérault); Domaine de Fontsainte, Domaine de Ciceron (Corbières AOC); Château des Nouvelles (Fitou AOC); Domaine Saint-Luc (Côtes du Roussillon AOC); Domaine de Mas Blanc of Dr Parcé (Collioure AOC).

Corsica

If research, experiment and progress were slow in coming to the Midi, they arrived even later in Corsica. The image of faded rosé, oxydized white and heavy red wine is under attack from a combination of improved grape selection (relying heavily on the local Niellucio and Sciacarello for reds and rosés, Vermentino for the whites) and controlled vinification. Domaines to look out for include Domaine Peraldi, Clos Nicrosi (one of the best white wines in Corsica), Domaine Gentile (including two superb VDNs, Muscat and Rappu) and Domaine de Torraccia.

Vins Doux Naturels

Contrary to what the name suggests, *vins doux naturels* are fortified wines, made in the same manner as port. They should not be confused with *vins liquoreux*, wines naturally sweet from the concentration of sugar resulting from the over-ripeness or botrytised condition *(pourriture noble)* of the grapes when harvested, the classic examples being Sauternes, Vouvray Moelleux or Alsace Sélection des Grains Nobles. A VDN is produced by halting fermentation by the addition of alcohol, before all the sugar has fermented out. This alcohol, a neutral grape brandy of a minimum of 90°, is added to the must while it still contains almost half its natural sugar. A wine intended to become a VDN must have at least 250 grams per litre of grape sugar (usually more), giving a potential alcohol content of 14°. The process of stopping the fermentation is called *mutage*, as it renders the bubbling young wine still or quiet (*muet*). The sweetness depends on two factors, the stage at which the alcohol is added, and the amount (not less than 6° or more than 10°). The same system of arresting the fermentation by fortification is used for the two *vins de liqueur* Pineau de Charentes and Ratafia, with the proviso that the former must be fortified with Cognac, the latter with *eau-de-vie de Champagne*.

Banyuls VDN

Red and tawny VDNs from the communes of Banyuls, Cerbère, Port-Vendre and Collioure in the Pyrénées-Orientales *département*. The Grenache Noir must represent at least 50%, accompanied by the Grenache Gris and Blanc, Maccabeo, Malvoisie and Muscat. The yield is a maximum of 30 hl/ha, rarely attained from these terraced hill vineyards, with a schistous soil that is very difficult to work. Banyuls must have a minimum of 21.5° alcohol plus sugar, with a maximum of 7% unfermented sugar. If the *mutage* is left until the wine is almost (or totally) fermented out, the taste will be dry. A good Banyuls should retain the rich, grapey flavour of the Grenache with a concentrated fruit taste and a sweet but not cloying finish, the natural product of a very sunny climate. Banyuls may be bottled young, or matured for several years in cask. Once bottled, however, Banyuls and all VDNs do not improve with further ageing. A **Banyuls Grand Cru** must be made with a minimum of 75% Grenache to have the *appellation*, be aged in wood for at least 30 months after the vintage, and must be submitted to two official tasting panels. **Banyuls Rancio** has been aged in wood, with the barrels taken out into the sun during the summer to give the wine the concentrated, slightly burnt Rancio flavour. These will be more tawny than red, as they lose colour in cask and rival the tawny ports. The finest Banyuls comes from individual properties such as Le Mas Saint-Louis and Le Mas Blanc of Dr Parcé. About 6 million bottles are produced, only 20% of the best quality. Price B–C.

Côtes d'Agly VDN
Maury VDN
Rivesaltes VDN

Grenache-based red and rosé VDNs, with Muscat, Malvoisie and a little Maccabeo for the whites. The same rules of *appellation* apply as for Banyuls, which they resemble, while being slightly sweeter. The best examples are the late-bottled wines which will state 'Vieux' or 'Rancio' on the label. Price A.

Muscat de Beaumes-de-Venise VDN

Made from the Muscat de Frontignan grape, planted on stony, sandy soil high above the town of Beaumes-de-Venise overlooking the Dentelles de Montmirail in the Vaucluse *département*, this is one of the finest 'white'

VDNs. The grapes must ripen to provide a potential of at least 15° alcohol, to leave a total not exceeding 21.5° after *mutage*. The Muscat de Beaumes-de-Venise has a lovely pale-golden colour, an extraordinarily heady scent of fresh Muscat grapes with overtones of apricots or ripe peaches, an explosive grapy, concentrated fruit taste and a rich, unctuous but lively finish. It is not honey-sweet, in the style of a Sauternes, and is best drunk in the year or two following the vintage. Muscat de Beaumes-de-Venise should be drunk very cold but not iced, as an aperitif or *digestif*, as it is too aromatic to go with food, except some fruit desserts. Most of the production comes from the excellent Cave Coopérative, where Vidal-Fleury and Paul Jaboulet purchase some good *cuvées*, while of the growers bottling their own wine, Domaine des Bernardins and Domaine Durban are very fine. Production is almost 1 million bottles. Price B.

Muscat de Frontignan VDN

A white VDN from the local Muscat de Frontignan grape planted on exposed, arid, stony vineyards running right down to the Mediterranean a few kilometres east of Sète in the Hérault *département*. This is the best known of the VDN Muscats and is even richer than the equally fine Muscat de Beaumes-de-Venise. The grapes are late-harvested for the highest possible concentration of sugar and flavour, and the *mutage* only enhances the explosive Muscat fruit, to leave a wine that is golden in colour, rich, unctuous, with concentrated floral aromas and sweet, honeyed taste. Despite its richness, Muscat de Frontignan has great finesse, is never cloying and is also supposed to have great restorative qualities. Almost all of the wine is made at the Cave Coopérative and is sold in a special bottle with carved fluting up the sides. Production is around 2 million bottles. It has led a revival in recent years for the other Muscats from the Midi – **Muscat de Lunel**, **Muscat de Miréval**, **Muscat de Rivesaltes**, **Muscat de Saint-Jean-de-Minervois**. These share the same golden colour, the heady 'musky' bouquet and grapey-raisiny flavour. They are perhaps a little less impressive than the Muscat de Frontignan and less fine than the Muscat de Beaumes-de-Venise, and consequently are less expensive. Price A (all).

Rasteau VDN

Made from the Grenache grape planted in the Côtes du Rhône commune of Rasteau north-east of Orange, Rasteau VDN may either be 'white' (a deep gold) or 'red' (more like tawny), depending on the length of time the skins ferment with the must. The grapes are picked with exceptional ripeness to make one of the best and rarest VDNs in France. The finest is the wood-aged Rasteau Rancio from the Domaine Bressey-Masson. Price B.

Bordeaux

The vineyards of Bordeaux are situated entirely in the *département* of the Gironde in the South-west of France, covering both banks of the Gironde estuary and the rivers Garonne and Dordogne. Red, rosé, dry, semi-sweet and *liquoreux* white and sparkling wines are made. With some 100,000 hectares under vines, producing around 500 million bottles of wine a year, all AOC, Bordeaux is the largest vineyard of fine wines in the world. The generic *appellations* – Bordeaux, Bordeaux Supérieur, even the 1ères Côtes de Bordeaux – do not come into the scope of this book. The fine wines of Bordeaux, without exception, come from individual estates in the more prestigious *appellations*. The more

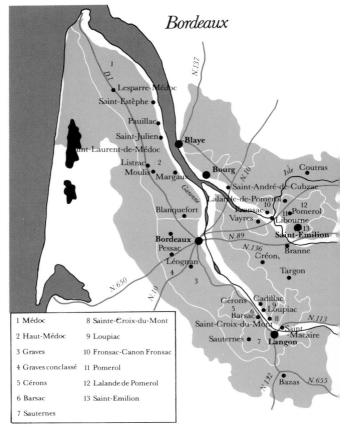

Bordeaux

1 Médoc	8 Sainte-Croix-du-Mont
2 Haut-Médoc	9 Loupiac
3 Graves	10 Fronsac-Canon Fronsac
4 Graves conclassé	11 Pomerol
5 Cérons	12 Lalande de Pomerol
6 Barsac	13 Saint-Emilion
7 Sauternes	

important of these are assessed within their own *appellations* in the pages that follow. The balance of the different grape varieties is given in abbreviated form, as follows: red, Cabernet Sauvignon (CS), Cabernet Franc (CF), Merlot (Me), Malbec (Ma), Petit Verdot (PV); white, Semillon (Se), Sauvignon (Sa), Muscadelle (Mu).

The Médoc

The region known as *le Médoc* comprises virtually the whole of the left bank of the Gironde estuary, an area of 80 kilometres running from Blanquefort, 12 kilometres north of Bordeaux, to Soulac, at the tip of the estuary. Only red wines may carry the *appellation*, the very few whites and even fewer rosés produced being sold as Bordeaux or Bordeaux Supérieur. The grapes planted on a predominantly gravelly soil are the classic Bordeaux varieties: Cabernet Sauvignon (usually dominant), Cabernet Franc, Merlot and small amounts of Petit Verdot and, very rarely, Malbec. A Médoc should have a fine ruby colour, a slightly briary fruit bouquet, with overtones of oak and spice and a concentrated fruit on the palate, often austere when young, but with good balance and a clean refreshing finish. It is this balance and dryness, despite the fruit, that makes it the perfect wine with food. The region is divided into the following *appellations*: Médoc (10° minimum alcohol from 50 hl/ha), Haut-Médoc (10°, 48 hl/ha), and the superior communal *appellations*: Margaux, Moulis, Listrac, Saint-Julien, Pauillac, Saint-Estèphe (10.5°, 45 hl/ha). Within these *appellations*, the majority of the finer châteaux have been awarded Cru Classé or Cru Bourgeois status.

The 1855 Classification

This famous classification was conceived for the 1855 Exposition Universelle in Paris and prepared by the *courtiers* or wine-brokers of Bordeaux, based on the quality and price of the major Châteaux of the Médoc and Sauternes at that time. Since the idea of a 'Château X' is basically that of a recognized *marque commerciale* or brand name, and the only official control of quality on the wine are the controls imposed by its *appellation* (unknown in 1855), what this selection classified were the names of the Châteaux and in no sense a precise *terroir*. The many changes in ownership of these Châteaux before and since 1855, and in the quality, desirability and price of these wines, have tended to bring into question the validity of the classification. The fact that a Château may purchase (or sell) vines in its own *appellation* (and outside, in the case of Lafite–Rothschild) does not affect its status, and neither does the actual condition of the vineyard, *encépagement*, age of vines, or quality of wine-making, which means that the real relative quality of these brand names must constantly be under review. The INAO attempted a reclassification in 1960, which met with strong opposition. Alexis Lichine has proposed a very well-researched classification, to include the Graves, Pomerol and Saint-Emilion. Meanwhile, today as in 1855, real quality tends to be reflected in the price. In the text, the Châteaux are listed as in the 1855 classification.

The Crus Bourgeois

The Crus Bourgeois were first classified in 1932, reclassified in 1966 and again in 1978. Today there are 240 Châteaux with the right to put Cru Bourgeois on their label, representing, in terms of each *appellation*: Médoc 50%, Haut-Médoc 70%, Listrac 70%, Moulis 80%, Margaux 25%, Saint-Julien 15%, Pauillac 10%, Saint-Estèphe 50%. The Syndicat des Crus Bourgeois has subdivided the Châteaux into 3 categories: Grand Bourgeois Exceptionnel (only Haut-Médoc, Château-bottling obligatory); Grand Bourgeois (barrel-ageing obligatory); Bourgeois (minimum 7 hectares of vines, vinified separately, subject to tasting). While some of the finest *non-classé* wines do not belong to the Syndicat – Siran, d'Angludet, Lanessan, de Pez – its role in encouraging and promoting quality in the Médoc is undeniable.

Haut-Médoc AOC

Red wine only from the southern part of the Médoc, between Blanquefort in the south and Saint-Seurin-de-Cadourne a little north of Saint-Estèphe. The communal *appellations* (pages 118–37) benefit from a soil of light gravel that historically has produced the finest wines, including all but 5 of the 61 Crus Classés. Of the 15 communes that make up the Haut-Médoc *appellation*, those with the highest incidence of gravel in the soil (logically those nearer the Gironde river) – Blanquefort, Parempuyre, Ludon, Macau, Arcins, Lamarque, Cussac and Saint-Seurin-de-Cadourne – tend to produce wines that have an edge of finesse over the more solid wines from the inland communes – Le Taillan, Le-Pian-de-Médoc, Avenson, Saint-Laurent-du-Médoc, Saint-Saveur, Cissac and Vertheuil.

The Crus Classés of the Haut-Médoc

Château La Lagune

3ème GCC (55 ha; CS 55%, CF 20%, Me 20%, PV 5%)

The nearest Cru Classé to Bordeaux, the vineyards of La Lagune are planted in the light, sandy gravel of the commune of Ludon. In 1958, when it was bought and reconstituted by Georges Brunet (qv Château Vignelaure Coteaux d'Aix en Provence), there were only 4 hectares under vines. In the early 1960s the wine was very supple and rich, misleadingly Burgundian in style, but with the vineyard maturing, it has taken on a deeper colour and firmer structure, while keeping its particular velvety smoothness. All new oak is used for every vintage. La Lagune is particularly appealing in light years and in great vintages should be kept 12–15 years. Production 25,000 cases. Price D.

Château La Tour Carnet

4ème GCC (32 ha; CS 53%, CF 10%, Me 33%, PV 4%)

The vineyards, in the commune of Saint-Laurent, due west of Saint-Julien, were almost entirely replanted in 1962 by the current owners, and until 1975 the wine, although charming, was not of Cru Classé standard. The clayey-sandy soil imparts body and robustness which is now underlined by the greater age of the vines, and the wine now has good colour, structure and pure Médoc style. A further 13 hectares are to be planted. La Tour Carnet is relatively quick-maturing, needing 6–8 years in good vintages. The second label is 'Le Sire de Camin'. Production 16,000 cases. Price high C.

Château Cantemerle

5ème GCC (25 ha; CS 45%, CF 10%, Me 40%, PV 5%)

The second most southerly Cru Classé in the Médoc, north-west of La Lagune, Cantemerle was sold in 1981 to Cordier and, judging by the 1982, the wine has regained its position as the equivalent of a 3ème Cru. The light, sandy soil and high proportion of Merlot give Cantemerle a rich charming fruit that is intensified and stiffened by the Cabernets and by two years in barrel. Cordier will double the land under vines, bringing it back to its original size. In good vintages, Cantemerle should be kept 10–15 years. Production 9,000 cases. Price D.

Château Belgrave

5ème GCC (44 ha; CS 40%, CF 20%, Me 35%, PV 5%)

The vines of Belgrave are in a sole block to the west of Saint-Julien, the same commune as La Tour Carnet and Camensac. The estate changed hands in 1979, and intensive investment in the vineyards, especially drainage, and in the *cuvier* and *chais*, had an immediate result in an attractive 1980 and a deep-coloured, fruity 1982. Belgrave is made to be drunk at 6–8 years. Production 25,000 cases. Price C.

Château Camensac

5ème GCC (60 ha; CS 60%, CF 20%, Me 20%)

One of the four Crus Classés in Saint-Laurent, west of Saint-Julien, Camensac was largely replanted in 1965 and has been making deep-coloured, well-structured wines since the mid-1970s. It lacks the elegance and style of the better Crus nearer the Gironde, but is very reliable. At its best at 8–10 years. Production 20,000 cases. Price C.

The Crus Bourgeois of the Haut-Médoc

Whereas in the four superior communes of Margaux, Saint-Julien, Pauillac and Saint-Estèphe, the Crus Bourgeois tend to be overwhelmed by the importance of the Crus Classés, the Châteaux in the Haut-Médoc provide an extraordinary concentration of high-quality wines of great individuality. While only obsessive care in the vineyards and in the *chais* will regularly produce a fine wine, the *terroir* still gives the wine its basic character. The better Crus Bourgeois are discussed from the south of the *appellation* to the north. The nearest property to Bordeaux is **Château de Taillan**, owned by the Cruse family, producing a light, supple red wine and a dry white called **Château La Dame Blanche**. At Blanquefort, **Château Dillon**, grown on a sandy soil, is an elegant, attractive, medium-weight wine, while due north at Parempuyre, **Château Ségur** is in the same style but with more depth. Le Pian, inland, harbours **Château Sénéjac**, back on form thanks to financial reinvestment and a brilliant young *maîtresse-de-chai* from New Zealand, and is making fine, intensely fruity, classic wines (1983), and **Château de Malleret**, regularly firm and elegant. Nearer to the river at Ludon, **Château Ludon-Pomies-Agassac** is owned by and usually contains the *déclassements* of Château La Lagune, **Château d'Agassac**, a moated, fairy-tale château, produces extremely elegant wine of Margaux quality and style, while those of **Château d'Arche** are almost as fine. **Château Maucamps** and **Château Biré** at Macau (better known for Château Cantemerle) are aromatic and stylish. Just south-east of Moulis, the clayey undersoil at **Château Citran** (Avensan) adds a finesse and subtlety to a rather firm wine, while **Château Villegorge**, with vines in Moulis and Soussans (Margaux) and a high percentage of Merlot, is altogether richer and smoother. The *appellation* Margaux separates Avensan from Arcins, where the newly rebuilt **Château d'Arcins** as well as **Château Barrèyres** produce a vast amount of correct wine, but are outclassed by the depth and breed of **Château Arnauld**, under the same ownership of Poujeaux-Theil. Further north, at Lamarque, **Château Lamarque** is serious and satisfying, pure Haut-Médoc with good colour and fruit, and **Château Malescasse** is stylish but more reserved. The commune of Caussac is at the southern edge of Saint-Julien, which the wines strongly resemble: **Château Lanessan**, owned by the Bouteillier family of Pichon-Baron, has a striking bouquet and great depth and firmness of flavour that is regularly of Cru Classé standard; **Château Beaumont** is making excellent wine, deep-coloured, full of fruit, classic, but quicker to mature; **Châteaux Aney, Fort Vauban, La Tour du Haut Moulin** and **Moulin Rouge** are interesting, but do not have the quality of Lanessan and Beaumont. West of Saint-Julien at Saint-Laurent, the largest estate in the Médoc, **Château Larose-Trintaudan**, produces 70,000 cases of smooth, well-made wines with fruit and character, while those of **Château Caronne-Sainte-Gemme** are more traditional, meaty and tannic. At Saint-Saveur inland from Pauillac, **Château Peyrabon** (also sold as Château Pierbone) is known for rounded, elegant wines, aiming at the Lafite style; **Châteaux Ramage-la-Batisse** and **Touteran** have a rich, supple fruit and may be drunk young, **Château Hourtin-Ducasse** is fine and elegant while **Château Liversan** is more of an old-style Médoc. Slightly north at Cissac, **Château Cissac** makes a deep-coloured, fruity wine in the Pauillac style, **Château Hanteillan** is elegant and softer, more typically Saint-Julien, and **Château du Breuil**, less fine than these, has the firmness and austerity of a Saint-Estèphe. **Châteaux le Bourdieu, Meynieu** and **Reysson** at Vertheuil, on the south-west borders of Saint-Estèphe, are all correct and well made. The most northern commune of the Haut-Médoc, Saint-Seurin de Cadourne, has the fine, gravelly soil of the best parts of the *appellation*. The wine is uniformly deep-coloured, vigorous and long-lived. **Château Sociando-Mallet** stands out as the 'Latour' of the commune, with dark, intense wines from a high percentage of Cabernet Sauvignon; opposite in style is **Château Coutran**, planted in Merlot, rounder and quicker to mature; **Château Bel-Orme-Tronquoy-de-Lalande** is firm and fruity, but slightly austere, as is **Château Verdignan**; **Château Léstage-Simon** has a richer concentration of fruit and **Châteaux Bonneau, Charmail, Grand-Moulin** and the Coopérative **La Paroisse** are firm and reliable. Price A, mostly B, C.

Médoc AOC

Red wines only from the northern part of the vineyards on the left bank of the Gironde, from north-west of Saint-Estèphe to Soulac. While all the wine should share the characteristics of the *appellation* – fine ruby colour, firmness of fruit on bouquet and palate and a harmonious finish – some of the many hundred Châteaux are making wine that better expresses the possibilities of soil and climate than others. In general, these have been recognized and are classified Crus Bourgeois (qv). Since the element of *terroir* is primordial in Bordeaux, as in all fine-wine regions, some of the more successful wines are listed below with the names of their communes, from south to north.

The Crus Bourgeois of the Médoc

The most southern commune of the Médoc is Saint-Germain d'Esteuil, where **Châteaux Hauterive, du Castéra** and **Livran** produce well-made wines. To the north and inland, Ordonnac is dominated by the excellent wine from **Château Potensac**, which, with its other labels, Château Gallais-Bellevue, Château Goudy-la-Cardonne and Cru Lassalle, are owned by Michel Delon and made with the same care as his Léoville-Las Cases. Potensac is regularly the finest wine of the Bas-Médoc. Due north at Blaignan, **Château La Cardonne** (Rothschild) produces a large amount of eminently drinkable Médoc, **Château Blaignan** is almost as large but less fine, while **Château La Tour-Haut-Caussac** has more depth and *terroir*, in the more complex Haut-Médoc style. Nearer the estuary at Saint-Yzans, the splendid vineyards of **Château Loudenne** run down almost to the Gironde, producing a supple, beautifully balanced red wine with a marked element of new oak and a fine, crisp, dry white; also at Saint-Yzans, **Château Sigognac** is as delicate as Loudenne is stylish, but ages well. North-west at Couquèques is the soft, attractive **Château Haut-Canteloup** and the very impressive **Château Les-Ormes-Sorbets**, a wine with intensity of fruit, character and ageing potential. The most important commune in the *appellation* is Bégadan, with **Château La Tour de By** (second label La Roque de By) making consistently fine wine, deep-coloured, aromatic, with great depth of fruit, pure Médoc, somewhat in the Pauillac style; **Château Patache d'Aux** is equally well regarded, but has less finesse; **Château Greyssac**, light and elegant, is quicker maturing than these, as is **Château Laujac**, while solidly fruity but fine wine comes from **Châteaux La Clare, du Monthil** and **Vieux-Ch.-Landon**. A little more inland, **Château Bournac** at Civrac is becoming known for its deep-coloured wines, packed with fruit and Médoc character, and at Saint-Christoly, **Châteaux Saint-Bonnet, La Tour Saint-Bonnet, Le Bosq, Lavallière** and **La Tour Blanche** are well made, but lack the intensity and assurance of the better wines from Bégadan. At Queyrac, **Château Carcannieux** is lightish, but stylish and smooth, while nearer to the estuary at Valeyrac, **Château Bellerive** produces a meaty, concentrated Saint-Estèphe style, and **Château Bellevue** a smoother, more aromatic, quicker-maturing wine. In the very north of the *appellation*, still largely unplanted, **Château Sestignan** looks like becoming a classic Médoc. Price A–B.

Margaux

Red wine only from an *appellation* covering the five communes of Margaux, Cantenac, Labarde, Arsac and Soussans, an area of almost 1,100 hectares. At Margaux itself, the soil is lighter and finer and the wines have a corresponding edge of elegance over the other communes. The style of Margaux has been summed up by Alexis Lichine in three words: finesse, elegance, subtlety. To this may be added the brilliant, deep colour and the capacity for ageing. Margaux is often thought of as the most feminine wine from Bordeaux, an idea contradicted by the sturdiness of some of the Crus Classés. They should, however, be most fragrant and refined.

The Crus Classés of Margaux

Château Margaux

1er GCC (Red: 75 ha; CS 75%, Me 20%, PV 5%. Bordeaux blanc: 10 ha; Sa 100%)

This world-famous wine is the only Premier Cru Classé from which the *appellation* which it represents to perfection, is named. The characteristics of finesse, elegance and subtlety are backed by a firmness that only heightens the whole. After a series of unspectacular vintages from the late 1960s, Margaux was sold to M. André Mentzenopoulos in 1977 and the current splendid quality of the wine is the result of massive and much-needed investment in the vineyards and the *chais*. The better vintages (1979, 1981) should be kept for 12 to 15 years. The second wine, Pavillon Rouge du Château Margaux, and lighter vintages may be drunk at 6–8 years. The white wine, made in a separate *chai* with the most modern equipment, is dry, with a flinty, floral persistence and can be drunk young or kept for 3–4 years. Production 20,000 cases red, 3,000 white. Price F (white), FF (red).

Château Rausan-Ségla

2ème GCC (45 ha; CS 51%, CF 11%, Me 36%, PV 2%)

Although the vineyards border those of Margaux and Palmer, Rausan-Ségla does not seem to justify its place as top of the 2ème Crus Classés. It is fragrant but sometimes lacking in intensity. Recent vintages (1975, 1978, 1982) have been of good quality. Production 14,000 cases. Price C–D.

Château Rauzan-Gassies

2ème GCC (30 ha; CS 40%, CF 23%, Me 35%, PV 2%)

The smaller part of the old Rauzan estate, making correct wines, if lacking a little finesse, not really of 2ème Cru standard. In the 1980s, the guidance of Professeu Peynaud has resulted in improved quality, with woodiness being replaced by a smoother fruit. Due to the low proportion of Cabernet Sauvignon and a relatively short period of vinification and ageing, the wine can be drunk at 6–10 years. Production 10,000 cases. Price C–D.

Château Durfort-Vivens

2ème GCC (19 ha; CS 82%, CF 10%, Me 8%)

With the exception of a small parcel of vines almost encircled by Château Margaux, the vines of Durfort-Vivens are in Cantenac, near Brane-Cantenac, both properties owned by Lucien Lurton. The higher proportion of Cabernet Sauvignon lends Durfort a firmness and leanness that needs ten years to soften. The second wine is Domaine de Curebourse. Production 6,000 cases. Price high D.

Château Lascombes

2ème GCC (93 ha; CS 46%, CF 8%, Me 33%, PV 12%, Ma 1%)

An extremely parcellated vineyard, now one of the largest in the Médoc, making deep-coloured, fruity wine, almost beefy for a Margaux, but smooth and attractive. Lascombes is reliable, even in light vintages, and its roundess allows it to be drunk at 6–10 years. The second wine is Château la Gombaude. Production 35,000 cases. Price D.

Château Brane-Cantenac

2ème GCC (85 ha; CS 70%, CF 13%, Me 15%, PV 2%)

Large property with vines planted on light, gravelly soil with a chalk base. The relatively young vines led to a succession of quick-maturing vintages in the 1970s (with the exception of a magnificent 1975), while in the 1980s the wines have more colour and intensity, with a distinctive finesse and flavour. Another Paynaud-advised property. There are two second labels: Château Notton and Domaine de Fontarney. These may be drunk at 5 years, while the *grand vin* needs 10. Production 29,000 cases. Price D–E.

Château Giscours

3ème GCC (75 ha; CS 66%, Me 34%)

The most southern of the Margaux Crus Classés, Giscours is an immaculately run property making extremely reliable, deep-coloured, concentrated wine, that has more robustness than delicacy, but great style. 1975 was the last of the very tannic vinifications, and current vintages now have a smooth density of fruit and softer tannins and can be drunk at 8–10 years. Production 25,000 cases. Price D.

Château Kirwan

3ème GCC (35 ha; CS 31%, CF 31%, Me 33%, PV 5%)

A well-run property in Cantenac and one of the last of the Crus Classés to adopt château-bottling, Kirwan has been considerably replanted since 1972. The wine used to be rather light and mean, but in 1975, 1979 and 1982 produced deep-coloured, firm, long-lived wines, relatively tough for a Margaux. Production 11,000 cases. Price C–D.

Château d'Issan

3ème GCC (32 ha; CS 80%;, Me 20%)

A magnificent moated Château with almost all its vines in a single block on the Cantenac-Margaux borders, d'Issan is one of the most typical Margaux, with a fragrant bouquet and soft, lissom fruit. The very high percentage of Cabernet Sauvignon gives depth and complexity, while a shortish vinification prevents the wine becoming too tannic. D'Issan has been very good indeed since the middle 1970s. At its best at 8–12 years. Production 11,000 cases. Price D.

Château Maléscot Saint-Exupéry

3ème GCC (30 ha; CS 55%, CF 10%, Me 30%, PV 5%)

A wine of intensity and finesse, without the charm of Margaux or Palmer, but with great breed, one of the most respected Crus Classés. It is hard and lean when young and needs ten years or more to show at its best. Production 12,000 cases. Price D.

Château Cantenac-Brown

3ème GCC (32 ha; CS 75%, CF 18%, Me 15%, PV 2%)

Traditionally made wines, that make up in body and structure what they lack in delicacy. Quality has been uneven and Cantenac-Brown seems only to give of its best in classic years like 1970, 1975 and 1978, when the wine can be very long-lived. Production 15,000 cases. Price C–D.

Château Palmer

3ème GCC (35 ha; CS 45%, CF 5%, Me 40%, PV 10%)

The most prestigious property in Margaux after Château Margaux itself, and in the last two decades often the best wine of the commune. The vineyards cover the best soil of the *appellation* and the particular *encépagement* produces a deep-coloured, intensely fruity wine, with a soft, plummy flavour, firm finish and great finesse and distinction. The absence of hard tannin allows Palmer to be enjoyed young, while good vintages can last 20 years. Production 11,000 cases. Price E.

Château Desmirail

3ème GCC (11 ha; CS 80%, CF 9%, Me 10%, PV 1%)

Desmirail was parcelled and sold in 1939 to Palmer and Brane-Cantenac. The latter's owner, Lucien Lurton, has decided to recreate the property from parcels of vineyards in Cantenac and has the right to add a further 7 hectares. The 1982 was very successful. To maintain the quality of the *grand vin*, there is a second wine, Château Baudry. Production 3,000 cases. Price D.

Château Ferrière

3ème GCC (4.13 ha; CS 46%, CF 8%, Me 33%, PV 12%, Ma 1%)

Since 1960, the vines of Ferrière are leased to Château Lascombes who make the wine in the same way: fruity, plummy, quite quick-maturing. Production 1,000 cases. Price high C.

Château Marquis d'Alseme Becker

3ème GCC (9 ha; CS 29%, CF 29%, Me 29%, PV 13%)

Small property to the north of the Margaux *appellation* in Soussans making big, meaty, distinctive wines. The high percentage of Petit Verdot adds colour and fruit in good years and balances the low percentage of Cabernet Sauvignon. The wines are very carefully made in a new *cuvier* and last 10–15 years. Production 4,500 cases. Price C–D.

Château Boyd-Cantenac

3ème GCC (18 ha; CS 67%, CF 8%, Me 20%, PV 5%)

Small property making sturdy, rather old-fashioned wines from old vines. The low-yielding vines, addition of 15% *vin de presse* and ageing for 24 months in barrels of which only a few are new, results in a wine that contrasts to the feminine, delicate image of a Margaux, but is pure Médoc. Production 6,500 cases. Price high C.

Château Pouget

4ème GCC (8 ha; CS 85%, Me 10%, PV 5%)

Small property next door to Kirwan and Brane-Cantenac, Pouget was made at Boyd-Cantenac until 1983 (same ownership). The wine is similar in style, deep-coloured, full-bodied, serious, underlined by the high proportion of Cabernet Sauvignon and the absence of Cabernet Franc. The very successful recent vintages should be kept 10–15 years. Production 3,500 cases. Price C.

Château Prieuré-Lichine

4ème GCC (58 ha; CS 52%, CF 12%, Me 31%, PV 5%)

Extremely parcellated property with vines in all the best parts of the *appellation*, making one of the less weighty Margaux, with purity of style and great finesse. The experience of Alexis Lichine combined with the advice of Professeur Peynaud have produced a run of successful vintages including a very fine 1983. The second label, from vats declassified by MM Lichine and Peynaud, is Château de Clairefont. Production 28,000 cases. Price high C.

Château Marquis de Terme

4ème GCC (30 ha; CS 45%, CF 15%, Me 35%, PV 5%)

Robust, dark-coloured wine (with up to 20% *vin de presse* added) for long-term drinking. Recent vintages are as full-bodied, but less hard than the 1970 and 1975, and can be drunk at 10 years. The property sells a second wine, Domaine des Gondats, under the *appellation* Bordeaux Supérieur. Production 11,500 cases. Price high C.

Château Dauzac

5ème GCC (45 ha; CS 70%, CF 5%, Me 20%, PV 5%)

Bordered by Châteaux Siran and Giscours in the commune of Labarde, Dauzac is under new management since 1978, the vineyard has been expanded and replanted and the *cuvier* rebuilt. The style of the wine is accessibly round and fruity and recent vintages are encouraging. Production 15,000 cases. Price high C.

Château du Terte

5ème GCC (45 ha; CS 80%, CF 10%, Me 10%)

The vineyards of du Terte are set apart from the other Crus Classés, in the commune of Arsac. The property is managed by the owner of Calon-Segur and since the mid-1970s the wine, dark-coloured with a fine, concentrated fruit, has been of high quality. 1982 was exceptional. The wines of Château du Terte can be drunk at 6–10 years. Production 14,000 cases. Price C-D.

The Crus Bourgeois of Margaux

Since Margaux possesses the largest number of Grands Crus Classés, it is not surprising that the Crus Bourgeois are to be found on the perimeter of the *appellation*, where the wines are a little sturdier and less delicately balanced. There are, however, four properties that stand out from the rest, whose wines are regularly of Cru Classé standard: **Château Siran**, in Labarde, whose vines touch those of Giscours and Dauzac, makes extremely fine, deep-coloured, suave-wine, pure Margaux and quite exceptional in great years (1961, 1970, 1975); **Château d'Angludet**, in Cantenac, set apart from but almost surrounded by Crus Classés, with all the *sève*, elegance and length one expects from a Margaux, has been very successful in recent vintages; **Château Bel-Air-Marquis-d'Aligre**, in Margaux and Soussans, with its particular *encépagement* of one-quarter each of CS, CF, Me and Ma, on a chalky soil, produces wines of arresting elegance, style and depth; **Château La Tour de Mons**, at Soussans, is full-bodied, with high extract and acidity, a slow-maturing wine with a great deal of fruit. Nearly on the level of these four is **Château Labégorce-Zédé**, at Soussans which has more breed and elegance than the good but rather rich **Château Labégorce**. Also at Soussans, **Château Tayac** is rather lean but quite distinguished, and **Château Paveil de Luze** is smoother and more straightforward. At Margaux itself, **Château Charmant** is as delicious as its name suggests, **Château Canuet** is soft and elegant and **Château La Gurgue** is improving. At Cantenac, the iron content in the soil produces wines that are more muscular and tannic, such as **Château Montbrun** and the well-situated **Château Pontac-Lynch,** while **Château Martinens** is suppler and of good quality. At Arsac, to the south of the *appellation*, **Château Montbrison** used to be part of **Château Desmirail** and produces wines with much finesse, and **Château d'Arsac**, although classified Haut-Médoc, is a large, well-run property. Price C, high C for the Crus Exceptionnels.

Saint-Julien

Red wine only from the smallest of the finer *appellations* of the Médoc, with 775 hectares under vines, of which 75% were classified in 1855. The soil is the same *graves* as at Margaux, but deeper and with more clay, and the wines are correspondingly richer. The vineyards nearer to the estuary, Beychevelle, Ducru-Beaucaillou, the Léovilles, produce wines of great breed and finesse, while those further inland, Talbot, Gruaud-Larose, La-grange, are meatier. Saint-Julien is 'quintessential Claret'.

The Crus Classés of Saint-Julien

Château Léoville-Las Cases

2ème GCC (80 ha; CS 65%, CF 13%, Me 17%, PV 5%)

The largest and most prestigious of the three Léovilles. The soil is slightly lighter than at Latour, but none the less, Léoville-Las Cases is the firmest of the Saint-Juliens, blending the austerity of Pauillac with the charm of Saint-Julien. It is a top-class wine of great breed and distinction, whose better vintages need at least 10 years. The high-quality second wine is Clos de Marquis and Domaine de Bigarnon (France only). Production 30,000 cases. Price D–E.

Château Léoville-Poyferré

2ème GCC (53.4 ha; CS 65%, CF 5%, Me 30%)

The middle part of the Léoville estate, Léoville-Poyferré has improved since 1975, with the wine again showing some of the elegance and class of a 2ème Cru. During the next few years, the vineyard will be enlarged by 15 hectares. The wines are less fragrant than Léoville-Barton but are now very well made. The second label is Château Moulin-Riche. Production 23,000 cases. Price D.

Château Léoville-Barton

2ème GCC (40 ha; CS 70%, CF 7%, Me 15%, PV 8%)

The smallest, most traditional and most Saint-Julien of the Léovilles, Léoville-Barton is a ripe, elegant wine, understated when young but blossoming out to show a fragrant, rose-like bouquet with great purity and length of flavour. Recent vintages have been very successful. There is no second wine, although in some years Ronald and Anthony Barton declassify the lighter wines into a generic Saint-Julien. Production 16,000 cases. Price low D.

Château Gruaud-Larose

2ème GCC (78 ha; CS 63%, CF 9%, Me 24%, PV 3%)

A large property set well back from the Gironde, producing dark, rich, full-bodied but classic Saint-Julien from a high proportion of old vines. The wine (and that of Talbot) showed a certain lack of elegance from the mid-1960s which has been reversed recently, coinciding with the return to the traditional Bordeaux bottle from the Cordier bottle in 1979. Gruaud-Larose is fruity enough to be drunk at 5-6 years, but needs 10–12 to show at its best. The excellent second wine, since 1979, is Le Sarget de Gruaud-Larose. Production 32,000 cases. Price D.

Château Ducru-Beaucaillou

2ème GCC (45 ha; CS 65%, CF 5%, Me 25%, PV 5%).

A very fine property, with most of the vines situated between Beychevelle and the Gironde, making a wine that only Léoville-Las Cases can rival. Ducru is a little more open and softer than Las Cases, with a great depth of fruit, impeccably made by Jean-Eugène Borie (Châteaux Grand-Puy-Lacoste, Haut-Batailley). The second wine, for much earlier drinking, is Château La Croix. Production 20,000 cases. Price D–E.

Château Lagrange

3ème GCC (50 ha; CS 58%, Me 40%, PV 2%)

Set well back, between Gruaud-Larose and the Haut-Médoc vineyards of Belgrave, Lagrange has made a considerable effort to improve its vinification. The high proportion of Merlot gives the wine a softness that allows it to be drunk at 5–6 years. The property was sold in 1982 to a Japanese group. Production 20,000 cases. Price high C.

Château Langoa-Barton

3ème GCC (20 ha; CS 70%, CF 7%, Me 15%, PV 8%)

The château at which Léoville-Barton is made and whose vines are in the heart of the *appellation*. A traditional vinification produces a ruby-coloured, finely bouqueted wine, slightly more round than the Léoville and with equal balance. At 10–12 years Langoa is delicious, but good vintages may last much longer. Some lighter *cuvées* are sometimes sold as generic Saint-Julien. Production 8,000 cases. Price C–low D.

Château Saint-Pierre-Sevaistre

4ème GCC (18 ha; CS 63%, CF 15%, Me 20%, PV 2%)

A small property well situated between Talbot, Gruaud-Larose and Langoa-Barton making deep-coloured, meaty, rather old-fashioned (very little new oak) wines from old vines. In 1983 Saint-Pierre changed hands, with Jean-Eugène Borie of Château Ducru purchasing the *cuvier* and *chais*, in which to make his Cru Bourgeois Château Lalande-Borie, and Henri Martin of Gloria purchasing all the vines except two small parcels enclaved by Gruaud-Larose, which went to Cordier. The very reliable second wine, Château Saint-Louis-le Bosq, may be discontinued. Production 8,000 cases. Price C.

Château Branaire

4ème GCC (48 ha; CS 60%, CF 10%, Me 25%, PV 5%)

Very well run property with some vineyards opposite Beychevelle, the rest parcellated across the centre of the commune, making extremely elegant wine with good colour, relatively light in body but not in flavour, one of the most harmonious wines of the Médoc. Branaire (Duluc-Ducru) seems to typify Saint-Julien. May be drunk at 8–10 years. Production 20,000 cases. Price high C.

Château Talbot

4ème GCC (87 ha; CS 70%, CF 5%, Me 20%, PV 5%)

One of the largest estates in the Médoc, the largest in a single block, with vines running from Léoville-Poyferre to Gruaud-Larose, Talbot produces a full-bodied, richly textured Saint-Julien. While it often lacks the elegance of the Léovilles, it is very satisfying, particularly in recent (1979, 1981, 1982) vintages. It is slightly quicker-maturing than its Cordier-owned stable-mate, Gruaud-Larose. Five hectares are planted with white grapes (Sa 80%, Se 20%) to make the attractive, dry 'Caillou Blanc', and the whole vineyard is to be expanded by a further 25 hectares. The second wine, since 1979, is Le Connétable de Talbot. Production 38,000 cases. Price low D.

Château Beychevelle

4ème GCC (70 ha; CS 72%, CF 3%, Me 24%, PV 1%)

A splendid estate, with wines separated from the Gironde by those of Ducru-Beaucaillou, making fine, elegant wines, as typically Saint-Julien as those from Branaire opposite, and rather fatter. After over 100 years in the Achille-Fould family, the Château was sold in 1983 to an insurance company. The second wine, for early drinking, is Réserve de l'Amiral. Production 30,000 cases. Price D–E.

The Crus Bourgeois of Saint-Julien

With most of the commune occupied by the Crus Classés, there are few Crus Bourgeois in Saint-Julien. The largest is **Château Gloria**, regularly on a par with the Crus Classés and often beating them in blind tastings, with two second labels, Château Haut-Beychevelle-Gloria and Château Peymartin. Only a little smaller, sometimes unreliable and less distinguished is **Château du Glana**. **Château Terrey-Gros-Caillou** produces a delicate, supple wine, **Château Hortevie** is fuller-bodied and very good, and **Château Moulin-de-la-Rose**, almost entirely surrounded by Crus Classés, is more concentrated and more tannic. **Château Lalande-Borie**, often erroneously described as the second wine of Ducru-Beaucaillou, is naturally of high quality, **Château Teynac** used to be part of Saint-Pierre-Sevaistre and still makes good wine, and **Château La Bridane** is reliable. On the borders of Pauillac, Michel Delon of Léoville-Las Cases produces the very elegant wines of **Château du Grand-Parc.** Price high B–C.

Pauillac

Red wines only from the second-largest fine-wine-producing commune in the Médoc, with 900 hectares under vines. The soil is a deep gravel with some clay and chalk in the base, becoming heavier towards the west of the *appellation*. The wines of Pauillac should share a dark, garnet colour, an intense fruit with an almost metallic hardness when young that never really softens out and is known as *le goût de capsule* or 'lead-pencil taste'. Pauillacs, Lafite-Rothschild excepted, are seldom feminine or delicate, but possess a structure and 'presence' that is most classic in fine Claret. The fragrance of Lafite, the severity of Latour and the sumptuousness of Mouton are all characteristic of *les premiers vins du monde*.

Château Lafite-Rothschild

1er GCC (90 ha; CS 70%, CF 5%, Me 20%, PV 5%)

One of the finest and most prestigious wines of Bordeaux, justifiably back at the top since the middle 1970s. The vineyards of Lafite are at the northern edge of the commune, bordering Mouton-Rothschild. A small parcel of vines is actually in Saint-Estèphe. The wine is made as carefully as possible: long vinification in wooden vats, 2½ years in new oak. Rigorous selection at bottling (two-thirds of the 1980 vintage was declassified), and the age of the vines and the intentional low yield add to the quality that comes from the gravelly, slightly chalky soil. Lafite has the most fragrant bouquet of the Pauillacs, where the aroma of violets is unmistakable, and despite great delicacy, can be firm and long-lived. Lighter vintages are charming and can be drunk at 7–8 years after the vintage, the better wines needing 10–15. The second wine is Le Moulin des Carruades. Production 25,000 cases. Price FF-FFF.

Château Latour

1er GCC (50 ha; CS 75%, CF 10%, Me 10%, PV 5%)

The most consistently great wine of Bordeaux, Latour has its vineyards in the southern part of the commune, on the borders of Saint-Julien, with the vines running down towards the Gironde. Everything that can be done to improve and maintain the quality of the wine is done, in the vineyards as in the *chai*, and only the very best goes into the *grand vin*. In style, Latour is massive, with an immense colour and terrific structure, perhaps the only wine in the Médoc that is not approachable in great vintages until 15 years, yet its power does not result in heaviness, but breed and depth. The second wine, Les Forts de Latour, comes from vines outside the walled vineyard of Latour, and from younger vines within it, and is very much in the Latour style, the quality being that of a 2ème Cru Classé. Production 20,000 cases. Price FF-FFF.

Château Mouton-Rothschild

1er GCC (1973) (80 ha; CS 85%, CF 10%, Me 5%)

Producing one of the most spectacular wines of Bordeaux, the vineyards of Mouton-Rothschild adjoin those of Lafite in the north of the commune. The wine is the result of the most single-minded dedication to quality at all costs in the history of the Médoc, over a period that now spans 60 years. Due to the very high percentage of Cabernet Sauvignon leading to an intense concentration of flavour, the wine more resembles Latour, but is flamboyant where Latour is severe. Except in very tannic years (1961, 1970, 1975) this rich concentrated *feu d'artifice* from low-yielding old vines will begin to open up at 10 years; the greater vintages need 20. There is no second wine from Mouton-Rothschild. Production 25,000 cases. Price FF-FFF.

Château Pichon-Longueville-Baron

2ème GCC (30 ha; CS 75%, Me 23%, Ma 2%)

The smaller of the two Pichons, with vines opposite Latour on the west of the Médoc road, making deep-coloured, sturdy wines that repay keeping. The high percentage of Cabernet Sauvignon and absence of Cabernet Franc emphasizes the structure of this wine that has been rather less fashionable than Pichon-Comtesse. 1978, 1979 and 1982 are excellent, among the best wines of the commune. Production 11,000 cases. Price high D.

Château Pichon-Longueville-Comtesse

2ème GCC (55 ha; CS 45%, CF 12%, Me 35%, PV 8%)

An exceptionally stylish wine from the larger of the Pichons, from vineyards touching those of Latour, Pichon-Baron and the commune of Saint-Julien. Although the château is actually in the Latour vineyards, the style of wine is more Saint-Julien, with the suppleness of the Merlot and the charm of the Cabernet Franc pointing up a contrast to the more dense and unyielding Pauillacs. Vintages since the 1970s have been very successful, combining quality with quantity. Despite their smooth fruit, good vintages should be kept at least 10 years. The second wine is La Réserve de la Comtesse, on a par with a 5ème Cru. Production 17,500 cases. Price D–E.

Château Duhart-Milon-Rothschild

4ème GCC (40 ha; CS 70%, CF 5%, Me 20%, PV 5%)

A vineyard purchased by the Lafite-Rothschilds in 1964 and completely replanted, and since 1976 producing top-class wines with both body and elegance. The situation of the vineyards, back from Lafite and Mouton, the same *encépagement* as Lafite, the same intentional low yield (20 hl/ha) from the still young vines and very careful vinification result in a wine of exceptional promise. The second label is Moulin de Duhart. Production 15,000 cases. Price D.

Château Pontet-Canet

5ème GCC (75 ha; CS 70%, CF 8%, Me 20%, Ma 2%)

A large estate due south of Mouton-Baronne-Philippe with one of the highest productions in the Médoc. From 1964 to 1974 the wines were unimpressive, but since 1975 things have improved under the administration of Guy Tesseron and the recent vintages (1979, 1981, 1982) have been very good. Production 35,000 cases. Price D.

Château Batailley

5ème GCC (45 ha; CS 70%, CF 5%, Me 22%, PV 3%)

The larger of the two Batailleys, separated in 1942. The vineyards are set well back from the Gironde in the south-west of the commune and the wine is deep-coloured and firm, lacking in charm, but quite satisfying. Recent vintages have had an excellent fruit and less rustic tannin so may be drunk at 8–10 years. Production 20,000 cases. Price C–D.

Château Haut-Batailley

5ème GCC (20 ha; CS 65%, CF 10%, Me 25%)

The smaller of the two Batailleys, owned by the same family as Ducru-Beaucaillou and Grand-Puy-Lacoste, making a very elegant, supple wine slightly in the Saint-Julien style. The comparison is similar between Batailley-Haut-Batailley and Pichon-Baron-Pichon-Comtesse: sturdy versus stylish Pauillacs. Professeur Peynaud is consultant to the two latter estates. The second label is Château La Tour d'Aspic for drinking at 4–5 years. Production 6,000 cases. Price D.

Château Grand-Puy-Lacoste

5ème GCC (35 ha; CS 75%, Me 25%)

This excellent property, separated from the Gironde by the Bages plateau, was purchased in 1978 by the Borie family (qv) from the remarkable Raymond Dupin. The wine, very dark in colour, with the Pauillac *goût de capsule* or 'lead-pencil' impression on the palate, has remained one of the most striking wines of the *appellation*, equal in quality to a 2ème Cru. The better vintages should wait for 10 years before drinking. A second wine was introduced in 1982, Château Lacoste-Borie. Production 12,000 cases. Price D.

Château Grand-Puy-Ducasse

5ème GCC (32 ha; CS 70%, Me 25%, PV 5%)

A parcellated estate with vines near Pontet-Canet, Lynch-Bages and Batailley, now under the same ownership as Chasse-Spleen and Rayne-Vigneau. The young vines are high yielding and the wine spends only one year in wood, which makes for a pleasant wine that can be drunk at 5–8 years. Production 14,000 cases. Price C.

Château Lynch-Bages

5ème GCC (70 ha; CS 70%, CF 10%, Me 15%, Ma + PV 5%)

The vineyards consist of five parcels across the Bages plateau, where the soil makes for dark, full-bodied wines. The high proportion of Cabernets, the age of the vines and the low yield at Lynch-Bages underline this to make a wine packed with an intense fruit that dominates the natural austerity of Pauillac. Very reliable wines, both for quality and ageing. The second wine, with 4 hectares of its own, is Château Haut-Bages-Avérous. A very little Sémillon-based dry white is made. Production 25,000 cases. Price D.

Château Lynch-Moussas

5ème GCC (22 ha; CS 70%, CF 5%, Me 25%)

The furthest inland of the Crus Classés, surrounded by woods on the borders of the *appellation*, Lynch-Moussas is undergoing a renaissance under the same ownership as Batailley next door. The wine is still relatively *petit* for a Cru Classé, but is improving with each vintage. Further replanting is envisaged. Production 8,500 cases. Price C.

Château Mouton-Baronne-Philippe

5ème GCC (50 ha; CS 65%, CF 5%, Me 30%)

The old Mouton d'Armailhac estate, renamed Mouton-

Baron-Philippe in 1956 and Mouton-Baronne-Philippe in 1974, runs between Mouton-Rothschild and Pontet-Canet. The light, sandy soil would lead the style of wine towards the latter, but the low-yielding vines and exemplary vinification give it a depth and polish that is associated with the former. Can be drunk at 5–8 years. Production 15,000 cases. Price E.

Château Haut-Bages-Libéral

5ème GCC (22 ha; CS 78%, Me 17%, PV 5%)

A small property with the majority of its vines just north of Latour, but on a lighter soil. The very high percentage

of Cabernet Sauvignon and the absence of Cabernet Franc result in a deep-coloured, chewy, slow-maturing wine that has shown very well in recent vintages. Production 8,000 cases. Price C.

Château Pédesclaux

5ème GCC (20 ha; CS 70%, CF 10%, Me 20%)

The vineyards of Pédesclaux are split into two main parcels, one to the west of the town of Pauillac near Lynch-Bages, the other to the north

by Pontet-Canet and Mouton. The wines are firm and complete, very successful and long-lasting in the classic vintages. Wine not sold as Pédesclaux goes into the owner's two Crus Bourgeois, Châteaux Bellerose and Grand-Duroc-Milion. Production 8,000 cases. Price C.

Château Clerc-Milon

5ème GCC (28 ha; CS 70%, CF 20%, Me 10%)

An estate in the north of the commune adjoining Lafite and Mouton, purchased by Baron Philippe de Rothschild

in 1970, Clerc-Milon produces firm, complete wine, less supple but more structured than Mouton-Baronne-Philippe. Classic vintages like 1975, 1978, 1982 will repay 15 years ageing. Production 9,000 cases. Price D–E.

Château Croizet-Bages

5ème GCC (21 ha; CS 37%, CF 30%, Me 30%, PV + Ma 3%)

With vines between Lynch-Bages and Grand-Puy-Lacoste, the *encépagement* and vinification of Croizet-Bages does not correspond to its neighbours. The wine is more muted, with less intensity of fruit, and, until 1979, rather woody. A very marked improvement was seen in the 1981, as with the sister-Château, Rauzan-Gassies. Can be drunk at 6–8 years, but will improve for longer. Production 8,000 cases. Price C.

The Crus Bourgeois of Pauillac

With twelve 5ème Crus in the commune, not to speak of the three 1er Crus, the Crus Bourgeois of Pauillac tend to be overshadowed by their grander brothers. Apart from the many Cru Classé Châteaux who use their Cru Bourgeois properties for the second wine, there are some fine individual properties: **Château La Couronne**, owned by the Borie family and adjoining Haut-Batailley, produces a perfectly balanced, stylish wine; **Château Fonbadet** is firm, fruity and distinguished, a true Pauillac; **Château Haut-Bages-Montpelou**, part of Duhart-Milon until 1948 and now owned by the Castéjas of Batailley, is softer, but very correct; **Château La Fleur-Milon**, well situated next to Clerc-Milon, makes some firm, meaty wine that deserves to be better known; **Château Pibran** and **Château La Tour Pibran**, touching Pontet-Canet and Grand-Puy-Ducasse, produce deep-coloured wine with good acidity; **Château Colombier-Montpelou** is less lively, but a serious wine made by the owner of Pédesclaux; finally, **Château La Bécasse** is not a Cru Bourgeois, but due to its high percentage of Cabernet Sauvignon and lavish use of new oak, has been described as 'a mini-Mouton-Rothschild'. Price C.

Saint-Estèphe

Red wines only from the largest of the fine-wine *appellations* in the Médoc, with 1,100 hectares under vines. The vineyards are more hilly than in the communes to the south, and the soil, while still predominantly gravel, has more clay. In style, Saint-Estèphe is always sturdy (a delicate Saint-Estèphe is a contradiction in terms), with a firm fruit and great staying power. It is far away, geographically and in character, from Margaux, near to Pauillac, and what it lacks in charm it makes up in 'wineyness'. When young, or from unsunny years, the wines tend to be tough, even astringent, but with recent progress in vinification, fruit now tends to dominate wood and tannin.

The Crus Classés of Saint-Estèphe

Château Cos d'Estournel

2ème GCC (57 ha; CS 50%, CF 10%, Me 40%)

The vines of Cos d'Estournel occupy a stretch of rising ground overlooking those of Lafite. The property belongs to the Domaines Prats, also owners of Petit-Village in Pomerol. The grapes are picked as late as possible to ensure high sugars and avoid harsh tannin and acidity, while the long fermentation captures the maximum amount of colour and bouquet. This, helped by the high percentage of Merlot, makes Cos a deep-coloured, rich, plummy wine, with great breed and elegance, that relies on intensity of fruit rather than tannin for its long life. Lesser *cuvées* are destined for Bruno Prats's nearby Cru Bourgeois, Château de Marbuzet. Production 20,000 cases. Price D–E.

Château Montrose

2ème GCC (64 ha; CS 65%, CF 5%, Me 30%)

A fine estate to the north of Saint-Estèphe, with its vines planted in a single block on an easy slope towards the Gironde. The more temperate climate due to the proximity to the estuary limits the risk of spring frost and aids the grapes to ripen early (1964), but the secret of Montrose is in the classic *encépagement* and the determination to make a *grand vin*. The wine has great colour, structure and integrity, while the packed fruit can take over 15 years to emerge. It is Saint-Estèphe at its most vigorous. One of the best 1982s. The lesser *cuvées* are reserved for the personnel (1,800 cases a year) and the second label, Château Demereaulement. Production 24,000 cases. Price D–E.

Château Calon-Ségur

3ème GCC (50 ha; CS 50%, CF 25%, Me 25%)

The most northern Cru Classé and the one with the lowest altitude (2–12 metres above sea-level), with vines planted on a gravelly, chalky soil that adds a lightness to the Saint-Estèphe style. If not as consistently good as Cos d'Estournel and Montrose, Calon-Ségur is full of flavour and charm and can be strikingly elegant. Recent vintages have been very successful. Production 20,000 cases. Price D-low E.

Château Lafon-Rochet

4ème GCC (42 ha; CS 70%, CF 8%, Me 20%, Ma 2%)

The vineyard of Lafon-Rochet, which is just north of Lafite and Duhart-Milon, and south-west of Cos d'Estournel, was entirely replanted in the early 1960s by Guy Tesseron who bought the estate (and rebuilt the château) in 1961. The high percentage of Cabernet Sauvignon and a long vinification results in a deep-coloured, intense, austere wine with a rich fruit that repays 10 years keeping. Recent vintages, as the vines age and the style Saint-Estephe-Pauillac is confirmed, have been very good. Production 15,000 cases. Price C–D.

Château Cos Labory

5ème GCC (15 ha; CS 35%, CF 25%, Me 35%, PV 5%)

A small vineyard, with parcels adjoining Cos d'Estournel and Lafon-Rochet, but far from these in style, Cos Labory is fruity and supple rather than firm and intense. The roundness of the wine approaches Moulis or Saint-Julien, and it may be drunk at 5-6 years. Production 6,000 cases. Price C.

The Crus Bourgeois of Saint-Estèphe

With over 1,000 hectares under vines and only five Crus Classés, the idea of a Cru Bourgeois Château comes into its own in Saint-Estèphe. If one estate has to be singled out as producing consistently fine wines in the Médoc outside the 1855 classification, it might be **Château de Pez**. These are perfectly made, with every quality one could desire in a Saint-Estèphe: colour, bouquet, firmness and depth of fruit, elegance and ageing potential. From the same village comes **Château Les Ormes-de-Pez**, owned by the Cazes family of Lynch-Bages, rich and rounded and very good. Nearer to the river are **Château Phélan-Segur**, with finesse, elegance and style, **Château Capbern-Gasqueton**, an excellent, well-structured wine under the same ownership as Calon-Ségur, **Château Meyney**, a strikingly rich, concentrated wine owned by Cordier, and **Château Haut-Marbuzet**, whose use of new barrels gives the wine a polish and enhances the fruit. In the southern part of the *appellation* are **Château de Marbuzet** (qv Cos d'Estournel), **Château Macarthy**, with good depth, **Château le Crock**, more supple and elegant, and **Château Andron-Blanquet**, which is made at Cos Labory. In the centre, **Châteaux Pomys** and **la Haye** are quite full-bodied and complex, **Château Houissant** tends to be lean at first but softens out, **Château Laffitte-Carcasset-Padirac** is a large estate with a good reputation, and **Château Tronquoy-Lalande** produces dark, plummy wines almost in the style of Meyney. The excellent Cave Coopérative, **Le Marquis de Saint-Estèphe**, has its *chais* in this part of the *appellation*. To the north, around the village of Saint-Corbian, are **Château Beausite** and **Château Beausite-Haut-Vignoble**, the former full and round, the latter firm and reserved, **Château Morin**, **Château Domayne** and the excellent **Château Boscq**, the last vineyard before the *appellation* ends and the Médoc begins. Price B–C.

Moulis

Red wines only from 390 hectares of vines inland from the Gironde, on a highish plateau north-west of Margaux. The gravelly soil is heavier than in the vineyards nearer the river, but an underlying current of chalk gives the wines a smoothness and roundness that are characteristic of the *appellation*. In style, the best have good fruit, body and finesse and are mid-way between Margaux and Saint-Julien, the less good are rather rustic and lean. Depending on vinification and ageing (the more prestigious Châteaux treat their wines in the same way as the Crus Classés), Moulis can be drunk at 3–4 years and last 12–15. The Crus Exceptionnels and the better Crus Bourgeois are the most long-lived and attain the price of the minor 5ème Crus. The finest wines come from the more gravelly soil around the village of Grand Poujeaux: **Châteaux Chasse-Spleen** is certainly of Cru Classé standard, with a very deep colour and great depth, style and complexity with a judicious use of new oak; **Château Poujeaux-Theil** is even darker and more powerful with a suave plumminess and slight austerity that needs ageing; **Château Maucaillou** is in the same vein, always impressive but less *grand*; **Château Gressier-Grand-Poujeaux** is more traditional and very fine after 7–8 years; **Château Dutruch-Grand-Poujeaux** is a Cru Exceptionnel of great weight and consistency, **Château Branas-Grand-Poujeaux** is more elegant, pure Médoc, **Château La Closerie-Grand-Poujeaux** is equally solid and powerful, while **Château Ruats-Petits-Poujeaux** is light and pretty and can be drunk at 2–3 years; **Château Bel-Air-La-Grave**, with a high percentage of Cabernet Sauignon, is consistently fruity and firm. Nearer the village of Moulis-en-Médoc the wines are slightly lighter: **Château Brillette**, whose pebbly soil reflects the light, hence the name, and **Château Biston-Brillette** have great charm yet age well; **Châteaux Moulin-à-Vent**, **Duplessis** and **Duplessis-Fabre** (under the same ownership as Fourcas-Dupré) are satisfying, medium-weight wines; **Château Mauvezin**, the largest estate in the *appellation*, with modern installations, is firm and aromatic, while **Château Moulis**, once the largest estate, is smooth and carefully made. Price B–C.

Listrac

Red wine only from vineyards covering 570 hectares to the north-west of Moulis. The gravelly soil has a limestone-chalk base which, while it cannot produce wines as fine as the purer gravel soils near the Gironde estuary, encourages a deep colour and a muscular firmness that can be immeasurably improved by good vinification. Listrac lacks the suave fruit of Moulis, but possess a 'grip' that can be compared to Saint-Estèphe or Canon-Fronsac. The wines are typically Médoc, with a rather hard fruit and lack of aimiability at first, and become extremely satisfying if allowed to age for 7–8 years. Until the late 1970s, the finest wines in the *appellation* were without doubt the two Fourcas, **Châteaux Fourcas-Dupré** and **Fourcas-Hosten**. The former, with a little part of its vines in Moulis, regularly achieves the colour, depth of fruit and complexity of the Crus Classés, and has had a series of excellent vintages; while the Crus Classés are progressively bringing out second labels, Fourcas-Dupré has brought out a *tête-de-cuvée* beginning with the 1975 vintage. The latter, with a high percentage of Merlot and impeccable vinification makes a wine that is less vigorous but more polished, especially for a Listrac. The newcomer, determined to produce wine equal to the best in the Médoc, is **Château Clarke-Rothschild** (CS 62%, Me 33%, PV 5%), whose first vintage was 1978. Immense investments and the advice of Professeur Peynaud have resulted in a very fine, deep-coloured 1982 and an exceptional 1983, with the vines at 10 years of age. Rare for a Cru Bourgeois, Clarke has a second label, Les Granges de Clarke, and also makes a rosé. **Châteaux Fonreaud** and **Lestage**, under the same ownership and both with recognizable red labels, are very large properties on the Moulis side of the *appellation*, producing fruity, well-structured wines with a certain smoothness. **Château La Bécade** and the co-owned adjoining **Château Lafon** have good colour and relatively rounded fruit, while **Châteaux Pierre Bibian**, **Gobinaud** and **Moulin de Laborde** are in the more old-fashioned, tough style. The Borie family own **Château Ducluzeau**, which is lightish and elegant, and attractive, supple, well-made wines come from **Châteaux Peyredon-la-Gravotte** and **Cap de Léon Veyrin**. Price B-C (Château Clarke-Rothschild).

Graves

The Graves *appellation* extends from where the Médoc ends, at La Jalle de Blanquefort, north of Bordeaux, to south of Langon, where it surrounds the *appellations* of Cérons, Barsac and Sauternes. The actual area is 60 kilometres long and about 15 kilometres wide, but most of the vineyards close to Bordeaux (with the exception of Châteaux Haut-Brion, La Mission-Haut-Brion and Pape-Clément) have been sold for building land. The region takes its name from the nature of the soil, gravel on a sandy base with a little clay, generally flat but with excellent drainage. As in the Médoc, with a similar soil and a climate influenced by the Atlantic, the Cabernet Sauvigon flourishes, and is the major grape variety of all but one of the Crus Classés. The *appellation* is unique in Bordeaux in that it covers both red and white wine, with the latter being dry or *demi-sec*. Production of red wine has recently overtaken white, and this trend seems confirmed. The white, with almost no *demi-sec* made these days, is at its finest in the north, where certain Crus Classés make an extremely fine wine that is a little understated at first and repays ageing, while the wines south of Léognan can be elegant and fruity, but are less interesting and may be drunk young. Red Graves has the same clean, dense fruit as a Médoc, a similar austerity when young and a soft charm with sometimes a hint of roses in the bouquet. They are perhaps less striking than the grand Médocs, come round a little earlier, but are their equal in finesse. The red must be at least 10° and the white 11° from a maximum yield that was increased in 1983 from 40 hl/ha to 50 hl/ha.

The Grands Crus Classés of Graves

These are all situated in the north of the *appellation*, to the west and south of Bordeaux. The two most prestigious wines, from the communes of Pessac and Talence, actually have their vineyards surrounded by the western suburbs of Bordeaux, and as a result enjoy a warmer climate than their colleagues in Léognan, Villenave d'Ornon, Cadaujac and Martillac. Of these, Léognan is the most extensive, with 6 of the 14 Crus Classés and a *cave-exposition-vente* in the town itself. Only Château Haut-Brion was classified (Premier Grand Cru Classé) in the 1855 classification, the remaining Châteaux being temporarily classified in 1953, with a final, official classification taking place in 1959. There is no official order of quality.

Château Haut-Brion

(44 ha; CS 55%, CF 20%, Me 25%; Pessac)

The doyen of the Bordeaux châteaux, well known since the 17th century, Haut-Brion produces wines of great elegance and breed, with a fine sweetness of fruit and harmonious finish. Even in great years (1975, 1979, 1982) the wine may be drunk after only 7–8 years, due to the softness of the tannin, but reaches its peak at 15 years. Haut-Brion was the first property in Bordeaux to instal stainless-steel vats to control the vinification better (1960). The second wine, Château Bahans-Haut-Brion, used only to be a non-vintage blend using only young vines, much lighter than the *grand vin*. However, since 1976, a proportion of Bahans-Haut-Brion has carried a vintage date, and this wine is much closer in style to Haut-Brion itself. Under 1,000 cases of very fine white wine are made at Haut-Brion (Se 50%, Sa 50%), with the panache and *sève* of a Montrachet and just as expensive. Production of red 12,000 cases. Price FF.

Château La Mission-Haut-Brion

(12 ha; CS 60%, CF 5%, Me 35%; Talence)

For many years the great rival of Haut-Brion, La Mission-Haut-Brion was purchased by Haut-Brion in 1983. The style of wine is quite different: much darker in colour, as dark as the most intense Médoc, more tannic with a rich spiciness that is very particular. The 1975 and 1982 are quite exceptional. Slow maturing, the best vintages need 20 years. Production 4,800 cases. Price F (F).

Château La Ville-Haut-Brion

(5 ha; Se 60%, Sa 40%; Talence)

The white wine of La Mission-Haut-Brion. The high proportion of Sémillon gives the wine a richness and *sève* that surpasses other white Graves, and permits it to age beautifully. Fermentation and ageing in new wood leave a marked impression on the young wine. Of its type, the best dry white wine in Bordeaux. Should be drunk at 1–2 years or after 10. Production 1,200 cases. Price F.

Château La Tour-Haut-Brion

(8 ha; CS 65%, CF 5%, Me 35%; Talence)

Similar to La Mission-Haut-Brion in colour and tannin (more *vin de presse* is used), very firm, but showing less of the rich spiciness. With the exception of years like 1975, it matures earlier than La Mission. Production 3,200 cases. Price E.

Domaine de Chevalier

(15 ha; CS 65%, CF 5%, Me 30%; Léognan)

A vineyard unique in the Graves, with all the vines planted in a single square block, surrounded by woods. The soil is light and gravelly, the vines intentionally low-yielding, and a long fermentation gives a deep colour and firm structure to the wine which has great purity of style and incomparable finesse. It is often more successful than other Châteaux in poor years, and can be drunk at 7–8 years, but good years are better at 10–15. The Domaine de Chevalier 1981 is the finest wine of that vintage. Two hectares are devoted to white wine (Sa 70%, Se 30%) which is barrel-fermented and then barrel-aged for 18 months before bottling. It is firm and delicate at the same time and is for many the finest dry white wine produced in Bordeaux. In 1983 the Ricard family sold the Domaine to the Bernard family of Bordeaux. Production, 5,000 cases of red, 600 of white. Price E.

Château Pape-Clément

(27 ha; CS 66.5%, Me 33.5%; Pessac)

The oldest vineyard in the Graves, created in 1300 by Bertrand de Goth who became Pope Clément V. The wine is not one of the deepest coloured Graves, yet it possesses a rich, supple fruit and a harmonious softness. In certain vintages (1955, 1962, 1970, 1978) it is spectacular, at its best after 12 years, while lighter vintages may be drunk at 5–6 years. There is a tiny amount (1,500 bottles) of *non-classé* white that is not commercially available. Production 10,000 cases. Price low E.

Château Haut-Bailly

(23 ha; CS 34%, CF 16%, Me 26%, 24% old vines mixed; Léognan)

Very stylish wines (red only), with a purity of fruit, a deceptive suppleness on the palate and the classic 'faded-roses' Graves finish. After a few light vintages in the 1970s, Haut-Bailly returned to form with a fine 1977 (100% Cabernet), an excellent 1978 and an exceptional 1979. The wine is attractive quite young, at 6–7 years, but good years should be kept twice as long. The second wine, La Parde de Haut-Bailly, is a lighter, quite delicious reflection of the *grand vin*. Production 8,500 cases. Price D.

Château Bouscaut

(32 ha; Me 60%, CS 35%, CF 5%; Cadaujac)

The high proportion of Merlot (unique in the Graves) produces a wine that is firmer and more tannic than in Saint-Emilion or Pomerol, with good structure but perhaps lacking in finesse. Since 1978 the wines are richer and better balanced and Bouscaut's recent (1980) acquisition by Lucien Lurton (Châteaux Brane-Cantenac, Durfort-Vivens, Climens) and the increasing interest of Jean-Bernard Delmas, *directeur-oenologue* at Haut-Brion should see this trend continue. The Cru Classé white comes from 6 ha planted 70% Se, 30% Sa, is barrel-fermented and wood-aged to produce a wine of good quality that can age well. Production 10,000 cases of red, 2,500 of white. Price C.

Château Carbonnieux

(Red: 35 ha; CS 50%, CF 10%, Me 30%, Ma + PV 10%. White: 35 ha; Sa 65%,

The largest property of the Graves, Cru Classé Carbonnieux is divided equally between the production of red and white wine, the latter being better known. The red has a good colour, is never overly fruity and is sometimes a little tart when young, but softens after 7–8 years. The white ferments in stainless steel and spends 3 months in wood before being bottled in May or June the year after the vintage. It is very fresh but a little closed when young and needs 2–3 years in bottle to show some complexity. Production 15,000 cases of both red and white. Price C.

Château de Fieuzal

(22 ha; CS 75%, Me 20%, Ma + PV 5%; Léognan)

With its high proportion of Cabernet Sauvignon and controlled fermentation at high temperatures to extract deep colour and with no hard tannins, Fieuzal is almost more Médoc than Graves. The 1978, 1979, and 1982, were particularly successful. The rich fruit allows it to be drunk at 5–6 years, but the wine is not at its peak in good vintages until after 10 years. Under 1,000 cases of non-*classé* white comes from 60% Sa and 40% Se, the grapes being cold-fermented, for drinking young or keeping. Production 7,000 cases (increasing). Price high C.

Château Malartic-Lagravière

(14 ha; CS 50%, CF 25%, Me 25%; Léognan)

A small *vignoble* covering a single block of land around the Château with the highest yields per hectares of all the Crus Classés. The wine has a strikingly pretty deep carmine colour, a high proportion of new wood in recent vintages and is one of the most successful 'modern' wines made under the influence of Professeu Peynaud. It is very good at 5–8 years, to appreciate the fruit. The white, from 100% Sa planted on under 2 ha, is bottled in the spring following the vintage after a few months in new oak, and seems to defy the generalization that Sauvignon on its own does not age well. Production 6,000 cases of red, 600 of white. Price C.

Château La Tour-Martillac

(Red: 19 ha; CS 65%, CF 6%, Me 25%, Ma+PV 4%. White: 4 ha; Se 50%, Sa 45%, Mu 5%; Martillac)

The high proportion of old wines (average age 30 years, with some from the late 1920s) and old-fashioned vinification produces a full-bodied wine that is rather rough at first, but quite quick to mature and at its best at 10 years. The 1975 was exceptional and the 1979 very fine. The high proportion of Sémillon gives the white the traditional Graves style that improves with age. The Château has been in the hands of the Kressmann family since 1930. Production 7,500 cases of red, 1,500 of white. Price C.

Château Smith-Haut-Lafitte

CF 11%, Me 16%; Martillac)

Much recent replanting as part of an expansion programme by the owners (Louis Eschenauer & Co., *négociants* and also owners of Château Rauzan-Ségla) has resulted in a wine of clean fruit and charm that is good to drink at 5–8 years. The 1975 was richer than many wines of that year and the 1978 very complete. The white, *non-classé*, is 100% Sauvignon, crisp and dry for early drinking. Production 20,000 cases of red, 2,500 of white. Price C.

Château Olivier

(Red: 15 ha; CS 65%, CF 15%, Me 20%. White: 14 ha; Se 65%, Sa 33%, Mu 2%; Léognan)

The proprietor, M. de Bethmann, has left the running of this estate to Louis Eschenauer & Co., who have undertaken a programme of replanting, especially for the less well-known red. The wines are well made, with a fine colour, clean fruit and pleasantly tannic Graves finish. The 1978 and 1981 are very successful, and can both be drunk at 7–8 years. As the vines mature, the wine will perhaps need more time. The white is much better than in the past, and, despite a high percentage of Sémillon, should be drunk quite young. Production 9,000 cases of red, 9,000 of white. Price C.

Château Couhins

(White: 6 ha; Sa 50%, Se 50%; Villenave-d'Ornon)

The property is owned by the Institut National de la Recherche Agronomique (INRA), who took back the running of the vineyards from André Lurton in the late 1970s. The vines are very young and the wine is straightforward modern-style Graves. 1983 was the first vintage that the wine was vinified at the Château. Production 1,600 cases red *non-classé*, 550 white. Price C.

Château Couhins-Lurton

(1.75 ha; Sa 50%; Se 50%; Villenave-d'Ornon)

This beautifully made, aromatic yet dry white wine is made by André Lurton at Château La Louvière. The 1982 was almost Californian in its strikingly modern, clean, fruity oaky style. Drink young, at 1–3 years. Production 850 cases. Price C.

The Non-Classified Graves

While the finest wine is undoubtedly made by the conscientious Crus Classés, and the wines from the north generally have more bouquet, style and concentration than those from the south, there are some excellent *non-classé* wines made in the Graves from the more southern communes of Portets, Podensac, and, south of the Sauternais, of Langon and Saint-Pierre-de-Mons. They may be considered the equivalent of the Crus Bourgeois of the Médoc. The following take great care to produce wines of high quality, and are listed north to south: **Château Les Carmes Haut-Brion**, a neighbour of Haut-Brion, with a high proportion of Merlot that gives it a softer style; **Château La Louvière**, a large and immaculately kept property owned by André Lurton, with a deep-coloured, firm, Cabernet-Sauvignon based red and a classic, slightly austere white from mainly Sauvignon, both of Cru Classé standard; **Château du Cruzeau**, another Lurton property, with similar wines to La Louvière, the red being meatier but less fine;

Château de France, adjoining Château de Fieuzal, makes deep-coloured, supple reds; nearby, at **Château Gazin** (90% CS), the wine is intensely fruity but still classic; **Château Larrivet-Haut-Brion** is light and elegant; **Château Haut-Bergey**, also from Léognan, has a pronounced bouquet of roses; further south, at Castres, **Château Ferrande** produces some solid, well-made red and some good white; at Portets, **Château Rahoul** and **Domaine La Grave**, both managed by Peter Vinding-Diers, produce quite exceptionally aromatic and stylish whites through cold fermentation, and some strikingly good 'modern' red; **Chateau Millet**, next door, is a very big property making more old-fashioned wines; **Château de Chantegrive** at Podensac makes some light, fruity red and some very interesting white; near Langon, Christian Médeville vinifies some excellent dry whites and sturdy reds at **Château Respide**, while **Château de Respide** at Langon produces lighter wines altogether; Langon is also the headquarters of Pierre Coste, the person most responsible for the success of the clean, fruity, 'modern' Graves, and the wines from his properties **Château Chicane** and **Domaine de Gaillat** exemplify this style; finally, at Saint-Pierre-de-Mons, **Château Magence** makes clean, fruity red and white wine with equal success. Price A–B.

The Sweet White Wines of Bordeaux

The sweet white wines of Bordeaux, or *vins liquoreux* as they are called, come from vineyards on the left bank of the Garonne, from Podensac in the Graves to Langon, and from the slopes opposite on the right bank. The sole grape varieties planted are the Sémillon (always dominant), Sauvignon and Muscadelle (to a very small proportion, and often omitted). The particular micro-climate of the region, with coolish, misty mornings during the harvest, with the sun burning off the moisture during the day, will precipitate and encourage the development of a fungus called the *botrytis cinerea* (*pourriture noble* or noble rot), which attacks the grapes and reduces the volume of water in each berry with the consequent increase in sugar and potential flavour. If the weather during the vintage is too cold (1974, 1977), the botrytis will not appear; if it is too sunny and dry (1976, 1978), there is not enough moisture in the air, and the bunches will become roasted (*rôti*) and not *pourri*; finally, if the noble rot sets in well and the weather breaks (1964, 1982), anything not harvested before the rain is lost.

The actual picking is often spread over several weeks, during which the pickers make successive *tris*, passing many times over the same vineyard to pick the bunches most affected by rot. Fermentation is longer and more difficult than for a dry white or a red wine, where residual sugar is neither required nor allowed, and short cuts, by over-chaptalization or over-sulphuring, are only too evident in the bottle. A fine Sauternes should have a yellow-golden colour, a pronounced floral, fruity, honeyed aroma, a rich, luxurious flavour, clean and not cloying, and a refreshing finish. Barsac is less intensely sweet than Sauternes, although it may sell under the same *appellation*. The minimum alcohol content is 12.5°, and most Sauternes will aim for a minimum of 14° alcohol plus 3–4° unfermented sugar. The low yield of 25 hl/ha is almost never reached owing to the natural concentration due to the *pourriture noble*, and the risks inherent in its appearance.

Sauternes *AOC*
Château d'Yquem

1er GCC (102 ha; Sé 80%, Sa 20%; Fargues)

Château d'Yquem is the greatest of all the sweet white wines of France, a vineyard of almost mythical reputation, the most extreme in the Bordelais in its search for quality and perhaps the most notable example of what is meant by 'fine wine'. In modern terms, everything is exaggerated at Yquem: the length of the harvest, sometimes lasting into December, with up to eleven *tris*, the refusal to enrich the wine by chaptalization, the minute yield averaging one glass of wine per vine at 8 hl/ha, the use of only new barrels for fermentation and the three and a half years ageing, even the simplicity of the label. The result is a wine of great richness and perfect balance, an extraordinary mixture of fruit, alcohol and residual sugar that develops into a true work of art as it matures. Great vintages are still stunningly young after 40 years. In certain villages, Yquem will produce a dry wine sold under the name of Y (Ygrec) made from 50% Sé, 50% Sa, with some affinity to Laville-Haut-Brion due to the heady Sémillon nose and roundness of flavour. The *appellation* Sauternes is naturally disallowed, and Ygrec is sold as a Bordeaux Supérieur. The Lur Saluces also own **Château de Fargues**, which is less opulent than Yquem, but is none the less a wine of exceptional quality (average production 1,000 cases, price F). At Yquem total production averages 5,300 cases (2,000 of Ygrec, price F), price FFF.

Château Guiraud

1er GCC (70 ha; Sé 50%, Sa 45%, Mu 5%; Sauternes)

The sale of Guiraud to Canadian owners in 1981 has arrested a decade of decline for this property famous for its rich, racy, honeyed Sauternes. Heavy investment in vinification equipment, rigorous selection at the harvest and after fermentation should swiftly restore Guiraud's reputation. The *grand vin* should be drunk at 5–15 years, the second wine, Le Dauphin de Lalagüe, at 3–6. There is some excellent, deep-coloured, soft red wine made at Guiraud and some crisp Sauvignon-style dry white. Production 7,500 cases. Price D.

Clos Haut-Peyraguey

1er GCC (15 ha; Sé 88%, Sa 10%, Mu 2%; Bommes)

This tiny property occupies some of the best *terroir* in Sauternes, and the wine is made with great care. The Sauvignon is harvested when ripe but not botrytized and the Sémillon when fully botrytized (when the year permits), to produce a wine allying bouquet, richness, and elegance. It can be drunk young, but ages well, up to 15 years for exceptional vintages like 1975. The Pauly family also own **Château Haut-Bommes**, well situated next door to Yquem, which makes excellent wine. Production 2,500 cases. Price C.

Château Lafaurie-Peyraguey

1er GCC (20 ha; Sé 98%, Sa 2%; Bommes)

A small but parcellated property belonging to the Cordier family, Lafaurie-Peyraguey produces elegant Sauternes that is rather pale in colour, not overly sweet but firm and long-lasting. No wine was bottled in 1974, but otherwise quality has been high if not particularly outstanding. It is best drunk at 8–12 years. Production 3,500 cases. Price D.

Château La Tour Blanche

1er GCC (27 ha; Sé 72%, Sa 25%, Mu 3%; Bommes)

Donated to the State in 1912, La Tour Blanche doubles as a producer of Sauternes and a School of Viticulture and Oenology. The vineyards are on the borders of Barsac, and the wine is correspondingly lighter than many other 1er Cru Sauternes. It is also sometimes lacking in personality, and may be drunk at 5–6 years. Production 6,000 cases. Price C.

Château Rabaud-Promis

1er GCC (30 ha; Sé 80%, Sa 18%, Mu 2%; Bommes)

The vineyards of Rabaud-Promis represent the larger part of the Château Rabaud estate classified in 1855, due to a separation in 1903. The wines are rich but sometimes rather weighty and lacking complexity, spending 3–4 years in vat before final selection and bottling. No Rabaud-Promis was bottled in 1972, 1973, 1974 and 1977. The 1975 was excellent and the 1979 very good. They are at their best at 5–10 years. Production 3,750 cases. Price C.

Château Rayne-Vigneau

1er GCC (66.5 ha; Sé 65%, Sa 30%, Mu 5%; Bommes)

One of the largest properties in Sauternes, Rayne-Vigneau was much modernized in the early 1970s and now produces a pleasant *vin liquoreux* and a crisp dry wine from the highest-yielding vines in the *appellation*. It is rare among 1er Crus in that it is regularly found in supermarkets in France. Should be drunk at 4–5 years. Production 16,500 cases. Price C.

Château Rieussec

1er GCC (55 ha; Se 74%, Sa 24%, Mu 1%; Fargues)

The vines of Rieussec cover the highest point in the same commune as Yquem, to make a very stylish wine that is a little less rich than their neighbour's. The 1976 was untypical, being rather caramelized, but 1975 and 1979 were classic. A *cuvée* *spéciale*, corresponding to the old *appellation 'crème de tête'*, was introduced in 1975, while the less concentrated *cuvées* sell under the second label, Clos Labère. A dry white wine is also made at Rieussec, called 'R' de Rieussec, from the first *tri* of non-botrytized grapes. It is more Sémillon in style than the other dry white Sauternes, with the exception of 'Y'. Production 6,500 cases. Price D.

Château Sigalas Rabaud

1er GCC (14 ha; Se 75%, Sa 25%, Bommes)

The smaller part of the Rabaud property, making wines of greater finesse than Rabaud-Promis, Sigalas Rabaud is one the lighter, but most elegant and aromatic Sauternes. The floral, peach-like bouquet is preserved by ageing in vats rather than barrels and the wine can be drunk with pleasure after 4–5 years. Production 2,500 cases. Price C.

Château Suduiraut

1er GCC (70 ha; Se 80%, Sa 20%; Preignac)

Suduiraut is generally recognized as being potentially the second-greatest wine in Sauternes after Yquem. It is one of the most rich wines, both in colour and flavour, of the *appellation* which in great years (1967, 1976) comes near to perfection. Three years were totally declassified (1973, 1974, 1977), and the final selection produced only 4,160 cases in 1975 and 2,900 in 1976. Suduiraut ages well and is at its best at 10–20 years. Production 8,500 cases. Price D.

Château d'Arche

2ème GCC (30 ha; Se 80%, Sa 15%, Mu 5%; Sauternes)

Well made, rich and honeyed wine from a property situated between La Tour Blanche and Guiraud. The 1980 is remarkable for the vintage. A tiny amount of *crème de tête* is selected in successful vintages, the most recent being 1967, 1971 and 1975. Until 1980, the second wine was sold under the label **Château d'Arche-Lafaurie**, an adjacent property. Lesser *cuvées* are now sold to the Bordeaux trade. Production 6,500 cases. Price low C.

Château Filhot

2ème GCC (60 ha; Se 65%, Sa 32%,
Mu 3%; Sauternes)

The most southern of the
Crus Classés, Filhot has
family connections with the
Lurs Saluces at Yquem, but
the wine is quite different in
style, being much less
opulent. The light sweetness
and marked finesse of flavour
allow the wines of Château
Filhot to be drunk relatively
young, at 3–4 years, while the
best vintages (1976, 1979) are
very fine at 10 years old.
Production 6,500 cases.
Price C–D.

Château Lamothe

2ème GCC (8 ha + 11 ha; Se 70%,
Sa 20%, Mu 10%; Sauternes)

The 8-ha portion of Lamothe
owned by M. Despujols
produces a straightforward
Sauternes with no ambitions
to rival the 1er Crus.
Production 1,700 cases. Price
low C. The 11 hectares
purchased by the Guignard
family after the death of the
owner (M. Bastit Saint-
Martin of Château d'Arche)
in 1980 will produce their first
wine from the 1981 vintage
under the Lamothe-Guignard
label.

Château de Malle

2ème GCC (24 ha; Se 75%, Sa 22%,
Mu 3%; Preignac)

Château de Malle appears to
be one of the sweetest
Sauternes, rich, golden and
unctuous, with not quite the
complexity of a 1er Cru. The
same property makes some
very fruity red Graves,
Château de Cardaillan and a
dry white, Chevalier de
Malle. The second wine of de
Malle is Domaine de Saint-
Hélène. Production 5,000
cases. Price C.

Château Romer du Hayot

2ème GCC (15 ha; Se 69%, Sa 30%,
Mu 1%; Fargues)

The wine from this property,
which adjoins Château de
Malle, is well balanced and
fruity, but (in common with
all but the finest *vins liquoreux*)
it takes a fine vintage (1975,
1979) for it to achieve great
richness and complexity and
to last for more than 5–6
years. Production 4,000 cases.
Price C.

Crus Bourgeois

As the image of Sauternes improves and the 1er Crus Classés begin
to sell at a realistically high price, more notice is being taken of a
few fine wines in the *appellation* that were less well known through
lack of classification and their sales being concentrated on the
home market. The *régisseur* at Château d'Yquem, Pierre Méslier,
owns **Château Raymond-Lafon**, making luscious, stylish wines;
Château Bastor-Lamontagne is a large property, well situated at
Preignac, of which **Château de Pick** used to be a part, both now
making fine Sauternes; **Château Haut-Bergeron**, also at Preig-

nac, has a part of its vines next to Yquem, and practises a rigorous selection; **Château Saint-Amand** makes wine worthy of a 2ème Cru; **Domaine d'Arche-Pugneau** is entirely surrounded by 1er Crus; finally, at **Château Gilette**, the Médeville family have been making outstanding Sauternes since the 1930s. The 1937 *crème de tête* rivalled the Yquem and Climens of that year and the 1953 is no less extraordinary. At Gilette different *cuvées* are produced of varying degrees of richness, which will be stated on the label. It is, quite justifiably, almost a 'cult' wine in France. The Médeville's second wine is **Château les Justices**. Price B–C.

Barsac AOC
Château Climens

1er GCC (30 ha; Se 85%, Sa 15%)

Climens shares with Coutet the privilege of being one of the two 1er Crus in Barsac. It is the richest, most complete of the Barsacs, and in some years (1937, 1947, 1971) has been compared favourably with the wines of Château Yquem. Under the ownership of Lucien Lurton Climens remains dedicated to quality: 4 *tris* during the vintage, fermentation and two years' ageing in barrel, careful final selection. The wines are rich and complete and develop their full potential over 10–20 years. Production 6,000 cases. Price E.

Château Coutet

1er GCC (37 ha; Se 80%, Sa 15%, Mu 5%)

Climens's rival in Barsac, producing smooth, stylish wines, with less power but equal finesse. The slight hint of a lemony acidity after the honeyed taste is pure Barsac. Coutet is fermented and aged in wood, bottled after two years and is at its best at 8–10 years. A tiny amount of *crème de tête* is produced in great years, 1971 and 1975 each producing 75 cases, named Cuvée Madame, after the late owner, Madame Rolland-Guy. The current owner, M. Baly, will continue this practice. Production 8,500 cases. Price D.

Château Doisy-Daëne

2ème GCC (14 ha; Se 100%)

The best known of the three 'Doisy' vineyards, Doisy-Daëne is the only Cru Classé in Barsac-Sauternes to be planted 100% in Sémillon.

Pierre Duborddieu vinifies in stainless steel and ages with wine for one year in new oak, to produce a lively *vin liquoreux* of great style and finesse. A very clean and aromatic dry white wine is made with the *appellation* Graves. Production 2,500 cases. Price C.

Château Doisy-Védrines

2ème GCC (21 ha; Se 80%, Sa 20%)

A very traditional property, like Climens and Coutet, fermenting and ageing in barrel and making rich, long-lived wine from a small yield, 1975 was exceptional, 1976 and 1980 both very fine.

Doisy-Védrines can be drunk at 5–6 years but repays keeping. A clean, crisp dry white wine, Le Chevalier de Védrines, is made in some quantity, as well as a red wine, Latour-Védrines, reducing the average production of Doisy-Védrines to 2,000 cases. Price C.

Château Doisy-Dubroca

2ème GCC (3.3 ha; Se 90%, Sa 10%)

This tiny property, purchased by Lucien Lurton in 1971 at the same time as his purchase of Climens, is sandwiched between Doisy-Daëne and

Doisy-Védrines. Professeur Peynaud oversees the vinification here, as at Climens, and the result is a harmonious balance of roundness and long-lived richness. Production 500 cases. Price D.

Château Broustet

2ème GCC (16 ha; Se 60%, Sa 30%, Mu 10%)

Broustet is owned by M. Eric Fournier (also proprietor of Château Calon in Saint-Emilion) who makes a rich,

smooth Barsac. No wine was bottled in 1974, 1976 and 1977, but 1979 and 1980 promise well. The lesser wines (all 1976, for example) are sold under the label Château de Ségur. Production 2,000 cases. Price B–C.

Château Nairac

2ème GCC (15 ha; Se 90%, Sa 6%, Mu 4%)

Perhaps the first example of the new confidence in the future of the wines of Barsac was the purchase in 1971 of

Nairac by Tom Heeter and his wife Nicole *née* Tari. Since then the best possible wine has been made when possible (there was no Nairac in 1977 or 1978), and the dedication to quality is on a par with the finest of the 1er Crus. Production 2,000 cases. Price high C.

Château Caillou

2ème GCC (15 ha; Se 90%, Sa 10%)

The vineyards of Caillou touch those of Climens and the now defunct Château

Myrat and produce a wine with good fruit and rich flavour that spends 2-3 years in wood before bottling. It is a concentrated, long-lived wine, with a loyal French clientele. Production 5,000 cases. Price C.

Château Suau

2ème GCC (6.5 ha; Se 85%, Sa 15%)

A straightforward, rather sweet Barsac with no pretensions to rival the 1er Crus, but of reliable quality. Production 1,650 cases. Price B.

Crus Bourgeois

Perhaps since there are only two 1er Crus Classés in Barsac, the Crus Bourgeois have not been so overshadowed in repute as they have in Sauternes. Next door to Climens and Doisy-Védrines, **Château Roumieu** produces 3,000 cases of excellent wine, and Simone Dubourdieu makes a Barsac with great *sève* at **Château Roumieu-Lacoste**; the wines from **Château Piada**, a 13th-century vineyard, are successful, as are the fine, aromatic wines of **Château Liot**; **Château Cantegril** is lightly sweet, with a lemony edge, **Château Guiteronde-du-Hayot** is well made, **Château de Ménota** is less sweet but more fruity, with a high proportion of Sauvignon; **Château du Mayne**, owned by Jean Sanders of Haut-Bailly is in the classic mould, while **Château Padouen**, directed by Peter Vinding-Diers of Rahoul, uses cold fermentation and new barrels to produce a small quantity of exciting wine; **Château de Rolland** has a large production of pleasant wine, the smaller **Château Saint-Marc** and **Château Simon** are reliable, and an old Lur-Saluces property, **Château Pernaud**, has been recently replanted. Price B.

Cérons AOC

Dry and sweet white wines produced in the commune of Cérons between Pondensac and Barsac on the left bank of the Garonne. In recent years, the volume of Cérons has diminished in favour of a dry wine, which may take the *appellation* Graves, or Cérons sec, although in the latter case the wine must correspond to the 12.5° of alcohol and 40 hl/ha limit imposed at Cérons instead of the 11° and 50 hl/ha for Graves. The classic Cérons is a fully sweet wine, but less luscious than a Sauternes, and even less rich than a Barsac, Loupiac or Sainte-Croix-du-Mont, with a clean honeyed fruit and a pleasant touch of acidity in the finish. The finest of these sweet (*moelleux* rather than *liquoreux*) wines are the **Grand Enclos du Château de Cerons**, a wine of great raciness and finesse, and the **Château de Cérons**, while the wines produced by **Château Haura, Château Mayne-Binet** and **Château Archambeau** are very good. Price A.

Loupiac AOC

Sweet white wine only from a small *appellation* between Cadillac and Sainte-Croix-du-Mont on the right bank of the Garonne, opposite Barsac. The Sémillon, Sauvignon and Muscadelle grape varieties are late-picked to make a smooth, honeyed wine in the style of a minor Sauternes. Many Châteaux make only a small proportion of their wine in this manner, preferring the more commercial quality of a dry wine. For many years the finest wines, rivalling the best Sauternes, were the *crèmes de tête* of **Château de Ricaud**, which should now re-emerge under new ownership, and fine wines are made at **Château Loupiac, Château du Cros, Clos Jean** and **Château Mazarin**. Price A.

Sainte-Croix-du-Mont AOC

Sweet white wine from hillside vineyards on the right bank of the Garonne opposite Sauternes. The Sémillon, Sauvignon and Muscadelle grapes ripen well into the autumn to produce a small quantity of *vin liquoreux* often comparable to a good Sauternes. In common with Loupiac, the minimum degree must be 12.5° from a yield (much higher than in Sauternes, but very seldom reached) of 40 hl/ha, leading many growers to pick early and make a Bordeaux blanc sec. In good years, however, a well-made Sainte-Croix-du-Mont can be extraordinarily fine. Such wines may come from **Château Loubens**, the acknowledged '1er Cru' of the *appellation*, **Château La Rame**, **Château de Tastes** and the excellent **Château Lousteau-Vieil**. Price A–B.

Pomerol

With only 725 hectares in production (out of a possible 785), Pomerol is the smallest of the regions of Bordeaux producing fine wine. It is also the most parcellated, with 172 growers, one-third of whom own less than one hectare. The *appellation* is bordered by Lalande-de-Pomerol and Néac to the north, Saint-Emilion to the east and the town of Libourne to the south. The soil is perfect for vines, a flinty, clayey gravel mixed with sand on a hard clay and iron base, the iron giving Pomerol its particular richness. The wine is a mixture of velvety softness, richness and firmness, much nearer in style to a Saint-Emilion than a Médoc and with some affinity with good Burgundy. The dominant grape is the Merlot, aided by the Cabernet Franc rather than the Cabernet Sauvignon and a very little Malbec or Pressac. The soft fruit of the Merlot and the liveliness of the Cabernet Franc (known locally as the Bouchet) combine to give Pomerol an immediacy that is not found in Cabernet Sauvignon-based wines. However, while a fine Pomerol is very attractive and open 5 years after the vintage, it will, unless the vines have over-produced wildly, last 10-15 years more. All Pomerol is red, with a minimum alcohol content of 10.5° from a maximum yield of 42 hl/ha. Production varies, since the Merlot can be a very prolific (1973, 1979, 1982) or suffer from cold and rot (1977), but the average is 4 million bottles a year.

There has been no official classification of Pomerol. Pétrus is universally recognized as an honorary 1er Grand Cru Classé, followed by a handful of châteaux on a par with the 1er Grands Crus Classés B of Saint-Emilion or the 2ème or 3ème Crus Classés of the Médoc. Two dozen or so properties that are not quite in this league also make very fine wine.

Château Pétrus

(11.5 ha; Me 95%, CF 5%)

An extraordinary wine from the most perfectly kept property, managed and part-owned by the J.-P. Moueix family. The soil contains more clay than elsewhere in the *appellation*, with a thin sandy top-soil. The grapes are harvested at their optimum ripeness by an army of pickers who can finish the *vendange* in three afternoons, thus avoiding possible dilution of the wine by the morning dew. Vinification, in cement tanks, extracts a deep colour and the wine spends 20 months in new oak casks before bottling. Pétrus is generally a huge wine, very dark in colour, with plummy, blackcurranty flavours and great richness, structure and 'presence'. It can be drunk at 7–8 years, but the better vintages demand and deserve much more time. Despite the high proportion of old vines, production is a respectable 4,000 cases, a tribute to the health of the vineyard. Price FFF.

Château La Conseillante

(13 ha; Me 45%, CF 45%, Ma 10%)

The vineyard lies on the Saint-Emilion side of the *appellation*, between Pétrus and Cheval Blanc. The Malbec adds firmness to the fragrance of the Cabernet Franc and the soft fruit of the Merlot. It is a wine of deep, silky elegance, a Chambolle-Musigny of Pomerol, and is harmonious enough to last 10–15 years. Production 4,500 cases. Price E.

Château L'Evangile

(13 ha; Me 67%, CF 33%)

Situated, like La Conseillante, right on the edge of Saint-Emilion, L'Evangile makes a sturdier, meatier wine, with less finesse but more structure. It has much the same weight and tannin as Trotanoy, but is less intensely rich. Good vintages (1979, 1971, 1975, 1982) need over 10 years to develop their potential. Production 4,500 cases. Price E.

Château Lafleur

(4 ha; Me 50%, CF 50%)

A tiny property on the Pétrus plateau making exquisite, deep-coloured wines with a strikingly floral bouquet and great purity of flavour. Lafleur is a beautifully made, long-lasting wine from a high proportion of old vines. Production 1,200 cases. Price D–E.

Château La Fleur Pétrus

(9 ha; Me 75%, CF 25%)

A Moueix-owned property, near Pétrus and Gazin. Old vines and the gravelly-clay, iron-based soil produce a fine, firm Pomerol with good colour and structure, but less plummy and intense than either Pétrus or Trotanoy, perhaps more Médoc in style. Very good at 8–12 years. Production 3,500 caess. Price D.

Château Gazin

(24 ha; Me 60%, CF 20%, CS 20%)

One of the largest properties, in the north-east of the *appellation*, Gazin produces well-made wines that lack balance and sweetness in light years. Recent vintages (1979, 1982), with more colour, body and fruit, will last well. Production 10,000 cases. Price D.

Château Nenin

(25 ha; Me 50%, CF 30%, CS 20%)

The vineyards lie on the southern slope of Pomerol, towards Libourne, where the soil has more gravel and less sand. The style of Nenin is straightforward, full-bodied and satisfying, but without the depth and panache of the finest crus. The wines mature well. One of the rare châteaux in Pomerol to make enough wine to have a second label, Château Saint-Roch. Production 10,000 cases. Price D.

Château Petit-Village

(11 ha; Me 80%, CF 10%, Ma 10%)

This property is extremely well run by Bruno Prats, of Clos d'Estournel, who makes a wine almost more Médoc than Pomerol, complicated and rather firm, not a wine to drink young. The best vintages are after 1975. Production 4,500 cases. Price D.

Château Trotanoy

APPELLATION POMEROL CONTROLÉE

CHÂTEAU TROTANOY
POMEROL
1964
SOCIÉTÉ CIVILE DU CHÂTEAU TROTANOY
PROPRIÉTAIRE A POMEROL ·GIRONDE·
MIS EN BOUTEILLES AU CHATEAU

(9 ha; Me 85%, CF 15%)

The second star in the Moueix stable, after Pétrus, Trotanoy produces a deep-coloured, intensely flavoured wine with perfect structure from some of the oldest vines in Pomerol. While it is not the firework display that is Pétrus, it is perhaps a more serious wine, needing more time, totally satisfying. In light years (1974, 1980) it is stylish and elegant and can be drunk at 4–5 years; in great vintages (1964, 1970, 1982) it can last 20 years. A splendid wine. Production 3,000 cases. Price high E.

Vieux Château Certan

(13.5 ha; Me 50%, CF 25%, CS 20%, Ma 5%)

One of the most famous properties in Pomerol, whose wines are relatively Médocain in style, due to the presence of Cabernet Sauvignon and ageing in new barrels. The wood and the briary fruit of the Cabernets can dominate the young wine, giving an impression of astringency, but (in years of restrained production) Vieux Château Certan will acquire a smoothness and depth of fruit that make it one of the most elegant wines in Bordeaux. Production 6,500 cases. Price E.

The Crus Bourgeois of Pomerol

The following châteaux may be considered equal in quality terms to some of the 5ème Crus Classés of the Grands Crus Bourgeois of the Médoc. **Château Beauregard**, a full-flavoured wine of great charm, due to the high proportion of Cabernet Franc, elegant, supple and quite quick to mature. **Château Certan de May** (also known as **Château de May-de-Certan**), is across the road from Vieux Château Certan and produces some fine, meaty, long-lived wines. **Château Certan-Giraud** has vines situated on the highest part of the plateau de Certan, and one could wish for more finesse from this deep-coloured, generally satisfying, sturdy wine; **Château Certan-Marzelle** is under the same ownership and the wine is made at Certan-Giraud and is of the same style; **Château Clinet** produces sturdy wines with a certain leanness from the Cabernet Sauvignon, firm and long-lasting but lacking the plumminess of a classic Pomerol; Georges Audy also owns **Château la Croix-du-Casse**, which is softer, slightly sweeter and quicker maturing. **Clos du Clocher**, owned by J.-B. Audy, *négociants* at Libourne, is deep-coloured and smooth and full-bodied, reliable rather than exciting. **Clos de l'Eglise** has very old vines which give a rich wine with a lot of flavour, impressive and typically Pomerol. Under the same ownership, **Château Plince** is lighter and less interesting. **Château l'Eglise-Clinet**, a small property, well situated on a clayey-gravelly soil near the church, producing well-made wines, more generous and more stylish than Clinet. **Château l'Enclos**, situated just north of Clos René, produces a serious wine with deep fruit and warmth of flavour which ages well. **Château La Croix**, a large property for Pomerol, touching Nenin, Petit-Village and Beauregard, owned by J. Janoueix and Co. of Limbourne, who also own **Château La Croix Saint Georges**; these straightforward, meaty wines are made together. **Château La Croix de Gay**, from the northern part of Pomerol towards Néac, produces carefully made, deep-coloured, solid wines. **Château La Vraie Croix de Gay**, a small property near the best Crus of Pomerol (Le Gay, Lafleur), making delicious, racy wine with a bouquet of violets and truffles. **Château Feytit-Clinet**, with its vines planted on the best gravelly-clay, iron-based soil and the vinification of Jean-Claude Berrouet, the wine-maker for all the J.-P. Moueix properties, is a lightish, but elegant and stylish Pomerol. **Château La Fleur-Gazin**, another property managed by Moueix, next door to Gazin, Lafleur and La Fleur Pétrus, produces fairly intense wines of great elegance. **Château Le Gay**, under the same ownership as Château Lafleur, produces deep-coloured, rich, classic wines from very low-yielding vines. **Château La Grave-Trigant-de-Boisset**, owned by Christian Moueix, is one of the most stylish, vibrant and seductive Pomerols, impeccably made, a lovely wine. **Château Lagrange**, another J.-P. Moueix property on some of the best soil in Pomerol, produces firm, racy wines. **Château Latour-à-Pomerol**, owned by Mme Lacoste-Loubat, part-owner of Pétrus, and vinified by Jean-Claude Berrouet of J.-P. Moueix, is a richly textured wine with the elusive bouquet of truffles. **Château Mazeyres**, a well-kept property on the far west border of the *appellation*, making fine, if rather lean wines. **Château Moulinet**, one of the larger and older châteaux, produces a velvety, soft, very accessible Pomerol. **Château La Pointe**, a big property on the outskirts of Libourne, where the sandy soil gives a less intense colour and fruit than the more clayey, iron soil of the Pétrus plateau; well-made wines, good structure. **Clos René** produces solid, consistently well-made wine with a deep colour and plummy, long-lived fruit; including **Château Moulinet-Lasserre**, part of the same property. **Château Rouget,** from the north of the *appellation* near Néac, was classified as the fifth finest Pomerol in 1868; dark-coloured, powerful wines with long life. **Château de Sales**, the largest property in the *appellation*, produces very sound, fruity, slightly earthy wines that give great pleasure. **Château La Violette**, with most of the vines next to Nenin, produces a pretty wine with a soft fruit and the expected aroma of violets.

Saint-Emilion

Saint-Emilion is by far the largest fine wine *appellation* in Bordeaux, with over 5,000 hectares under vines, not counting the 3,000 hectares in the 'Satellite' Saint-Emilions to the north-east of the main *appellation*. The vineyards are to be found on the right bank of the Dordogne in the region known as the 'Libournais', named after Libourne, the country town that is the capital of the right-bank wine industry. Grapes planted are principally the Merlot, with the balance being made up of Cabernet Franc, and a little Cabernet Sauvignon and Malbec (Pressac). Consequently, the wine has a richness and suppleness, from the Merlot, that is a contrast to the rather hard intensity of the Cabernet Sauvignon-based Médocs. The wines of Saint-Emilion are divided into two styles by nature of the soil: the 'Graves', sandy, gravelly soil adjacent to Pomerol, with a pronounced bouquet and rich, almost sweet fruit; and the 'Côtes', undulating vineyards with a clayey soil on a limestone base, being rather firmer, close-knit and less easy when young. Both are quite robust, with a minimum alcohol content of 11° from a yield of 45 hl/ha, 11.5° for the Grands Crus from a lower yield of 40 hl/ha. There are many different styles of wine in the *appellation*, due to soil, *encépagement* and vinification, but if there is a Saint-Emilion type, it is a rich, full-coloured wine, with a warm concentrated fruit and an apparent sweetness due to a relatively low degree of tannin. They may be drunk younger than a Médoc or a Graves, the minor wines at 2–3 years, the better ones at 5–6, while, like all fine claret, the best wines need 10 years. Production varies greatly, but averages 25 million bottles.

The Classification of the Wines of Saint-Emilion

The *appellation* Saint-Emilion classified its wines in 1954, selecting two châteaux (Ausone and Cheval-Blanc) as 1er Grands Crus Classés 'A' and a further ten as 1er Grands Crus Classés 'B', these last being on a par with the 2ème or 3ème Crus Classés of the Médoc. Further down the scale come the Grands Crus Classés, the equivalent of the 5ème Cru or Cru Bourgeois, of which there are now 72 châteaux. These are followed by the Grands Crus, where the châteaux re-apply each year and their wine can be refused by a tasting panel. Everything else is plain Saint-Emilion. In 1984, however, thirty years after the first official classification, the system will be revised, reducing the different levels from four to two. From the 1984 vintage, there will be 90 Grands Crus Saint-Emilion, and then Saint-Emilion *tout court*. It is unlikely that this new legislation will have any effect on the 12 1er Grands Crus Classés.

The 1er Grands Crus Classés

Château Ausone

(7 ha; Me 50%, CF 50%)

The vines are planted on the edge of the town of Saint-Emilion, east-south-east-facing, on a clayey soil with a limestone base. The protection from the north and the west, the slope of the vineyards and the age of the vines combine to offer the finest raw material, which since 1975 has been complemented by the brilliant vinification of Pascal Delbeck. Ausone has a deep garnet-ruby colour, an intense, smooth flavour, with no hint of heaviness, and a long, harmonious finish. It is the most sophisticated of the Saint-Emilions. New barrels are used every year and the wine matures perfectly in the cellars, originally limestone quarries, and is bottled after 15 to 20 months with no filtration. It has no harsh tannins and may be drunk at 7–8 years, while the finer vintages last 15–20. Production 2,000 cases. Price FF.

Château Cheval Blanc

(35 ha; CF 66%, Me 33%, Ma 1%)

The other 1er Grand Cru 'A' of Saint-Emilion, from the Pomerol side of the *appellation* known as the 'Graves'. The soil, basically gravel, with sand and clay in parts, and the virtual absence of slope, is particularly suited to the Cabernet Franc, lending to this varietal a richness that is not found elsewhere in Bordeaux. Cheval Blanc is always a big wine, or potentially so, with a roundness, richness and certain plummy sweetness that is a pure contrast to Ausone. It is more often compared either to Pétrus, across the road in Pomerol, or to Figeac, of whose vineyard is used to be a part. Really great vintages (1961, 1975), where the low yield concentrates the flavour, will last 20-30 years, while the good ones may be drunk at 10–12. Production 11,500 cases. Prices FF.

Château Beauséjour-Bécot

(17 ha; Me 60%, CF 20%, CS 20%)

This represents the northern half of the Beauséjour vineyard, divided in 1869, which, 100 years later, Michel Bécot purchased from Dr Fagouet. The current estate includes the two adjacent properties of Château La Carte (4.5 ha) and Château Les Trois Moulins (5 ha) owned by M. Bécot, a slightly questionable merging which will no doubt be ratified by the new classification of 1984. The wine is firm, slightly lean when young, but ages well, a serious but not overly exciting wine. Production 9,000 cases. Price D.

Château Beauséjour-Duffau-Lagarosse

(7 ha; Me 50%, CF 25%, CS 25%)

The smaller part of the Beauséjour property, bordered to the north by Beauséjour-Bécot and to the south and west by Canon. The wines are classic Saint-Emilion, deep-coloured, high in alcohol and extract, with the rich fruit of the Merlot balanced by the firmness of the Cabernets. Good vintages (1979, 1982) need at least 10 years and the best wines will last 20 years or more. Production 3,300 cases. Price D.

Château Belair

(13 ha; Me 60%, CF 40%)

Under the same ownership and management as Ausone, of whose vineyards it is a north-western continuation, Belair is similar in style and has been extremely successful in recent vintages. The slightly higher percentage of Merlot, the ageing in barrels of which only one-third are renewed each year and the 'younger' vines (35 years average as opposed to 45 years at Ausone) tend to make a faintly less striking wine. The 1976 and 1979 however, are among the best of the *appellation*. At 10 years Belair is perfect. Production 4,000 cases. Price E.

Château Canon

(18 ha; Me 55%, CF 40%, CS 2.5%, Ma 2.5%)

Canon is entirely surrounded by other 1er Grands Crus Classés, the two Beauséjours, Clos Fourtet, Belair and Magdelaine, and corresponds to the archetypal Saint-Emilion 'Côtes': deep-coloured, aromatic, firm yet welcoming, with an admirable seriousness and length. The cellars, old limestone quarries, are the finest in Saint-Emilion, vinification is very traditional and the wine stays for 22 months in wood (two-thirds renewed each year) before bottling. It is ideal at 8–10 years, but the best vintages need longer. Production 8,000 cases. Price D–E.

Château Figeac

(38 ha; Me 30%, CF 35%, CS 35%)

One of the largest of the 1er Grands Crus Classés, situated in the 'Graves' Saint-Emilion, adjoining Cheval Blanc which, until the 1830s, was part of the Figeac estate. The gravelly hillocks that make up most of the vineyard at Figeac are particularly suited to the Cabernet, and the one-third of Cabernet Sauvignon gives the wine a length and *sève* that complements perfectly the natural sweetness of the Merlot. Figeac is less massive than Cheval Blanc, equally firm, but more seductive. Vinification is impeccable and the whole of the crop is aged in new barrels. The harmony and sweetness of Château Figeac allow the wine to be enjoyed young, and the same qualities do not fade with age. Production 12,500 cases. Price E–F.

Clos Fourtet

(17 ha; Me 60%, CF 20%, CS 20%)

The vines of Clos Fourtet are planted on the eastern edge of the town of Saint-Emilion on a clayey soil with a solid limestone base, from which the famous cellars have been hewn. The wine used to be hard and old-fashioned, often dried out before the tannin had had time to soften, but since the 1978 vintage, a more modern vinification extracts more fruit and less tannin. It fairly resembles Canon, with less intensity and quicker maturing. A forthright, well-made wine. Production 5,500 cases. Price (C)–D.

Château La Gaffelière

(20 ha; Me 65%, CF 25%, CS 10%)

The oldest vineyard in the *appellation*, created in the 4th century, and possibly, due to the discovery in 1969 of the ruins of a Roman palace complete with mosaics showing bunches of grapes, the site of Ausonius's house. The vines are planted away from the town, surrounded by Belair and Magdelaine to the north-west, Pavie to the east. The dominance of Merlot, mostly vines over 40 years old, and a long vinification give the wine a blend of richness and solidity which is typically Saint-Emilion. The recent successful vintages of La Gaffelière (1978, 1979, 1981) will be at their best at 10–12 years. Production 8,000 cases. Price D.

Château Magdelaine

(11 ha; Me 80%, CF 20%)

A small property with vines planted on south-facing slopes away from the town, flanked by Canon and Belair to the north and east. Magdelaine is owned by Ets. J.-P. Moueix of Libourne and the wine made by the Moueix oenologist Jean-Claude Berrouet. The high proportion of Merlot, the highest among the Grands Crus Classés, picked at optimum ripeness by a large team of *vendangeurs*, gives the wine a sweetness and suppleness that is almost Burgundian. It is the most feminine of the finest Saint-Emilions and, apart from naturally tannic vintages such as 1970, 1975, may be drunk at 6–8 years. Production 5,000 cases. Price E.

Château Pavie

(37 ha; Me 55%, CF 25%, CS 20%)

The largest (in production terms, but equal in size to Figeac) of the 1er Grands Crus Classés, Pavie occupies a superbly situated south-facing slope outside the town. It also possesses some 100-year-old vines, the most ancient of the *appellation*. A more modern vinification since the mid-1970s has combined with a run of good vintages for Saint-Emilion to put Pavie firmly in the front rank with a good 1978 and an exceptional 1979. It is less austere than Canon or even than Clos Fourtet, another Peynaud-advised estate. The current stylish fruitiness of the wines of Pavie make it difficult to wait the 10–12 years that they deserve. Production 13,000 cases. Price E.

Château Trottevieille

(10 ha; Me 50%, CF 25%, CS 25%)

The vineyard of Trottevieille is situated to the east of Saint-Emilion, set apart from the other 1er Grands Crus Classés 'Côtes', which are to the west and south. The wine always has a good colour and vigorous fruit but lacks sometimes finesse and intensity of flavour. It is reliable but not spectacular and shows best at 5–8 years. Production 4,200 cases. Price D.

The Grands Crus Classés

The last classification of the châteaux of Saint-Emilion was in 1969, which confirmed Grand Cru Classé status on 72 châteaux. Some of these are almost of 1er Grand Cru standard, others are definitely not. Most of the wines are very good at 5 years, at their best at 7–8 and fading after 12. In cases where production is pushed to the limit, the wines will be lighter and quicker to mature. Price is usually indicative of quality, and while some of the larger properties have acquired a reputation that ensures them a good price, the smaller estates often do as well by selling to a regular clientele of private buyers. Almost all the Grands Crus Classés are Price C. The list that follows is in alphabetical order.

The Saint-Emilion 'Côtes'

Château L'Angélus, large property below Beauséjour, round, full wines, quite expensive; **Château L'Arrosé**, well-made, concentrated wine with 40% Cabernet Sauvignon; **Château Balestard-la-Tonnelle**, rich, full-bodied wine with length, finesse and class; **Château Bellevue**, sound, quick maturing; **Château Bergat**, not far from Trottevieille, is managed and sold by Borie-Manoux; **Château Cadet-Bon**, small property with traditional, full-bodied wines; **Château Cadet-Piola**, smooth, elegant wines with good colour and one of the prettiest labels in Bordeaux; **Château Canon-la Gaffelière**, stylish, elegant wine, good but rather expensive; **Château Capdemourlin, Château Cap de Mourlin**, the wines are made separately but in the same cellar and are softer versions of Balestard-la-Tonnelle; **Château La Carte**, now integrated with Beauséjour-Bécot; **Château Chapelle-Madeleine**, a tiny 0.2-hectare property owned by Mme Dubois-Challon and now absorbed into Ausone; **Château Le Chatelet**, small property not far from Beauséjour with well-made wine; **Château La Clotte**, well-situated vineyard near to Pavie, lovely, elegant Merlot-style wines; **Château La Cluzière**, adjoins and owned by Pavie, but not so fine; **Château La Couspaude**, rather lean wines from a high percentage of Cabernet; **Château Le Couvent**, tiny vineyard actually in the town of Saint-Emilion; **Château Couvent-des-Jacobins**, excellent, meaty, high-quality wines, better than the **Clos des Jacobins**, a Cordier-owned vineyard where the wines are improving; **Château Curé-Bon-La-Madeleine**, excellent little property near to Belair and Canon making well-structured wines; **Château Faurie-de-Souchard**, well made, good soft fruit, quick maturing; **Château Fonplégade**, large property making very reliable, sturdy wine; **Château Fonroque**, owned by J.-P. Mouiex, dark, full-bodied, very different from Moueix's Magdelaine; **Château Franc-Mayne**, well-positioned property making soft, supple wines; **Château Grand-Mayne**, elegant wines from 50% Cabernets; **Château Grand-Pontet**, firm, fleshy wines, lacking in charm; **Château Grand-Murailles**, combines the vineyards of **Côte-Baleau** and **Clos Saint-Martin** just at the north edge of the town, an excellent, sweet-fruited wine; **Château Guadet-Saint-Julien**, a small property near Montagne-Saint-Emilion; **Château Haut-Sarpe**, owned by the Janoueix family, making serious, complex wine; **Château Laniote**, a Merlot-dominated property next door to Fonroque; **Château Larcis-Ducasse**, an excellent property just east of Pavie, full-bodied, concentrated wines from old vines; **Château Larmande**, Capdemourlin ownership and Professor Peynaud's advice in the cellar is producing some deep-coloured, stylish wine; **Château Laroze**, big property, with sandy soil, near to the 'Graves' in situation and style, well-made wines; **Clos La Madeleine**, tiny property beside Belair and Magdelaine, 50% Cabernets, should be very fine; **Château Matras**, next door to L'Angélus, with a low proportion of Merlot, fine, carefully made wines; **Château Mauvezin**, small property near to Soutard and Balestard-la-Tonnelle, making very solid wine from old vines, but now replanting; **Château Moulin-du-Cadet**, well situated, just north of Saint-Emilion among the other Cadets, firm, stylish wine; **Clos de l'Oratoire**, largish property making fairly rich, straightforward wines; **Château Pavie-Decesse**, well-placed property above Pavie and under the same ownership since 1970, making firm, elegant, long-lived wines; **Château Pavie-Macquin**, traditionally made, Merlot-dominated wines with potential for expansion; **Château Pavillon-Cadet**, small property making fine wines with 50% Cabernet Franc; **Château Petit-Faurie-de-Soutard**, solid, high-class wines from a property managed by M. Capdemourlin; **Château Le Prieuré**, deep coloured, firm wines made by the same owner as Vraye-Croix-de-Gay (Pomerol) and Siaurac (Lalande-de-Pomerol); **Château Saint-Georges-Côte-Pavie**, well made, elegant wines from a vineyard next to La Gaffelière and Pavie; **Château Sansonnet**, small property near Trottevieille; **Château La Serre**, meaty wines from a Merlot-dominated property not too far from Ausone, under the same ownership as La Pointe; **Château Soutard**, classic, distinguished, long-lived wines from a large estate well situated just north-west of Saint-Emilion; **Château Tertre-Daugay**, well-placed vineyards adjoining Magdelaine and Belair, recently bought by the owner of La Gaffelière and being replanted; **Château Trimoulet**, serious, carefully made wine owned by the serious *négociant* Pierre Jean; **Château Troplong-Mondot**, one of the largest and the best of the Grands Crus Classés, owned by the Valette family of Pavie, producing consistently fine wine; **Château Villemaurine**, at the north-eastern edge of the town, producing sturdy, rather lean wines.

The Saint-Emilion 'Graves'

Château Chauvin, on the Saint-Emilion-Pomerol border, producing fleshy wines with a certain sweetness; **Château Corbin**, deep-coloured, meaty wine but lacking finesse; **Château Corbin-Michotte**, wines of exceptional quality and breed, painstakingly made by Jean-Noël Boidron; **Château Coutet**, smooth, well-constituted, satisfying wines; **Château Croque-Michotte**, situated between Cheval Blanc and Pomerol, making a full-bodied, plummy wine of good quality; **Château Dassault**, big property, where the wines are as elegant as the label; **Château La Dominique**, next door to Cheval Blanc, with rich, generous, stylish wine; **Château Grand-Barrail-Lamarzelle-Figeac**, big property opposite Figeac whose wine it resembles in a lighter, sweeter style; **Château Grand-Corbin**, big, chewy wine from old vines, in the same style as Corbin; **Château Grand-Corbin-Despagne** producing serious, deep-coloured wines of high quality;

Château Haut-Corbin, small property making smooth, modern Saint-Emilion; **Château Jean-Faure**, adjoining Cheval Blanc with impressive wine from the same high proportion of Cabernet Franc; **Château Ripeau**, next door to Jean-Faure, which it used to own, making smoother, softer wines; **Château La Tour-Figeac**, separated from Figeac in 1879, this is the best of the three La Tour-Figeacs; **Château La Tour-du-Pin-Figeac (Giraud)**, well-made wines but not up to the Figeac name; **Château La Tour-du-Pin-Figeac (A. Moueix)**, a more elegant, leaner wine from a high proportion of Cabernet Franc; **Château Yon-Figeac**, opposite Figeac, adjoining Grand-Barrail, making firm, consistent wine.

The Grands Crus

In many cases these wines are the equal of the Grands Crus Classés, but generally their quality is of good generic standard and the *appellation* Grand Cru is misleading. With 72 Grands Crus Classés already in existence and some 150 Grands Crus, it will be interesting to see which Châteaux the nine-man tasting commission will select to fill the 78 places available for Grand Cru status for the 1984 vintage. Listed alphabetically are some of the finer estates deserving serious consideration: Châteaux Bellefont-Belcier, Cardinal Villemaurine, Carteau Matras, Cormey-Figeac, Ferrand, La Fleur Pourret, Fombrauge, Franc Pourret, La Grâce Dieu, Grand-Corbin-Manuel, Haut Simard, Laroque, Magnan-La-Gaffelière, Monbousquet, Monlabert, Peyraud, Simard.

The 'Satellite' Saint-Emilions

The communes surrounding Saint-Emilion have the right to the *appellation* if it is preceded by the name of their commune. They share the same 45 hl/ha maximum yield (very often exceeded) as Saint-Emilion and the 11° minimum alcohol, and tend to be less concentrated but similar in style. With the merging of Sables-Saint-Emilion to the main *appellation* and Parsac-Saint-Emilion to Lussac-Saint-Emilion, there are now four:

Lussac-Saint-Emilion, soft, quick-maturing wines (Châteaux Lyonnat, de Lussac), **Montagne-Saint-Emilion**, more structured and robust (Châteaux Calon, Coucy, Corbin, Plaisance), **Puisseguin-Saint-Emilion**, with good colour and balance (Châteaux Bel-Air, Guibeau, Teyssier) and **Saint-Georges-Saint-Emilion**, producing generally the finest wines (Châteaux Calon, Saint-Georges.) Price B.

Wines of the Libournais

Lalande-de-Pomerol AOC
Néac AOC

Red wine only from two *appellations* north of Pomerol and bounded on the east by Montagne-Saint-Emilion.

Although the finest wines come from the *appellation* Néac, the more prestigious-sounding Lalande-de-Pomerol *appellation* is used, following a merger of the two areas in 1954. The vineyards are flat, with a gravelly soil in which is mixed clay or sand. The grapes planted are the Cabernet Sauvignon, Cabernet Franc, Merlot and Malbec, with Merlot dominant as in Pomerol. The wines have some similarities; a deep colour and rounded flavour, but Lalande-de-Pomerol tends to be tougher and leaner, with less of the soft Merlot charm, and requires some time in bottle to become attractive. There are just under 1,000 hectares under vines, producing 4–5 million bottles. Price B, some better wines C.

The oustanding wine of the *appellation* is **Château Tournefeuille**, from the Pomerol border, a firm long-lived wine with a concentrated fruit from low-yielding vines.

Canon-Fronsac AOC Fronsac AOC

Red wine only from the smaller but finer of the Fronsadais *appellations*, covering 300 hectares of hillside vineyards 2.5 kilometres north-west of Libourne. Of the Bordeaux grape varieties, the Merlot and the Cabernet Franc dominate, with Cabernet Sauvignon and Malbec used for balance and colour. The wines of Canon-Fronsac are the best of the 'minor' *appellations*, often outshining many Médocs, Saint-Emilions, Pomerols or Graves. They have a fine, deep colour, a clean, quite concentrated aroma of fruit with a little spice and the firm vigorous flavour of well-made wine. In general, they are very satisfying wines that have not been tempted into over-production, as have many wines from Saint-Emilion. They can be drunk at 4–5 years, but the better wines need 10 years to underline their complexity and high quality. Canon-Fronsacs are relatively sturdy, with a minimum of 11° alcohol from a yield of 47 hl/ha. Production is 1.6 million bottles. Price B.

Some of the finest, most elegant wine in the *appellation* comes from the tiny **Château Canon**; **Château Canon de Brem** and its second label Château Pichelebre produce classic, intensely flavoured wines that improve over 15–20 years; **Châteaux Coustolle**, **Vincent** and **Vrai-Canon-Bouché** are almost of this standard, while **Château Vrai-Canon-Boyer** is lighter and quicker maturing; other fine wines come from **Châteaux Haut-Ballet**, **du Gaby**, **du Gazin**, **Junayme**, **Mazeris**, **Haut-Mazeris** and **Moulin-Pey-Labrie**.

The wines of Fronsac come from the lower slopes. The grape varieties planted and the style of wine are similar to Canon-Fronsac, except that Fronsac may be lighter (10.5° minimum) and less intense, thus being ready to drink earlier. Many proprietors have châteaux in both *appellations*. The vineyards cover 700 hectares, producing 4 million bottles. Price A–B.

Decanting

There are three reasons for decanting: to separate an old wine from its sediment; to aerate the wine, also known as allowing it to breathe; and to enhance the appearance of the wine. Aesthetically, any wine will benefit from being served in a clear glass decanter or carafe, but it is not usually done for everyday wines nor for white wines, except in the grander houses in Bordeaux. When a wine has thrown a deposit, it is essential to decant, unless the bottle has been standing upright for some days beforehand, and it is very carefully opened and even more carefully served. The slightest backwash while serving will disturb the sediment, which will then mix with the wine. While decanting baskets are essential for taking a wine from the cellar, where it has been binned horizontally, to the dining-room, they in no way prevent the sediment from flowing into the wine if it is carelessly poured. The wine should be poured from the bottle into the decanter above a candle or lamp, to show when the sediment is reaching the neck of the bottle, which is the time to stop pouring. If the sediment has been disturbed, a fine coffee filter paper or a linen handkerchief may be used with a funnel or strainer.

The length of time a wine needs to breathe depends on the age and type of the wine. Certain experts insist that a wine does not need aeration, that the 'breathing' does not change the wine chemically and oxydizes the fruit. Other experts put less importance on the time the wine spends in the decanter and more on aeration in the glass. What is plain is that the act of pouring wine into a decanter or carafe wakes it up and allows the 'off' odours that may have accumulated after some years in bottle (known as 'bottle-stink') to disappear. The younger and sturdier the wine, the more it needs and can take aeration. Decanting an hour or so before the meal and replacing the stopper seems the procedure for mature wines, while very old wines should be decanted almost at the last minute and allowed to open up in the glass.

Order of Serving

1. White and rosé before red unless the white is a dessert wine.
2. Dry white before sweet white; the same applies to rosés.
3. Light red before full-bodied red.
4. Young wines before old wines.
5. Dry sparkling wines at the beginning of a meal, sweeter sparkling wines at the end.
6. Build up to quality, do not begin with it.

Alsace   Anjou   INAO

Bordeaux

Tastevin

Decanter

Champagne   Burgundy

Bottle sizes for Bordeaux and Burgundy

½ bottle 0.375 l
Bottle 0.75 l
Magnum 1.50 l 2 bottles

Double-magnum 3.00 l 4 bottles
Jéréboam 4.5 l 6 bottles
Impériale 6.00 l 8 bottles

Temperature of Serving

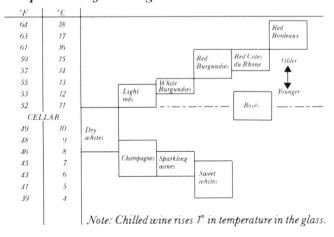

°F	°C						
64	18						Red Bordeaux
63	17						
61	16						
59	15				Red Burgundies	Red Côtes du Rhône	Older
57	14						
55	13			White Burgundies			
53	12		Light reds				Younger
52	11					Rosés	
CELLAR							
49	10	Dry whites					
48	9						
46	8						
45	7		Champagnes	Sparkling wines			
43	6				Sweet whites		
41	5						
39	4						

Note: Chilled wine rises 1° in temperature in the glass.

Regional Food and Wine

Dish

Aperitif: Champagne Crémant; Champagne Blanc de Blancs

Terrine de lapin en croûte *(Rabbit terrine in pastry)*
Boudin blanc *(Chicken, veal and pork sausage)*
Feuilleté d'escargots à la champenoise *(Snails in puff pastry with Champagne sauce)*

Matelote champenoise *(Eel, pike and carp stew)*
Truite aux amandes *(Trout with almonds)*

Paupiettes de saumon au Champagne *(Stuffed fillets of salmon with Champagne sauce)*

Potée champenoise *(Champagne pot au feu)*

Rognons de veau sautés à la crème *(Calves' kidneys with cream)*
Poulet au Bouzy *(Chicken in red wine)*
Cuissot de sanglier au genevièvre *(Roast leg of wild boar with juniper berries)*

Chaource
Carré de l'est
Pierre Robert

Poires à la champenoise *(Pear tart with frangipane)*

Digestif: Fine or Marc de champagne

Aperitif: Muscat d'Alsace

Foie gras d'oie en brioche *(Goose foie gras in brioche)*
Grenouilles au Riesling *(Sautéed frogs' legs)*
Tarte aux oignons *(Onion tart)*

Truite au bleu *(Trout poached in court-bouillon)*
Carpe farcie à l'alsacienne *(Stuffed carp)*
Sandre aux pommes *(Perch with apples)*

Choucroute garnie *(Sauerkraut with smoked pork and sausages)*
Rôti de cochon de lait *(Roast sucking pig)*
Cuissot de chevreuil aux poires *(Roast roe-deer with pears)*

Munster

Kugelhopf

Digestif: Marc de Gewürztraminer; Eau-de-vie Blanche

Aperitif: L'Etoile Mousseux; Crépy

Salade d'écrevisses *(Crayfish salad)*
Croustade jurassienne *(Cheese puff pastry turnovers)*
Pâté chaud au ris de veau *(Hot pâté with veal sweetbreads)*
Mousselines d'écrevisses *(Crayfish mousselines)*
Omble chevalier braisé *(Braised char)*

Coq au vin jaune *(Cockerel cooked with yellow wine)*
Perdreau aux fides *(Partridge with noodles, bacon and cheese)*
Escalope de veau belle comtoise *(Veal escalope with ham and cheese)*

Comté
Vacherin
Morbier

Gâteau grenoblois *(Walnut cake)*

Digestif: Vin de paille; Marc de Château d'Arlay

Aperitif: Kir; Kir Royale

Jambon persillé *(Parsleyed ham)*
Escargots à la bourguignonne *(Snails in garlic butter)*
Gâteau de foie de volaille *(Liver pâté)*

Pochouse *(Fresh-water fish stew with white wine)*
Quenelles de brochet *(Pike dumplings)*
Andouillette à la lyonnaise *(Fried chitterling sausage with onion and vinegar)*

Coq au Chambertin *(Cockerel in Chambertin sauce)*

Côtes de veau dijonnaise *(Veal chops with mustard)*
Boeuf bourguignonne *(Burgundy beef stew)*
Râble de lièvre *(Saddle of hare)*

Saint-Florentin
Epoisses
Montrachet

Sorbet de cassis *(Cassis sorbet)*

Digestif: Marc or Fine de Bourgogne

Champagne

Alsace

Jura and Savoie

Burgundy

Local Wines	Other Wines
Coteaux Champenois blanc Champagne Blanc de Blancs Champagne non-vintage	Montagny; Rully blanc Vouvray Chablis
Champagne non-vintage Champagne Blanc de Blancs; Champagne non-vintage Blanc de Blancs Crémant; Blanc de Blancs vintage	Meursault Riesling Chassagne-Montrachet blanc
Champagne 'monocrus'; Champagne non-vintage Champagne vintage; Champagne rosé Bouzy rouge; Coteaux Champenois rouge Champagne vintage, type Blanc de Noirs	Chinon; Chénas Beaune Savigny-lès-Beaune Pomerol; Hermitage
Coteaux Champenois rouge Champagne Blanc de Noirs	Volnay Mercurey Brouilly
Champagne demi-sec	Vouvray demi-sec

Local Wines	Other Wines
Tokay Riesling Sylvaner; Pinot Blanc	Sauternes; Jurançon Graves blanc Mâcon blanc
Pinot Blanc; Riesling Gewürztraminer; Tokay Pinot Blanc; Riesling	Puligny-Montrachet Chassagne-Montrachet blanc Pouilly-Fuissé
Pinot Blanc; Riesling Riesling; Tokay Riesling; Pinot Noir	Crémant d'Alsace Hermitage blanc; Saint-Julien Crozes-Hermitage rouge
Gewürztraminer	Juliénas
Tokay; Gewürztraminer Vendange Tardive	Champagne demi-sec

Local Wines	Other Wines
Côtes du Jura blanc; Seyssel Arbois blanc; Apremont Arbois blanc or rosé; L'Etoile Arbois blanc; Chignin Maréstel; Roussette de Savoie	Pouilly-Fumé Chablis; Rully blanc Meursault Champagne Crémant Bâtard-Montrachet
Arbois blanc; Côtes du Jura blanc Côtes du Jura rouge or rosé; Mondeuse Arbois rouge or rosé; Mondeuse	— Madiran Saint-Emilion
Côtes du Jura blanc or rouge Arbois blanc; Vin de Savoie blanc Arbois blanc; Chautagne Gamay	Médoc Pinot Noir d'Alsace Côte-de-Brouilly
Vin de paille	Tokay Vendange Tardive

Local Wines	Other Wines
Bourgogone Aligoté; Chablis Chablis; Bourgogne blanc Côte de Beaune blanc or rouge	Anjou blanc Ménétou-Salon Pouilly-Fumé
Meursault Saint-Romain; Corton Charlemagne Pouilly-Fuissé; Saint-Véran	Pinot Blanc d'Alsace Sancerre Vouvray sec
Chambertin; Gevrey-Chambertin; Morey-Saint-Denis Fixin; Mercurey; Morgon Pommard; Moulin-à-Vent Corton; Nuits-Saint-Georges	Châteauneuf-du-Pape Fronsac Cornas Hermitage rouge
Chablis Grand Cru Chablis Grand Cru; Irancy rouge Fleurie; Pommard	Arbois blanc Pinot Noir d'Alsace Bouzy rouge
—	—

Dish

Loire Valley

Aperitif: Vouvray Pétillant

Andouille/Rillettes/Rillons *(Mixed local meats)*
Mousse chaude de foies de volaille *(Warm mousse of chicken livers)*
Feuilleté d'asperges *(Asparagus in puff pastry with butter sauce)*

Saumon à l'oseille *(Salmon with sorrel)*
Brochet au beurre blanc *(Pike with white butter sauce)*
Petite friture *(Fried whitebait)*

Rôti de porc aux pruneaux *(Roast pork with prunes)*
Fricassé de volaille/lapin *(Fricassé of chicken/hare)*
Canard sauvage grillé *(Grilled wild duck)*

Crotin de chavignol
Port Salut
Sainte-Maure

Tarte tatin *(Caramelized upside-down apple tart)*

Digestif: Marc de Vouvray; Cognac

Rhône Valley

Aperitif: Saint-Péray Mousseux

Tomates provençales *(Grilled tomatoes with olive oil and garlic)*
Saucisson lyonnais aux pistaches et aux truffes *(Pork sausage with pistachio nuts and truffles)*
Melon rafraîchi *(Chilled Cavaillon melon)*

Chausson aux truffes *(Drôme truffle enclosed in puff pastry)*
Pavé de poisson *(Cold terrine of fish and shellfish)*
Encornets farcis *(Squid stuffed with tomato and rice)*

Perdreau aux choux verts *(Partridge casserole with cabbage)*
Sauté de lapin aux herbes *(Rabbit sauté with herbs)*
Gigot d'agneau en croûte *(Leg of lamb in pastry)*

Fromage de chèvre vieux
Mont d'or

Gâteau aux marrons glacés *(Chestnut cake)*

Digestif: Frigolet; Marc de Château Rayas

Provence and the Midi

Aperitif: Muscat de Beaumes-de-Venise

Pissaladière *(Onion, olive and anchovy tart)*
Ratatouille *(Provençal vegetable stew)*
Soupe au pistou *(Vegetable soup with basil)*

Loup de mer au fenouil *(Sea bass with fennel)*
Rouget à la niçoise *(Baked mullet with tomatoes and anchovies)*
Bouillabaisse *(Mediterranean rockfish soup)*

Canard aux olives *(Duck with olives)*
Poulet au riz au safran *(Chicken with saffron rice)*
Filet de boeuf froid à la niçoise *(Cold roast beef in tarragon aspic)*

Banon

Sorbet au citron *(Lemon sorbet)*

Digestif: Banyuls Rancio

Bordeaux

Aperitif: Champagne; Lillet blanc

Jambon de Bayonne *(Cured Bayonne ham)*
Terrine de gibier *(Game terrine)*
Foie gras de canard chaud aux raisins *(Hot duck liver with grapes)*
Huîtres et saucisses chaudes *(Hot oysters and sausages)*

Alose poché froid sauce verte *(Cold poached shad with green herb mayonnaise)*
Lamproies au vin rouge *(Eel stew with red wine)*
Cabillaud à la bordelaise *(Baked cod steaks)*

Entrecôte à la bordelaise *(Beef steak with marrow)*
Ris de veau aux truffes *(Sweetbreads with truffles)*
Salmis de pigeon *(Salmis of pigeon)*
Gigot d'agneau pré salé *(Leg of lamb from the salt marshes)*

Gouda
Roquefort

Pignola *(Pine nut cake)*

Digestif: Armagnac; Cognac

Local Wines	Other Wines
Anjou blanc; Quincy	Bourgogne Aligoté
Sancerre; Pouilly-Fumé	Chablis Premier Cru
Pouilly-Fumé; Vouvray sec	Riesling; Saint-Joseph blanc
Pouilly-Fumé; Savennières	Corton-Charlemagne
Anjou blanc; Vouvray sec	Bourgogne blanc
Sancerre; Pouilly-Fumé	Mâcon blanc; Entre-Deux-Mers
Chinon; Sancerre rouge	Côte de Beaune-Villages
Saint-Nicolas-de-Bourgueil; Champigny	Médoc
Chinon; Anjou rouge	Pomerol
Sancerre blanc	Beaujolais-Villages
Chinon	Saint-Amour
Sancerre; Bourgueil	Saint-Emilion
Quarts de Chaume; Coteaux du Layon	Jurançon doux
Lirac blanc	Graves blanc
Crozes-Hermitage blanc or rouge	Fleurie
Condrieu; Rasteau Rancio	Banyuls
Château Grillet; Hermitage blanc	Bâtard-Montrachet
Saint-Joseph blanc; Hermitage blanc	Graves blanc, Chablis
Tavel rosé; Lirac rosé	Provence rosé
Côte-Rôtie; Cornas	Aloxe-Corton
Côte-Rôtie; Côtes du Rhône-Villages	Bourgueil; Santenay
Châteauneuf-du-Pape rouge; Gigondas	Médoc
Cornas; Vacqueyras	Sancerre rouge
Lirac; Côtes du Rhône-Villages	Moulin-à-Vent
Muscat de Beaumes-de-Venise	Muscat de Frontignan
Provence blanc or rose	Sylvaner
Châteauneuf-du-Pape blanc; Tavel rosé	Crozes-Hermitage blanc
Provence blanc	Pinot blanc d'Alsace
Bellet blanc; Provence blanc	Hermitage blanc
Bellet rosé	Rosé des Riceys
Cassis blanc; Provence blanc	Graves blanc
Bandol; Provence rouge	Saint-Joseph rouge
Provence rosé; Tavel rosé	Rosé de Marsannay
Vin de Corse; Provence rouge	Lirac rouge
Coteaux d'Aix-en-Provence; Corbières	Côtes du Rhône-Villages
Muscat de Frontignan	Champagne demi-sec
Cahors; Madiran	Bourgueil
Fronsac; Pomerol	Crozes-Hermitage
Barsac; Sauternes	Tokay
Entre-Deux-Mers; Bordeaux blanc or rouge	Muscadet
Graves blanc	Savennières
Saint-Emilion; Graves rouge	Bouzy rouge
Graves blanc or rouge	Cassis blanc
Médoc; Graves rouge	Chinon
Margaux; Saint-Emilion	Volnay
Pomerol; Saint-Estèphe	Gigondas
Pauillac; Saint-Julien	Chambolle-Musigny
Médoc	Vosne-Romanée
Sauternes; Jurançon doux	Saint-Joseph rouge
Barsac; Loupiac	Vouvray demi-sec

Grape Varieties

The grape varieties permitted in the finer French wines are strictly controlled by the laws of *appellation*. Only Pinot Noir and Chardonnay may make Burgundy, these two grapes plus Pinot Meunier are the only grapes allowed in Champagne, Sancerre must come from the Sauvignon, Hermitage from the Syrah, and so on. In Bordeaux, the South-west of France and the southern Rhône valley, more than one varietal may be used in proportions consistent with the style of the *appellation* or responsible for a wine's differentness within its *appellation*. If a selection has been made over the centuries as to what grape may be planted where, it is due to the success or failure of different *cépages* in widely varying soils and climate. Certain 'local' varieties may make an interesting regional wine yet are not seen outside their area, while the *cépages nobles* are planted in wine-growing regions throughout the world, leading to the conclusion that while the grape variety does not always dominate the wine, it is the principal factor in determining the flavour.

Cépages Nobles (Red)

Cabernet Sauvignon

The principal grape of the Médoc, a late-ripening varietal with small, very dark berries producing a wine of intense colour, striking blackcurrant, bell-pepper aroma, hard, even austere tannin-backed flavour with great depth and ageing potential. The Cabernet Sauvignon is planted throughout the Bordeaux region and the South-west, and has spread up to the Loire valley and across to the Midi. It needs a relatively warm climate, is usually blended with Cabernet Franc and Merlot to offset its firmness, and benefits greatly from being allowed to age in wood and then in bottle. It is synonymous with high-quality red wine in Italy, Spain, Bulgaria, South Africa, Australia and North and South America.

Cabernet Franc

The lighter of the two Cabernets, making wine with a fine, deep carmine colour, delightful aroma of raspberries or violets and firm but not hard fruit finish. It is at its best in Touraine, Anjou, the Graves and Saint-Emilion regions of Bordeaux and northern Italy. It also makes a fine rosé.

Merlot

A dark-coloured grape, ripening relatively early, but very subject to rot in humid vintages, the Merlot is planted principally in Bordeaux (where it is the perfect foil for the Cabernet Sauvignon in the Médoc, and dominant in Saint-Emilion and Pomerol) and the South-west of France, northern Italy and with great success in California. The wine is rich in colour, with a plummy smoothness needing less ageing than the Cabernets.

Pinot Noir

The traditional grape of Burgundy and Champagne, also planted in Alsace and the Jura, Pinot Noir is a fragile grape that prefers a cool climate. The wine has a medium-deep colour, a rich strawberry-cherry-blackcurrant aroma and sweet, fleshy fruit and firm but not tannic finish. Except in Champagne, where it is pressed and the juice blended with that of Chardonnay and Pinot Meunier, it loses its character if blended with other grapes.

Syrah

Very dark-coloured grape suited to warm climates and making rich, powerful wine with a blackcurranty, spicy aroma and concentrated fruit flavour. It is at its best in the northern Rhône, adds backbone and style to the wines of the southern Rhône and is very successful in South Africa and Australia. If the yield is kept low (Hermitage, Côte-Rôtie), the wine is very intense and long-lived.

Grenache

Less fine than the Syrah, with a tendency to overripeness leading to high alcohol and low acidity, the Grenache flourishes in the warm climates of the southern Rhône, Provence and the Midi, Spain and California. It produces a full-bodied, fruity, 'warm' wine, and also makes a fine fleshy rosé and the best red *vins doux naturels*.

Mourvèdre

A late-ripening varietal making dark-coloured, firmly structured wines with a welcome acidity. It is the principal grape in Bandol and almost a necessity in Châteauneuf-du-Pape to add stature and ageing potential to the 'fat' wines of the Grenache. It is irregular in ripening and needs careful vinifying, but is a much underrated grape.

Cépages Nobles (White)

Chardonnay

The grape of white Burgundy and Champagne, Chardonnay prefers a lightish soil and coolish climate, but adapts remarkably well to different *terroirs*. The colour ranges from almost colourless yellow to a full gold, often with green tints, the aroma is elusive, with appley, buttery or nutty overtones, and the flavour is high in fruit, sometimes lean and sometimes rich, with good acidity. Complexity is added by the *terroir*, barrel fermenting and ageing and a year or two in bottle. It has been planted with great success, in all the fine-wine-producing countries in the world, and epitomizes fine, dry white wine.

Chenin Blanc

The underrated varietal produces the finest wines, in a range from a tart dryness to a luscious richness, in the Loire valley, where it is known as Pineau de la Loire. It is not planted elsewhere in France, but produces excellent wines, both dry and sweet, in South Africa, New Zealand and California. The high natural level of acidity permits the wines to age beautifully.

Riesling

One of the finest and most complex of the white wine grapes, with the range of the Chenin Blanc and the complexity of Chardonnay, Riesling has a distinctive fruit, purity of style and lemony acidity (even at its sweetness) that transcends differences in region and climate. This and the other *Cépages nobles* from Alsace are described on pages 30-3. Riesling is perhaps more closely allied to Germany than France, and is very successful in all the wine-growing countries of the New World.

Sémillon

The principal grape that makes the great sweet wines of Bordeaux, due to its ability to attain *pourriture noble*, and important in many white Graves and other white wines of the South-west of France. Its mellow softness has made it less fashionable than the less complex but crisper Sauvignon.

Sauvignon

Extremely versatile grape that ripens early but can attain *pourriture noble* in the right conditions, Sauvignon is at its most marked in the Loire valley where its aggressively fruity blackcurrant/gooseberry aroma and crisp acidic finish are typified by Sancerre and Pouilly-Fumé. In Bordeaux it is a minor grape in the *encépagement* for sweet wines, and is becoming the dominant grape in the dry wines of Graves and the South-west. It is also planted in northern Burgundy, the Midi and with great success in the New World where it is made both in dry, sweet, and late-harvest styles.

Viognier

A rare and very fragile varietal only planted in the northern Rhône valley, making the intensely aromatic, richly flavoured wines of Condrieu and Château Grillet. Some experimental plantings have been made in the Midi and California.

Glossary

Appellation communale the *appellation* covering a commune, e.g. Volnay, where there are different *crus* from specific vineyards.
Appellation régionale the *appellation* covering a sub-region of a main type of wine.
Cépage noble one of the few grape varieties that consistently make fine wines.
Climat specific vineyard, generally in Burgundy, not classified as Grand or 1er Cru.
En coteaux vines planted on slopes, usually making superior wine.
Crémant sparkling wine that is less sparkling than Champagne or *vin mousseux* but more sparkling than a *vin pétillant*. The pressure inside the bottle is between 3 and 4 atmospheres.
Cuvée a wine from a selected barrel or vat, generally superior to the norm. In Champagne it means the wine from the first pressing.
Cuverie where the wine ferments.
Demi-muid large oak barrel, generally 600 litres.
Demi-sec between sweet and dry, with the sweetness definitely discernible due

either to residual sugar or to *dosage*.

Elevage   the 'bringing-up' of a wine, usually in barrel, prior to bottling.

Encépagement   mix of different grape varieties in a wine.

Foudre   large wooden cask, immobile, for storing wine.

Gras   rich, full body, generally high in alcohol.

Lieu dit   see *Climat*.

Goût de terroir   distinctive taste or style imparted by the combination of grape variety and soil.

Macération carbonique method of vinification in which the grapes are placed whole in the vats to achieve rapid fermentation under pressure from their natural gases. Used to produce fruity red wines for early drinking, typically in the Beaujolais and now in the Loire and Midi.

Marc   either the 4,000 kilos of grapes in a Champagne press, or an *eau-de-vie* made from macerating spirit with the 'cake' of grape skins after pressing.

Mas   vineyard area or *climat* (qv) in the Northern Rhône.

Méthode champenoise   see pages 24–5.

Moelleux   very sweet, luscious white wines, between *doux* and *liquoureux*.

Oeil de perdrix   pale rosé, literally 'partridge-eye'.

Plafond limité de classement (PLC)   quantity of wine allowed to be declared above the permitted yield in a specific *appellation* (see page 11).

Pourriture noble   noble rot, or the fungus which attacks white grapes in specific vineyards in the Loire Valley and the South-West, essential to making a great sweet white wine.

Rosé de Noir   rosé made from black grapes only.

Rapé   percentage of wine discarded in Châteauneuf-du-Pape and Gigondas to maintain quality.

Saignée   process of drawing off fermenting juice of red grapes to make a rosé.

Sélection des grains nobles   very late picking of selected berries from botrytis-affected bunches, specific to Alsace.

Sève   sappy, racy, the inherent style and punch of a wine.

Terroir   the combination of soil and climate. The main element in the taste of a wine along with the grape variety.

Tête-de-cuvée   the finest casks or *cuves* of a particular vintage.

Tris   successive picking of a vineyard to harvest only the most ripe grapes.

Tuffeau   chalky-clay soil in the Saumur and Touraine regions on which some of the best wines are made.

Vendange tardive   late picking of very ripe grapes.

Vin gris   very pale rosé, result of shortened skin contact or particular grape (Gris Meunier).

Vin liquoreux   very sweet white wine, generally made from grapes affected by *pourriture noble*.

Vin ordinaire   wine with no regional origin.

Vin de presse   wine from the grapes pressed after fermentation has finished or, in Champagne, from further pressings.

Comités Interprofessionnels Vins et Spiritueux

Alsace
C.I.V.A., Comité Interprofessionnel des Vins d'Alsace, 8, place de-Lattre-de-Tassigny, 68000 Colmar.

Beaujolais
U.I.V.B., Union Interprofessionnelle des Vins du Beaujolais, 210, boulevard Vermorel, 69400 Villefranche-sur-Saône.

Burgundy/Mâcon
C.I.B.M., Comité Interprofessionnel des Vins de Bourgogne et Mâcon, Maison du tourisme, Boîte Postale 113, avenue du Maréchal-de-Lattre-de-Tassigny, 71000 Mâcon.

Côte d'Or/Yonne
C.I.B., Comité Interprofessionnel de la Côte d'Or et de l'Yonne pour les Vins A.O.C. de Bourgogne, Petite Place Carnot, 21200 Beaune.

Bordeaux
C.I.V.B., Conseil Interprofessionnel du Vin de Bordeaux, 1, cours du 30 juillet, 33000 Bordeaux.

Bergerac
C.I.V.R.B., Comité Interprofessionnel des Vins de la Région de Bergerac, place du docteur Cayla, 24100 Bergerac.

Champagne
C.I.V.C., Comité Interprofessionnel du Vin de Champagne, 5, rue Henri-Martin, B.P. 135, 51321 Epernay Cedex.

Côtes de Provence
C.I.V.C.P., Comité Interprofessionnel des Vins des Côtes de Provence, 3, avenue Jean-Jaurès, 83460 Les-Arcs-sur-Argens.

Côtes du Rhône
C.I.C.D.R., Comité Interprofessionnel des Vins des Côtes du Rhône, Maison du Tourisme et du Vin, 41, cours Jean-Jaurès, 84000 Avignon.

Fitou/Corbières/Minervois
Conseil Interprofessionnel des Vins de Fitou, Corbières et Minervois, R.N. 113, 11200 Lézignan-Corbières.

Gaillac
C.I.V.G., Comité Interprofessionnel des Vins de Gaillac, 8, rue du Père Gibrat, 81600 Gaillac.

Pays Nantais
C.I.V.O.P.N., Comité Interprofessionnel des Vins d'Origine du Pays Nantais, 17, rue des Étas, 44000 Nantes.

Touraine
C.I.V.T., Comité Interprofessionnel des Vins de Touraine, 19, square Prosper-Mérimée, 37000 Tours.

Anjou/Saumur
C.I.V.A.S., Conseil Interprofessionnel des Vins d'Anjou et de Saumur, 21, boulevard Foch, 49000 Angers.

Vins Doux Naturels
C.I.V.D.N., Comité Interprofessionnel des Vins Doux Naturels, 19, avenue de Grande-Bretagne, 66000 Perpignan.

Corsica
Groupement Interprofessionnel des Vins de l'Ile de Corse, 6, rue Gabriel-Péri, 20000 Bastia.

Bibliography

Benson, Jeffrey and Mackenzie, Alastair, *The Wines of Saint-Emilion and Pomerol*, Sotheby Publications, 1983.

Blanchet, Suzanne, *Les Vins du Val de Loire*, ed. Jema SA, Saumur, 1982.

Brejoux, Pierre, *Les Vins de la Loire*, ed. Revue du Vin de France.

Broadbent, Michael, *The Great Vintage Wine Book*, Mitchell Beazley, 1980.

Coates, Clive, *Claret*, Century, 1982.

Debuigne, G., *Dictionnaire des Vins*, ed. Larousse.

Dovaz, Michel, *Encyclopédie des Crus Classés du Bordelais*, Julliard, 1981.

Dovaz, Michel, *L'encyclopédie des Vins de Champagne*, Julliard, 1983.

Duijker, Hubert, *Grands Bordeaux Rouges*, Fernand Nathan, 1977.

Duijker, Hubert, *Les Bons Vins de Bordeaux*, Fernand Nathan, 1982.

Duijker, Hubert, *Les Grands Vins de Bourgogne*, Fernand Nathan, 1980.

Duijker, Hubert, *The Loire, Alsace and Champagne*, Mitchell Beazley, 1982.

Feret et Fils, *Bordeaux et ses Vins*, Bordeaux, 1982.

Forbes, Patrick, *Champagne*, Gollancz, 1967.

Hanson, Anthony, *Burgundy*, Faber, London, 1982; Boston, 1983.

Hugel, Jean, *Gastronomy and Wines of Alsace*, private printing.

Johnson, Hugh, *The Wine Companion*, Mitchell Beazley, 1983.

Johnson, Hugh, *The World Atlas of Wine*, Mitchell Beazley, London, 1977; Simon and Schuster, New York, 1978.

Lichine, Alexis, *Encyclopedia of Wines and Spirits*, Alfred A. Knopf, New York, 1974; Cassell, London, 1978.

Livingstone-Learmonth, John and Master, Melvyn, *The Wines of the Rhône*, Faber, London, 1983; Boston, 1983.

Penning-Rowsell, Edmund, *The Wines of Bordeaux*, Penguin, 1979.

Peppercorn, David, *Bordeaux*, Faber, 1982.

Poulain, René and Jacquelin, Louis, *Vignes et Vins de France*, ed. Flammarion.

Poupon, Pierre and Forgeot, Pierre, *The Wines of Burgundy*, Presses Universitaires de France, 1979.

Ray, Cyril, *Bollinger*, Heinemann, 1971.

Renvoisé, Guy. *Guide des Vins d'Alsace*, Solarama, 1983.

La Revue du Vin de France, ed. Leader, Paris.

Woutaz, Fernand, *Dictionnaire des Appellations*, ed. Litec, Paris, 1982.

Index

Acknowledgements

So much has been written on the fine wines of France, that merely consulting all the books would have prevented me from writing this concise guide. However, the picture changes all the time, and while the figures and facts have been collected from material already published, the opinions as to the taste and quality of the individual wines are my own. This said, I have relied heavily on my colleagues at L'Académie du Vin: Michel Dovaz through his books on the Bordeaux Crus Classés and on Champagne, Michel Bettane for his extraordinarily detailed articles on the finer French *appellations*, which have appeared regularly in the *Revue du Vin de France*, and Muriel de Potex and Isabelle Bachelard for last-minute research into the details that make up these *appellations*. My secretary, Jo Korngut, arranged for the majority of the wine labels, as I was not prepared to open a bottle of Chambertin or Condrieu just for the label, and special thanks must go to M. Philippe Guyonnet-Duperat, Directeur de l'Union des Grands Crus de Bordeaux, for the labels of Bordeaux Châteaux. Finally, the presence of Hugh Johnson's *Wine Companion* and Alexis Lichine's *Encyclopedia of Wines and Spirits* constantly reminded me what a slim volume this is.

Maps: pp. 19, 31, 36, 86, 95, 106, 112 © SOPEXA, redrawn by kind permission; pp. 21, 39 (both), 40 redrawn by kind permission of Cartes Larmat – *Revue du Vin de France*, 65 rue Montmartre, 75002 Paris (tel: (1) 236 20 83; telex Lidersa 220710 F).

Temperature chart (p. 165) reproduced by permission of M. Dovaz and Editions Vecchi.

Illustrations p. 165 by Rick Blakely.